FUN WITH FINANCE

RECENT TITLES IN TEACHER IDEAS PRESS' READERS THEATRE SERIES

Nonfiction Readers Theatre for Beginning Readers
Anthony D. Fredericks

Mother Goose Readers Theatre for Beginning Readers
Anthony D. Fredericks

MORE Frantic Frogs and Other Frankly Fractured Folktales for Readers Theatre
Anthony D. Fredericks

Songs and Rhymes Readers Theatre for Beginning Readers
Anthony D. Fredericks

Readers Theatre for Middle School Boys: Investigating the Strange and Mysterious
Ann N. Black

African Legends, Myths, and Folktales for Readers Theatre
Anthony D. Fredericks

Against All Odds: Readers Theatre for Grades 3-8
Suzanne I. Barchers and Michael Ruscoe

Readers Theatre for African American History
Jeff Sanders and Nancy I. Sanders

Building Fluency with Readers Theatre: Motivational Strategies, Successful Lessons, and Dynamic Scripts to Develop Fluency, Comprehension, Writing, and Vocabulary
Anthony D. Fredericks

American Folklore, Legends, and Tall Tales for Readers Theatre
Anthony D. Fredericks

Multi-Grade Readers Theatre: Picture Book Authors and Illustrators
Suzanne I. Barchers and Charla R. Pfeffinger

More Readers Theatre for Middle School Boys: Adventures with Mythical Creatures
Ann N. Black

FUN WITH FINANCE:

Math + Literacy = Success

Written and Illustrated by Carol Peterson

Readers Theatre

A Teacher Ideas Press Book

Libraries Unlimited
An Imprint of ABC-CLIO, LLC

A B C  C L I O

Santa Barbara, California • Denver, Colorado • Oxford, England

Copyright 2009 by Carol Peterson

All rights reserved. No part of this book may be reproduced in any form or by any electronic or mechanical means, including information storage and retrieval systems, without permission in writing from the publisher, except by a reviewer, who may quote brief passages in a review. An exception is made for individual librarians and educators who may make copies of portions of the scripts for classroom use. Reproducible pages may be copied for classroom and educational programs only. Performances may be videotaped for school or library purposes.

Library of Congress Cataloging-in-Publication Data

Peterson, Carol, 1953-
  Fun with finance : Math + literacy = success / written and illustrated by Carol Peterson.
      p. cm.
  "A Teacher Ideas Press Book."
  Includes bibliographical references and index.
  ISBN 978-1-59158-759-0 (hard copy : alk. paper) 1. Finance, Personal—Juvenile drama. 2. Readers' theater. 3. Drama in education. 4. Finance, Personal—Study and teaching (Elementary)—Activity programs. I. Title.
    PS3616.E84275F86   2009
    372.67'6—dc22   2009017338

13 12 11 10 9   1 2 3 4 5

This book is also available on the World Wide Web as an eBook.
Visit www.abc-clio.com for details.

ABC-CLIO, LLC
130 Cremona Drive, P.O. Box 1911
Santa Barbara, California 93116 1911

This book is printed on acid-free paper ∞
Manufactured in the United States of America

This book is dedicated to Jim, Doug, and Nicole, who have made my life richer than I could ever be through money alone. It is also dedicated to teachers and parents everywhere, in the hope that we will be able to train our children (financially) in the way they should go so that when they are grown they will not turn from it.

Contents

Introduction: Finance (and Math) CAN Be Fun! xiii

Chapter 1: Money Mania 1
    What Is Money? 2
    Setting/Props/Costumes 2
    Characters 2
        Suitcases Full of Money 3
    Glossary 18
    Doing to Understand 18
        Activity 1. Comparing Values of World Currencies 19
        Activity 2. World Money Game 21
        Activity 3. Decoding the U.S. Dollar Bill 22
        Activity 4. Board Game 23
    Think About 30
    Find Out More 30

Chapter 2: Work Wise 33
    What Is Employment? 34
    Setting/Props/Costumes 34
    Characters 34
        Jacob's Job 35
    Glossary 48
    Doing to Understand 48
        Activity 1. Payroll Deductions 49
        Activity 2. Create an Employment Package 50
        Activity 3. Job Interview 53
        Activity 4. Future Careers 55
        Activity 5. Board Game 56
    Think About 61
    Find Out More 61

Chapter 3: Booming Businesses 63
    What Is a Business? 63
    Setting/Props/Costumes 64
    Characters 64
        Monkey Business 65
    Glossary 73
    Doing to Understand 73
        Activity 1. Gross Wage 74
        Activity 2. Employee Taxes 75
        Activity 3. Insurance Deductions 76
        Activity 4. The Check Stub and Paycheck 77

Chapter 3: Booming Businesses (*Cont.*)
      Activity 5. Starting a Business ... 78
      Activity 6. Board Game ... 79
  Think About ... 84
  Find Out More ... 84

Chapter 4: Savings Savvy ... 85
  What Is Saving? ... 85
  Setting/Props/Costumes ... 86
  Characters ... 86
    Something Interest-ing ... 87
  Glossary ... 98
  Doing to Understand ... 98
      Activity 1. Calculate Simple Interest ... 99
      Activity 2. Calculate Compound Interest and Principal ... 100
      Activity 3. Compare Simple and Compound Interest ... 101
      Activity 4. Think About and Discuss ... 102
      Activity 5. Interest Rates ... 104
      Activity 6. Board Game ... 105
  Think About ... 111
  Find Out More ... 111

Chapter 5: Credit Chaos ... 113
  What Is Credit? ... 114
  Setting/Props/Costumes ... 114
  Characters ... 114
    Credit Chaos ... 115
  Glossary ... 126
  Doing to Understand ... 126
      Activity 1. Credit Reports ... 127
      Activity 2. Home Mortgages ... 128
      Activity 3. The Real Cost of Debt ... 130
      Activity 4. Another Cost of Debt ... 131
      Activity 5. Improving Your Credit Score ... 132
      Activity 6. Board Game ... 133
  Think About ... 139
  Find Out More ... 139

Chapter 6: Budget Bonus ... 141
  What Is a Budget? ... 142
  Setting/Props/Costumes ... 142
  Characters ... 142
    Planning to Spend ... 143
  Glossary ... 156
  Doing to Understand ... 156
      Activity 1. Create a Budget ... 157
      Activity 2. Career Goal ... 158

Contents   ix

           Activity 3. Balance Your Checkbook 159
           Activity 4. Board Game 162
   Think About 168
   Find Out More 168

Chapter 7: Real Estate Rush 169
   What Is Real Estate? 170
   Setting/Props/Costumes 170
   Characters 170
      Old House/New House 171
   Glossary 184
   Doing to Understand 184
           Activity 1. Comparing Home Prices 185
           Activity 2. Price Per Square Foot. 186
           Activity 3. Charting Information 187
           Activity 4. Board Game 188
   Think About 194
   Find Out More 195

Chapter 8: Stock Stuff 197
   What Is Stock? 197
   Setting/Props/Costumes 198
   Characters 198
      Stocking Up (and Down) 199
   Glossary 209
   Doing to Understand 210
           Activity 1. Paper Money Trade. 211
           Activity 2. Watch List 212
           Activity 3. Conduct a Fundamental Analysis 213
           Activity 4. Conduct a Technical Analysis 214
           Activity 5. Portfolio Management 215
           Activity 6. Chart Information. 216
           Activity 7. Board Game 217
   Think About 223
   Find Out More 223

Chapter 9: Building with Bonds 225
   What Are Bonds?. 225
   Setting/Props/Costumes 226
   Characters 226
      Bonding with Friends. 227
   Glossary 235
   Doing to Understand 235
           Activity 1. Understanding Savings Bonds 236
           Activity 2. Bank Bonds. 237
           Activity 3. Municipal Bonds 238
           Activity 4. Laddering. 239

x Contents

Chapter 9: Building with Bonds (*Cont.*)
      Activity 5. What Are Your Savings Bonds Worth? 240
      Activity 6. Board Game 241
  Think About 247
  Find Out More 247

Chapter 10: Commodity Commotion 249
  What Are Commodities? 249
  What Are Futures? 250
  Setting/Props/Costumes 250
  Characters 250
      Just Drop It 251
  Glossary 258
  Doing to Understand 258
      Activity 1. Create a List of Commodities 259
      Activity 2. Find Commodities 260
      Activity 3. Board Game 261
  Think About 267
  Find Out More 267

Chapter 11: Collecting Can Count 269
  What Is an Investment Collection? 269
  Setting/Props/Costumes 270
  Characters 270
      Quizy's Collection 271
  Glossary 279
  Doing to Understand 279
      Activity 1. Collections 280
      Activity 2. Value of Collections 281
      Activity 3. Collection Display and Catalog 282
      Activity 4. Board Game 283
  Think About 289
  Find Out More 289

Chapter 12: Future Focus 291
  What Is Future Focus? 291
  Setting/Props/Costumes 292
  Characters 292
      Thinking Ahead 293
  Glossary 302
  Doing to Understand 302
      Activity 1. Financial Goals 303
      Activity 2. Building a Portfolio 304
      Activity 3. Retirement 305
      Activity 4. Setting Goals 306
      Activity 5. Board Game 309
  Think About 315
  Find Out More 315

Appendix 1: Board Game Pieces 317
Appendix 2: Tables. 327
Appendix 3: Pie Charts. 329
Appendix 4: Line Graphs. 331
Appendix 5: Bar Graphs 333
Appendix 6: Curriculum Standards 335
Appendix 7: Books about Money or Math 337
Appendix 8: Readers Theatre. 339
Bibliography 343
Index 345

Introduction: Finance (and Math) CAN Be Fun!

THE PROBLEM WITH MATH ISN'T A MATH PROBLEM

No matter how sweetly you remind kids that one day they really *will* use math; no matter how calmly you explain that math only gets harder if they don't learn it now; no matter how loudly you nag them to just learn it—kids remain resolute in their belief that math is hard, boring, and *useless*!

We have seen how fragile our world economy is and how important it is for adults to responsibly manage their finances. Unfortunately we leave instructing kids about finance to parents, who themselves often have received inadequate training. How can we train a generation of financial stewards if our kids see math as something to be avoided and have no idea how to manage money or build wealth?

We do it by showing kids that the math they are learning has real value for their future. We do it by getting kids to identify math with wealth building. And, perhaps most important for kids, we do it by making it fun! Showing a fun side of math makes students more likely to look at the subject with eagerness. Consequently, they are also more likely to learn the principles better and retain them longer.

High schools often include a segment on personal finance or independent living in the senior year to help prepare students to enter adult society. By the time students are 17, however, they have little time left to master personal finance principles before they are thrust into adulthood. Furthermore, by that grade most students have completed all of the mathematics study they ever will. Thus a study of finance in high school may not adequately connect mathematics principles they learned five or six years earlier with personal finance that could lead to financial responsibility.

The time to make the most impact on young people in instilling the value of mathematics for real world skills is when those math principles are first introduced. In grades 4 to 6. *Fun with Finance* is intended for just that age, when students' reading ability and maturity level will ensure a successful readers theatre experience and mathematics principles do not exceed those introduced in this book.

All of us will learn a skill more readily when we know how it will be used or when we see that there will be a benefit from learning it. These readers theatre scripts, activities, and games are fun. Students may more eagerly apply the skills presented when math and finance are hidden within the framework of humorous story and game play.

From a teaching point of view, this book addresses multiplication; percentages; simple geometry; basic number sense; and an understanding of tables, charts, and graphs to help teachers address mathematics curriculum standards. As an added bonus, a readers theatre resource that focuses on a mathematical subject gives teachers an opportunity to address two areas of curriculum standards at once. In other words, math + literacy = success. For both kids and teachers.

THE STUCTURE OF THIS BOOK

Each chapter of *Fun with Finance* introduces students to a specific area of finance—from basic monetary systems and how to manage personal finances, to an introduction of various forms of investment as a way to build wealth and security. The book completes the study of finances with a chapter on goal setting, applicable to all areas of life, to get kids thinking about what they want for their future and show them how to create a plan to achieve it.

Within each chapter is a readers theatre script to encourage literacy and explain basic terms and theory of the financial principle. Each chapter also includes math-related activities to further enhance the understanding of the financial principle and ends with a board game. (There are reproducible handouts in each chapter and in appendix 1.) Also included in each chapter are a glossary; a simple narrative about each principle; and suggested Web sites, local resources, and ideas for careers in that area of finance.

Appendixes 2 through 5 provide age-appropriate illustrated narratives to introduce students to simple tables, charts, and graphs. Appendix 6 lists the curriculum standards addressed in this book by page number. Appendix 7 provides a list of math- and finance-related books for children and teachers. Appendix 8 explains the use of readers theatre, with ideas for rehearsal and presentation.

SUPPORTING CURRICULUM STANDARDS

Each state may list its specific curriculum standards differently, using varying terminology. All, however, generally follow similar guidelines. Each chapter in *Fun with Finance* indicates which standards it addresses. These are then cross-referenced in appendix 6, which lists each standard and the page number where it is covered. *Fun with Finance* focuses on the following curriculum standards:

Math Standards

> Number Sense: computing numbers; decimals; fractions; percents; positive and negative numbers
> Statistics, Data Analysis, Probability, Graphs, Mathematical Reasoning
> Measurement and Simple Geometry
> Rates, Proportions, Percentages

Literacy Standards

> Vocabulary and Concept Development
> Reading Comprehension
> Spelling

Written and Oral English Standards

> Writing Strategies: Organization and Focus, Research and Technology
> Listening and Speaking Strategies and Applications
> Verbal Communication

Social Studies Standards

> Chronological and Spatial Thinking
> Economics and Historical Interpretation (where applicable)
> Geography
> History and World Culture

Are you ready to begin the financial journey with your students? Maybe you, too, need a reminder that finance (and math) can be fun!

Enjoy the ride.

CHAPTER 1

෨ $ ෫

Money Mania

Subject Matter: World currency; economics

Math Standards Addressed:

Number Sense: computing numbers; multiplication; decimals; fractions

Data Analysis: tables, charts, graphs

Literacy Standards Addressed:

Vocabulary and Concept Development

Reading Comprehension

Spelling

Social Studies Standards Addressed:

World Cultures

Geography

U.S. History

Written and Oral English Standards Addressed:

Listening and Speaking Applications

Verbal Communication

Reseach and Technology

WHAT IS MONEY?

Money is what people use to buy and sell things. It includes both paper money and coins. Paper money is called currency. Money is part of a worldwide economic system. An economic system includes such things as the value of money, credit, loans, investments, natural resources, how businesses are doing in a country, and how people are employed in jobs. The worldwide economic system includes the money that governments of other countries use and how each of those sets of money interacts with other money systems in the world.

SETTING/PROPS/COSTUMES

This play has six scenes for seven readers. Brother and sister, Doug and Nicole, are with their friends Jacob and Chandra. Quizy (a friendly alien from another planet) is with them. They're discussing Doug and Nicole's upcoming trip with their family around the world. Props could include a globe or world map that the friends point to when they talk about different countries. Costumes could include items from the countries mentioned. Quizy's clothing and appearance is limited only by students' imagination!

Pronunciation guides may be provided in the script in square brackets. The words are divided into syllables. The syllable to be stressed is in capital letters. For example, the pronunciation guide for Quizy's name would be [QUIZ-ee]. The reader should use the pronunciation guide but not read it aloud.

CHARACTERS

NARRATOR 1

NARRATOR 2

DOUG

NICOLE

JACOB

CHANDRA

QUIZY (a friendly alien visitor who collects empty tissue boxes)

Suitcases Full of Money

Scene 1: The Big News

NARRATOR 1: Doug, Nicole, Jacob, Chandra, and Quizy are together.

NARRATOR 2: Doug and Nicole are brother and sister.

NARRATOR 1: Quizy is a friendly alien visitor who hangs out with the students at their school.

NARRATOR 2: Let's listen to what they're talking about.

DOUG: Yippee!

CHANDRA: Why are you so happy?

NICOLE: He's happy because we're going on vacation.

JACOB: Where are you going?

DOUG: Everywhere!

CHANDRA: Everywhere?

NICOLE: Well, not everywhere.

DOUG: But we are going to lots of different countries.

NICOLE: All over the world.

QUIZY: Like where?

DOUG: Like England. And France.

NICOLE: And Spain. And Germany.

DOUG:	And Russia. And China.
NICOLE:	And Japan. And Mexico. And Canada.
DOUG:	And Africa. And Australia.
JACOB:	That's a lot of places!
QUIZY:	Why are you going to all those places?
NICOLE:	Our family is going with Dad.
CHANDRA:	Why is he going to all those places?
DOUG:	He's going on a business trip.
JACOB:	What kind of business trip?
NICOLE:	He sells widgets for the company he works for.
CHANDRA:	That's interesting.
QUIZY:	Widgets are very interesting.
JACOB:	What is a widget?
DOUG:	I don't know.
NICOLE:	They are technical.
CHANDRA:	How much does one widget cost?
DOUG:	It depends.
JACOB:	It depends on what?
NICOLE:	On where you live.
CHANDRA:	What do you mean?
DOUG:	A widget costs different amounts depending on what country you live in.

Scene 2: Quizy Learns about Economies

NARRATOR 1: Wow, Doug and Nicole have some exciting news.

NARRATOR 2: Yes, but what did Doug mean that his dad's widgets cost different amounts depending on the country?

NARRATOR 1: I don't know.

NARRATOR 2: Let's find out.

JACOB: Why does a widget cost different amounts depending on what country you live in?

NICOLE: If you live in the United States, a widget costs $100.

CHANDRA: What if I live in England?

DOUG: Then you would pay for a widget in pounds.

QUIZY: How many pounds does a widget weigh?

NICOLE: He doesn't mean pounds of weight.

DOUG: No, I mean English pounds. Pounds are what they call their money.

JACOB: I heard England also uses euros.

QUIZY: You are oh, what?

CHANDRA: Not "you're oh," Quizy. It is spelled e-u-r-o. Euro.

QUIZY: What's a euro?

JACOB: It's a unit of money used by a group of countries in Europe.

QUIZY: Why would they do that?

DOUG: The countries think their economies will all be stronger if they are tied together.

QUIZY: What's an economy?

NICOLE: An economy is everything that has to do with a money system.

JACOB: It includes the money itself—like U.S. dollars and English pounds.

CHANDRA: And euros.

DOUG: It also includes how businesses are doing.

NICOLE: And how many people have jobs.

JACOB:	And how much things cost.
CHANDRA:	And how much money people borrow.
DOUG:	And how strong the government is.
QUIZY:	It sounds like a lot of things affect an economy.
NICOLE:	They do.
JACOB:	And each country in the world has an economy.
CHANDRA:	And each country's economy affects other countries' economies.
DOUG:	It's a small world.
QUIZY:	Yes, Earth is much smaller than my planet.

Scene 3: Quizy Learns about Currencies

NARRATOR 1:	An economy sounds a little complicated.
NARRATOR 2:	And each country has a different economy.
NARRATOR 1:	And all of the countries in the world make up a world economy.
NARRATOR 2:	No wonder Quizy is confused.
NARRATOR 1:	Maybe we can find out more about the world's money.
NARRATOR 2:	Let's listen.
QUIZY:	So does France use euros?
NICOLE:	Yes. And France also has money called francs.
QUIZY:	What about Switzerland?
JACOB:	They use euros, too.
CHANDRA:	And francs.
QUIZY:	French francs?
DOUG:	No, Swiss francs.
QUIZY:	What about Belgium?

NICOLE: Belgium uses euros and francs.

QUIZY: Swiss francs?

JACOB: No.

QUIZY: French francs?

CHANDRA: No, Belgian francs.

QUIZY: That's confusing.

DOUG: Sometimes.

QUIZY: What about Germany?

NICOLE: Germany uses euros.

JACOB: They also use marks.

QUIZY: Who is Mark?

DOUG: Not Mark, a person. Mark the money.

QUIZY: They mark down what they want to buy?

CHANDRA: No. A "mark" is the name of the money in Germany.

QUIZY: What about Russia? Do they use euros?

DOUG: No, they don't use euros.

NICOLE: In Russia they use rubles.

QUIZY: I thought India used rubles.

JACOB: No, India uses rupees [roo-PEES].

QUIZY: And euros?

CHANDRA: No, India doesn't use euros.

DOUG: India isn't in Europe.

QUIZY: Greece is in Europe. Does it use euros?

NICOLE: Yes.

JACOB: And Greece also uses drachmas [DRAHK-maz].

QUIZY: Does Japan use euros?

CHANDRA: No, Japan isn't in Europe.

QUIZY: What does Japan have?

DOUG: Japan has yen.

QUIZY: I thought China had yen.

NICOLE: No, China has yuan [won].

QUIZY: Like won ton?

JACOB: No, not like won ton.

QUIZY: That's too bad. I like won ton.

CHANDRA: I like won ton, too, Quizy!

DOUG: And don't forget Thailand.

NICOLE: What money does Thailand have?

DOUG: Bahts [bots].

QUIZY: Ro-bots?

JACOB: No, Thai bahts.

QUIZY: Too bad. I have lots of ro-bots.

DOUG: Hey Quizy, if you sold a robot to someone in Thailand, he could pay you in Thai bahts.

QUIZY: I like your thinking!

Scene 4: Earth as Seen by Quizy

NARRATOR 1: I like won ton, too.

NARRATOR 2: So do I. But I wonder where else Doug and Nicole are going.

NARRATOR 1: Let's find out.

JACOB: Where else are you going?

DOUG: Australia.

QUIZY: Australia is not in Europe, either.

NICOLE: You sure know about Earth's countries, Quizy.

QUIZY: I've seen them all from my spaceship.

JACOB: Oh, right.

QUIZY: Except that all your maps are wrong.

CHANDRA: How are they wrong?

QUIZY: From space, Earth doesn't have any of those lines between the countries.

DOUG: Thanks for explaining that, Quizy.

NICOLE: Quizy, we only draw lines on maps to think about where the countries are.

QUIZY: And the countries are not red and pink and purple, either.

JACOB: We know, Quizy.

QUIZY: Although SOME of the countries are green.

CHANDRA: Thanks, Quizy.

QUIZY: And some are brown.

DOUG: Thanks, Quizy.

QUIZY: And a few are yellow.

NICOLE: Are the oceans at least blue from space?

QUIZY: Yes! But you should really tell your mapmakers to get the country colors right.

CHANDRA: Thanks, Quizy. But let's get back to money.

QUIZY: OK. Australia doesn't use euros.

DOUG: No, Australia uses pounds.

QUIZY: Like England?

NICOLE: Yes, Australian money is called pounds, like English pounds.

JACOB: Except it is not the same money at all.

QUIZY: What do you mean?

CHANDRA: England and Australia are different countries.

QUIZY: But the same color except on maps.

DOUG: Yes, but because they're different countries . . .

NICOLE: An English pound doesn't equal the same amount as an Australian pound.

QUIZY: What about Canada? They have dollars, like the United States has.

JACOB: And both countries are on the same continent.

CHANDRA: They're both in North America.

DOUG: Yes, but Canadian dollars are different than U.S. dollars.

QUIZY: Why?

NICOLE: Because Canada and the United States are different countries.

QUIZY: So just because Canadian money is called dollars, they're not the same as U.S. dollars.

JACOB: Canadian money doesn't even look the same as U.S. money.

CHANDRA: Yes, Canadian money has the queen of England on it.

QUIZY: Why is the queen of England on Canada's money?

DOUG: Because Canada is politically related to England.

QUIZY: Then why doesn't Canada have pounds?

NICOLE: Because . . .

QUIZY: And the U.S. used to be owned by England, so why doesn't the U.S. use pounds or euros?

DOUG: Quizy, it's a long story, but the point is . . .

NICOLE:	Canada is a separate country and has separate money from England.
JACOB:	Just like the United States does.
CHANDRA:	And the money is different even if it's called the same thing.

Scene 5: More about Economies

NARRATOR 1:	I never thought about how different countries might use the same name for their money.
NARRATOR 2:	But the money is not the same.
NARRATOR 1:	It doesn't look the same.
NARRATOR 2:	And it isn't worth the same, either.
QUIZY:	Why is all the money worth different amounts even if it's called the same word?
DOUG:	Because the money is based on how that country's economy is doing.
QUIZY:	What's an economy again?
NICOLE:	An economy is how wealth is created, divided, and used among people in that country.
QUIZY:	But why is an economy different for different countries?
JACOB:	Because an economy is also affected by what the country sells to other countries and buys from other countries.
CHANDRA:	And how the government's laws relate to workers, business, taxes, and interest rates.
DOUG:	So if the people in a country are all out of work or are taxed too much, . . .
NICOLE:	Then they don't have enough money to pay for extra things.

JACOB: Or if the government makes it hard for businesses to make money, . . .

CHANDRA: The country's economy may do poorly.

QUIZY: So the money of that country then may not be worth as much as the money from a different country?

DOUG: That's right.

NICOLE: Quizy, have you run out of questions?

QUIZY: I'm just thinking.

JACOB: About what?

QUIZY: Suitcases.

CHANDRA: What about suitcases?

QUIZY: Your suitcase must be really big.

DOUG: Why?

QUIZY: For all the different kinds of money you'll have to take on your trip.

NICOLE: We're only taking U.S. dollars.

QUIZY: What happens when you go to the other countries?

DOUG: We'll exchange our money.

QUIZY: Exchange it for what?

NICOLE: For the money of the country we're in.

QUIZY: I thought the money from each country was different.

JACOB: It is.

QUIZY: Then how can you exchange it?

CHANDRA: Every country's money has an exchange rate with the money from every other country in the world.

QUIZY: What does that mean?

DOUG:	The exchange rate tells you, for example, how many euros one U.S. dollar is worth.
NICOLE:	Or how many English pounds one U.S. dollar is worth.
JACOB:	Or how many Australian pounds one U.S. dollar is worth.
QUIZY:	So your suitcase doesn't weigh too many pounds!
CHANDRA:	Right.
QUIZY:	Or how many English pounds equals one Australian pound?
DOUG:	Yes.
NICOLE:	Does that sound confusing?
QUIZY:	Do you have to take a chart so you know how much your dollars are worth everywhere you go?
JACOB:	No. That wouldn't work.
QUIZY:	Why not?
CHANDRA:	Because the exchange rate may change every day.
QUIZY:	Why would it change every day?
DOUG:	Because the economies of each country might change every day.
NICOLE:	So the comparison of one economy to another would be different.
QUIZY:	Good-bye.

Scene 6: Quizy's Plan

NARRATOR 1:	I wonder where Quizy is going.
NARRATOR 2:	Let's find out.
JACOB:	Where are you going, Quizy?
QUIZY:	I'm going to sit in my spaceship and never leave.

CHANDRA: Why?

QUIZY: Earth is too confusing.

DOUG: Wouldn't you like to see other countries?

NICOLE: And meet other people?

QUIZY: Are they as confusing as their money?

JACOB: Don't worry so much, Quizy.

CHANDRA: It's just money.

QUIZY: But money is different everywhere you go.

DOUG: Yes.

QUIZY: Don't you get confused?

NICOLE: Sometimes. But I like the money from other countries.

QUIZY: Why?

NICOLE: I collect it. Look.

QUIZY: That's money? It has pink and green pictures on it.

JACOB: Look at that one.

CHANDRA: It's beautiful!

DOUG: What are you doing, Quizy?

QUIZY: Making a list.

NICOLE: Of what?

QUIZY: What I want to bring home from each country.

JACOB: That's a short list.

CHANDRA: What is on your list?

QUIZY: A little bit of money from each country I visit.

DOUG: What are you going to do with the money?

NICOLE: Are you going to collect it, like I do?

QUIZY: No, I'm just going to save it.

JACOB: For what?

QUIZY: I'm going to trade it.

CHANDRA: For what?

QUIZY: For other money.

DOUG: What do you mean?

QUIZY: When the euro is worth more than the yen, I'll trade my yen for another euro.

NICOLE: Why?

QUIZY: The money I traded will be worth more.

JACOB: And when your franc is worth more than your pound?

QUIZY: Then I'll trade my pound for another franc.

CHANDRA: Quizy . . .

QUIZY: I know. I'm brilliant!

DOUG: Quizy . . .

QUIZY: I'll make a gazillion bucks before anybody knows what I'm doing.

NICOLE: Quizy . . .

QUIZY: Just don't tell anyone my secret!

JACOB: Quizy, trading money isn't something secret.

QUIZY: What do you mean?

CHANDRA: The Forex.

QUIZY: The 4 Xs?

CHANDRA: No, the F-o-r-e-x [FOR-x].

DOUG: It stands for "foreign exchange." For is short for "foreign." Ex is short for "exchange."

QUIZY: What IS the Forex?

NICOLE: It's like the stock market for money.

QUIZY:	What do you mean?
JACOB:	People can buy and sell foreign money.
CHANDRA:	Just like buying and selling stock.
QUIZY:	Then you CAN take a big suitcase full of money with you.
DOUG:	No, you don't actually trade dollar bills or paper pounds.
QUIZY:	What do you do?
NICOLE:	You know the stock market?
QUIZY:	Yes. You buy and sell little parts of companies.
JACOB:	But you never actually take the parts of the company home with you.
QUIZY:	You only have a paper that says you own part of it.
CHANDRA:	And do you know how you make money in the stock market?
DOUG:	You make money if the little part you own goes up in value.
QUIZY:	So how do you make money in Forex?
NICOLE:	You trade currencies based on whether you think the value of a country's money will go up or down.
QUIZY:	So you can even make money on money?
JACOB:	Yes, you can.
QUIZY:	OK, then I'll go.
CHANDRA:	Where?
QUIZY:	Everywhere on Earth.
DOUG:	Great.
QUIZY:	But I'm still going to bring home a little bit of money from each country.
NICOLE:	But Quizy, we told you . . .

QUIZY: I know what you told me. But I'm still bringing it home.

JACOB: Why?

QUIZY: Because it is so pretty.

CHANDRA: Yes, it is pretty.

QUIZY: Collecting money MIGHT even be better than collecting empty tissue boxes.

DOUG, NICOLE, JACOB, AND CHANDRA: Much better!

18 Chapter 1: Money Mania

GLOSSARY

Baht: The name of the monetary unit of Thailand

Currency: The money of a country; usually the paper money.

Dollar: The name of the monetary unit of the United States and Canada.

Drachma: The name of the monetary unit of Greece.

Economy: A financial system of a country or of the world.

European Union: Group of European nations that joined together to form an economic unit. In addition to a common form of money, the nations agree to certain trade regulations among all countries in the union.

Euro: Also called "euro dollar." The name of the monetary unit used by the European Union.

Exchange rate: The price of one currency in units of another currency.

Forex: Foreign Currency Exchange. The market for trading foreign currency

Franc: The name of the monetary unit of France, Switzerland, and Belgium.

Mark: The name of the monetary unit of Germany.

Pound: The name of the monetary unit of England and Australia.

Ruble: The name of the monetary unit of Russia.

Rupee: The name of the monetary unit of India.

Yen: The name of the monetary unit of Japan.

Yuan: The name of the monetary unit of China.

DOING TO UNDERSTAND

The following activities are included as handouts:

1. Comparing Values of World Currencies
2. World Money Game
3. Decoding the U.S. Dollar Bill
4. Board Game

ACTIVITY 1. COMPARING VALUES OF WORLD CURRENCIES

Each country's monetary system has a different value compared to each other country in the world. For example, what costs $1.00US in America might cost 1.50 euros or 5 of another country's monetary unit. List five or six items you might normally buy at the store and how much each item costs. Using the business section of a newspaper or an online currency calculator, figure out how much each item would cost in the monetary units of several countries discussed in the readers theatre script. Use the handout (p. 20) to create a chart of the prices. Study the results. How do the exchange rates of the countries compare with the U.S. dollar? If you visited each of the countries, would your U.S. dollars be worth more or less than they are here?

Look up each country listed on your chart on a world map. Discuss how the location of countries nearby would affect their economies and exchange rates. What kind of chart or graph could you create to show the information from this table?

HOW MUCH?

Create a table to compare the cost of items in different countries' currencies. Use a separate sheet for each item studied. Use an online currency converter and do the exercise again after several days or weeks. Did the cost of the item stay the same for each currency? What did you learn?

Item: _____

Date	Country	Currency	Cost

ACTIVITY 2. WORLD MONEY GAME

You can learn a lot about a country from its money. Using the following list of countries and creatures, answer the questions below the list. Then use the first letter of each answer to reveal the final answer. Find each country listed below on a world map. Note each country's latitude and longitude.

COUNTRIES
China
Australia
Netherlands
Australia
Rwanda
India
Egypt
Antarctica
Ecuador

CREATURES
Lion
Gorillas
Armadillo
Mermaid
Elephants

To find the first word in the final question, answer these questions:
1. Scientific groups on this continent print penguins on a $1.00 bill to raise money for research: _____
2. This half human/half fish is on a 100 shilling bill from Austria: _____
3. Coins from this country picture a sphinx, a half man/half lion: _____
4. Zebras are on 100 franc bills from this African country: _____
5. Peacocks are on the 10 rupee bill of this country, which is famous for the Taj Mahal: _____
6. The panda is on coins from this country, which grows bamboo: _____
7. Argentina pictures this scaly, armored animal on its 25 peso bill: _____
8. This country, famous for flowers and windmills, has a bee and a sunflower on its 50 gulden bill: _____

To find the second word in the final question, answer these questions:
1. Kenya's 1000 shilling bill pictures this large, tusked animal: _____
2. Kangaroos are on one-half penny coins from _____
3. These extra large primates (like monkeys and apes) are on money from several African nations, including Rwanda and Uganda: _____
4. Tanzania, off the coast of Africa, has this member of the cat family on its 100 shilling bills: _____
5. This country near the equator features turtles from Galapagos Island on its 5,000 sucres bills: _____

Now, using the first letters from the answers above, fill in the blanks below. What animal is on U.S. Money?

___ ___ ___ ___ ___ ___ ___ ___   ___ ___ ___ ___ ___

Answers to first section: 1. Antarctica; 2. Mermaid; 3. Egypt; 4. Rwanda; 5. India; 6. China; 7. Armadillo; 8. Netherlands / **Answers to second section:** 1. Elephant; 2. Australia; 3. Gorillas; 4. Lion; 5. Ecuador / **Final answer:** American eagle

From *Fun with Finance: Math + Literacy = Success* by Carol Peterson. Santa Barbara, CA: Libraries Unlimited. Copyright © 2009.

ACTIVITY 3. DECODING THE U.S. DOLLAR BILL

Money is often designed with symbols that stand for something important to the country or its history. Look at a $1.00 bill and find the following:

- The frame around President Washington is the Greek letter omega, which early Christians used as a symbol for the future. Symbolically, George Washington (part of America's past) is linked to the future of America.

- List all the symbols you see on a dollar bill. Research what some of them mean and report to the class.

- The number 13 represents the original 13 colonies. In the circle (called a roundel) with the eagle, find:

13 stars	13 letters in *E pluribus unum*
13 leaves on the olive branch	13 berries on the olive branch
13 arrows	13 vertical sections on the shield
13 horizontal sections on the shield	

- Look at the letters at the bottom of the pyramid: MDCCLXXVI. The letters are Roman numerals. The letters stand for numbers. Using the table below, add up the numbers. What is the total? What does that number refer to?

    The following are the values of the Roman numerals on the dollar bill:

    M 1,000
    D 500
    C 100
    L 50
    X 10
    V 5

- Find the following mottos:
    - *E pluribus unum* is Latin for "out of the many, one." This motto indicates that out of the separate 13 colonies, one nation was formed.
    - *Annuit Coeptis* is Latin for "He favors our undertaking." This motto indicates that God approved the nation's beginnings.
    - *Novus Ordo Seclorum* is Latin for "A new order of the ages." This motto indicates that the nation was a new way of doing things.

ACTIVITY 4. BOARD GAME

Suitcases Full of Money

The object of the Suitcases Full of Money board game is to have the most money at the end of the game. This game can be played in small groups of two to four. To play you will need:

    a calculator

    a pencil and paper

    small game pieces for each player

    1 die

    1 game board (see appendix 1) for each player

    1 center board (see appendix 1)

    1 bank board (see appendix 1)

    the Star, Moon, Sun, and Flash cards from the handouts (pp. 25–29)

    paper money (see appendix 1)

Set Up

Photocopy one set of cards for each game played. For example, a group of four players will need one set of Star cards, one set of Moon cards, one set of Sun cards (note that there are two pages of Sun cards for this game), and one set of Flash cards. Place the piles of cards facedown in their boxes on the center board. When players have drawn all the cards in one pile, they should be shuffled and replaced, facedown on the center board, to reuse.

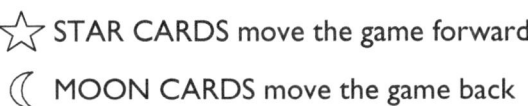

    ☆ STAR CARDS move the game forward

    ☾ MOON CARDS move the game back

    ☼ SUN CARDS help all players

    ⚡ FLASH CARDS speed a player ahead

Cut all cards and money along the lines.
Provide one game board for each player.
Photocopy enough money so there are four pages' worth for each player. At the beginning of the game, each player receives one of each of the following bills: $10, $20, $50, $100. The rest of the money is placed on the bank board for use during play.

Before starting the game, find out the currency exchange rate between the U.S. dollar and the euro, yen, and ruble for the day you are playing the game. Round that figure UP to the nearest half dollar. For example, if the euro is trading at 1 euro equals $1.75US, then round the euro up to $2.00; if the ruble is trading at 1 ruble equals $1.09US, then round it up to $1.50. Write those exchange rates down so they can be used during the game.

ACTIVITY 4. BOARD GAME (CONT.)

If the class does not have access to a computer, or for a simpler game, players can use the following rates, knowing that they do not reflect actual exchange rates:

ONE U.S. DOLLAR equals   2 euros
3 yen
4 rubles

To calculate how many euros one dollar equals, multiply 1 (dollar) x 2 (euros) for the simplified game or times the actual exchange rate if using a currency converter. In the game, that means if an item costs 3 euros, players must multiply 3 (euros) times 2 (the euro exchange rate for the simplified game) and pay $6.00US. Use pencil, paper, and calculators, if needed.

Play

Each player rolls the die to find out who plays first; whoever gets the largest number on the die plays first. Play then rotates counterclockwise.

Players travel around the board, moving forward the number of spaces on the die. If a player lands on a space with a symbol on it, that player takes a card from the pile with that symbol and follows the instructions on that card.

If a player lands on a "Flash" space and draws a card that sends him or her across the speed zone, the player moves through the center bar of the dollar sign to the next nearest shaded space at the end of the speed zone.

A player who does not have enough to pay the total owed must pay all he or she has to the bank and then skip one turn.

The game ends when the first person finishes a trip around the board and lands on "Finish." The player does not have to have an exact roll of the die to land on "Finish."

All players then count their money. The person with the most money (NOT the first player to finish) wins the game.

STAR CARDS FOR SUITCASES FULL OF MONEY GAME

(Photocopy, cut, and place facedown on center board.)

Sell your grandmother's teapot to someone in Russia for $20US. Multiply 20 times the ruble rate and receive that amount in U.S. dollars from the bank. ☆	Receive 50 yen from investment in Japan. Multiply 50 times the yen rate and receive that amount in U.S. dollars from the bank. ☆	Find sunken treasure while scuba diving in Greece. You are paid 200 euros by a Greek museum. Multiply 200 times the euro rate and receive that amount in U.S. dollars from the bank. ☆
Sell a Russian nesting doll to a collector in Russia for $100US. Multiply 100 times the ruble rate and receive that amount in U.S. dollars from the bank. ☆	Receive 100 yen for your family's recipe for sticky rice. Multiply 100 times the yen rate and receive that amount in U.S. dollars from the bank. ☆	Receive 100 euros for leading a backpacking tour of the Alps. Multiply 100 times the euro rate and receive that amount in U.S. dollars from the bank. ☆
Move ahead 1 space. ☆	Move ahead 1 space. ☆	Move ahead 1 space. ☆

MOON CARDS FOR SUITCASES FULL OF MONEY GAME

(Photocopy, cut, and place facedown on center board.)

Buy a jacket from Europe for 50 euros. Multiply 50 times the euro rate and pay the bank that amount in U.S. dollars.	Take a trip to Japan and spend 100 yen on dinner. Multiply 100 times the yen rate and pay that amount to the bank in U.S. dollars.	Buy a box of chocolate straight from France for 10 euros. Multiply 10 times the euro rate and pay that amount to the bank in U.S. dollars.
Buy a TV from Japan for 200 yen. Multiply 200 times the yen rate and pay that amount to the bank in U.S. dollars.	Buy a basket of French bread for 20 euros. Multiply 20 times the euro rate and pay that amount to the bank in U.S. dollars.	Buy a tin of Russian tea for 15 rubles. Multiply 15 times the ruble rate and pay that amount to the bank in U.S. dollars.
Have fresh sushi shipped from Japan for 100 yen. Multiply 100 times the yen rate and pay that amount to the bank in U.S. dollars.	Buy tickets to the Russian ballet for 50 rubles. Multiply 50 times the ruble rate and pay that amount to the bank in U.S. dollars.	Buy 2 train tickets on Eurail for 100 euros. Multiply 100 times the euro rate and pay that amount to the bank in U.S. dollars.

SUN CARDS FOR SUITCASES FULL OF MONEY GAME

(Photocopy, cut, and place facedown on center board.)

Each player receives $100US.	Each player receives 100 euros paid in U.S. dollars.	Each player receives 100 yen paid in U.S. dollars.
Each player receives 100 yen paid in U.S. dollars.	Each player receives 100 yen paid in U.S. dollars.	Each player receives $50US.
Each player receives 50 euros paid in U.S. dollars.	Each player receives 50 yen paid in U.S. dollars.	Each player receives 50 rubles paid in U.S. dollars.

From *Fun with Finance: Math + Literacy = Success* by Carol Peterson. Santa Barbara, CA: Libraries Unlimited. Copyright © 2009.

SUN CARDS FOR SUITCASES FULL OF MONEY GAME (CONT.)

(Photocopy, cut and place face down on center board)

Each player receives $20US.	Each player receives 20 euros paid in U.S. dollars.	Each player receives 20 yen paid in U.S. dollars.
Each player receives 10 euros paid in U.S. dollars.	Each player receives 20 rubles paid in U.S. dollars.	Each player receives $10US.
Each player receives 10 yen paid in U.S. dollars.	Each player receives 10 rubles paid in U.S. dollars.	Each player receives $5 in U.S. dollars.

FLASH CARDS FOR SUITCASES FULL OF MONEY GAME

(Photocopy, cut, and place facedown on center board.)

Advance to nearest speed zone. Cross zone and land on next STAR space after zone. Take a Star card AND receive $100US from the bank.	Advance to nearest speed zone. Cross zone and land on next STAR space after zone. Take a Star card AND receive $100US from the bank.	Advance 1 space.
Advance 1 space.	Advance 1 space.	Advance 3 spaces.
Advance 3 spaces.	Take an extra turn.	Take an extra turn.

From *Fun with Finance: Math + Literacy = Success* by Carol Peterson. Santa Barbara, CA: Libraries Unlimited. Copyright © 2009.

30 Chapter 1: Money Mania

THINK ABOUT

You may have heard someone say, "You can't take it with you." That means when you die, all the things you owned and all the money you saved stay here on Earth. Because we only have our money and things for the little while that we are alive, we might say we are just taking care of them. We should therefore be careful in managing everything we are responsible for while we are alive. That includes both money and possessions.

When we are good stewards (caretakers) of what we have, it helps develop our character. Two benefits of being good stewards of money are financial provisions for our needs and a better credit rating, which enables us to use other people's money for our own investments. Good stewardship can also lead to wealth, because the secret to being wealthy is to spend less money than you take in and then save and invest the rest.

That means handling money wisely. It also means not wasting other people's resources, such as not wasting electricity at the hotel just because someone else has to pay for it. It also means not borrowing something and returning it broken or worn out. It means not using more of the school's supplies than you really need. It also means not becoming a person who feels "entitled" to money or things just because they are available.

Different currencies have different values based on how a country's economy is doing. Just because other countries have "dollars" doesn't mean the currency is the same as ours. For example, Canada also calls its currency "dollars." Similarly, France, Switzerland, and Belgium all have a currency called "francs," although they now also use a non-country-specific currency called the "euro." In fact, euros are also called "euro dollars," but they are different from U.S. dollars!

Because the world economy works together, people who travel or do business internationally have to "exchange" money. That means they trade a certain amount of one type of currency for a certain amount of a different currency. The amount of each depends on the "currency exchange rate," which can change daily.

This currency exchange is another way some people invest. The currencies of different countries can be exchanged on a market similar to the stock market. Investors can look at such things as how good a country's economy is, how stable the country is politically, and what the interest rate is that is used by lenders in the country. They can then buy or sell that country's currency in the hope that the daily exchange rate will make money for them. This market is called "Forex," which is short for "foreign exchange."

FIND OUT MORE

Resources in Your Community

Find out whether a parent or family friend of a student works in the field of monetary systems, buys and sells currency, or collects foreign money. Ask that person to visit the class to share experiences or answer questions. For example, a bank representative might be able to explain how the U.S. Treasury selects money for destruction.

Web Sites

- Go to the U.S. Treasury Web site for information about the U.S. Mint, engraving, and Savings Bonds, at http://www.ustreas.gov/kids/.

- For an online currency converter, go to www.finance.yahoo.com/currency.

- For an online currency converter, go to www.forex-markets.com/currency-converter.htm.

- For information on individual countries, their currency, and their economies, go to the Central Intelligence Agency World Fact Book at www.cia.gov/library/publications/the-world-factbook/.

Careers

Related jobs include banker, loan officer, currency exchange trader, international politics specialist, and economist.

CHAPTER 2

෴ $ ෴

Work Wise

Subject Matter: Getting a job; employment from the point of view of an employee

Math Standards Addressed:

    Number Sense: computing numbers; multiplication; decimals; fractions

    Data Analysis: tables; charts; graphs

    Percentages

Literacy Standards Addressed:

    Vocabulary and Concept Development

    Reading Comprehension

    Spelling

Writen and Oral English Standards Addressed:

    Research and Technology

    Writing Applications

    Listening and Speaking Applications

    Verbal Communication

WHAT IS EMPLOYMENT?

Employment is when a person has a job and earns money for the work he or she does. Employment involves pride in work, doing a good job, being loyal to your employer (the person or company you work for), and having good ethics (being honest, for example). There are also practical things involved in having a job. For example, the employer is required by law to deduct certain amounts of money from your pay and must then deposit those amounts of money with the state and U.S. governmental tax authorities. These taxes are for your future benefit, but it is the employer's duty to make sure those taxes are deducted and paid for you.

SETTING/PROPS/COSTUMES

This play has six scenes for seven readers. Several friends—Jacob, Chandra, Doug, and Nicole—are together. Quizy (a friendly alien from another planet) is with them. They're discussing how Jacob would go about getting a job. Props could include paper and pencils. Costumes are not needed. Quizy's clothing and appearance is limited only by students' imagination!

Pronunciation guides may be provided in the script in square brackets. The words are divided into syllables. The syllable to be stressed is in capital letters. For example, the pronunciation guide for Quizy's name would be [QUIZ-ee]. The reader should use the pronunciation guide but not read it aloud.

CHARACTERS

NARRATOR 1

NARRATOR 2

JACOB

CHANDRA

DOUG

NICOLE

QUIZY (a friendly alien visitor who collects empty tissue boxes)

Jacob's Job

Scene 1: A Big Problem

NARRATOR 1: It looks like Jacob has a big problem.

NARRATOR 2: Let's find out what it is.

CHANDRA: What's wrong, Jacob?

DOUG: You look sad.

JACOB: I crashed my bike.

NICOLE: Are you hurt?

JACOB: No. But my bike is a wreck.

QUIZY: Will your parents buy you a new one?

JACOB: No. They're on a budget.

CHANDRA: What does that mean?

JACOB: They're trying to pay all their bills and get out of debt.

DOUG: My parents keep talking about bills.

NICOLE: I never want to ever get in debt.

QUIZY: I just want to have all the money I need to buy whatever I want.

JACOB: Dream on, Quizy.

CHANDRA: Maybe it's like that on your planet.

DOUG: That's not how it is here on Earth.

QUIZY: Well, it's possible.

JACOB: How?

From *Fun with Finance: Math + Literacy = Success* by Carol Peterson. Santa Barbara, CA: Libraries Unlimited. Copyright © 2009.

QUIZY:	I can work and save my money.
CHANDRA:	And budget.
QUIZY:	First you have to work.
DOUG:	That means a job.
NICOLE:	Then that's what you should do first, Jacob.
JACOB:	Good idea. I'll get a job and earn money for a new bike.
CHANDRA:	You'll have to save up.
JACOB:	Yes, it may take a while.
DOUG:	But then you'll have a new bike.
NICOLE:	How are you going to get a job?
QUIZY:	What can you do?
JACOB:	I'm good at math.
CHANDRA:	And you're strong.
DOUG:	And you're friendly.
NICOLE:	But you're only 12.
CHANDRA:	Who's going to hire you?
DOUG:	Have you ever had a job before?
JACOB:	No.
NICOLE:	Why would anyone hire you?
JACOB:	I think I need to figure this out.

Scene 2: Jacob's Skills

NARRATOR 1:	Too bad about Jacob's bike.
NARRATOR 2:	At least he wasn't hurt.
NARRATOR 1:	It's a good idea for him to earn money for a new bike.

NARRATOR 2:	I'd like to earn money, too.
NARRATOR 1:	Maybe we can find out how Jacob plans to earn money.
NARRATOR 2:	Let's listen.
CHANDRA:	How is the job hunting, Jacob?
JACOB:	No one wants to hire me.
DOUG:	How are you trying to get a job?
JACOB:	I go to a store and ask if they need help.
NICOLE:	What do they say?
JACOB:	They just look at me and say no.
QUIZY:	You need a plan.
NICOLE:	A plan to get a job?
DOUG:	Yes. When my brother graduated from college, he had a plan.
CHANDRA:	Did he get a job?
DOUG:	Yes, he did. And he is doing well.
JACOB:	I need a plan, too.
DOUG:	I watched what my brother did.
CHANDRA:	Can you help Jacob?
DOUG:	I'd love to.
NICOLE:	Let's make a list of what he needs to do.
CHANDRA:	I have paper.
DOUG:	Jacob, first you need to figure out what you're good at.
JACOB:	I'm good at math and spelling.
DOUG:	You're also strong.
CHANDRA:	And friendly.

NICOLE: And you're polite.

JACOB: But I've never had a job before.

QUIZY: No job that anyone paid you for.

JACOB: Except my mom and dad.

DOUG: But you have done work, right?

JACOB: I guess so.

CHANDRA: Like what?

JACOB: I mow the lawn every week.

QUIZY: So you could help a landscape company or a nursery or a park.

JACOB: I wash dishes every night.

QUIZY: So you could work in a restaurant.

JACOB: I helped my grandmother hold a yard sale.

QUIZY: So you could sell yards?

NICOLE: Quizy, a yard sale is like a garage sale.

QUIZY: So he could sell garages?

CHANDRA: It's sometimes called a tag sale.

QUIZY: So he could sell tags?

NICOLE: No, Quizy.

CHANDRA: A yard sale and a garage sale and a tag sale are just events where people sell things they no longer want.

QUIZY: Do they ever sell empty tissue boxes?

NICOLE: No, Quizy, I think you're the only one who likes empty tissue boxes.

DOUG: So when Jacob helped his grandmother, he learned how to count money and sell things.

CHANDRA: And you helped move furniture for your neighbors, Jacob.

JACOB: I guess I have more experience than I thought.

Scene 3: Thinking Through Jacob's Skills

NARRATOR 1: Jacob has lots of skills.

NARRATOR 2: He hasn't been paid for all of them.

NARRATOR 1: So would someone still want to hire him if he wasn't paid for his work?

NARRATOR 2: I'm not sure. Let's listen.

JACOB: Won't someone want to hire a person who has actually had a paying job before?

CHANDRA: Good question. I heard that employers want to hire people who have proven they're good employees.

NICOLE: That would mean having a paid job.

QUIZY: How would anyone ever get his first job if he had to have already had a job to prove he was good?

DOUG: I think employers know that everyone has to have a first job.

JACOB: What does that mean for me?

DOUG: It means that if you can show you're capable . . .

CHANDRA: And show that you're a hard worker . . .

NICOLE: And show that you've been helpful in different ways . . .

QUIZY: Then someone might give you a chance.

DOUG: If they see that you're eager and willing.

JACOB: I AM eager and willing.

CHANDRA: What should Jacob do next?

JACOB: Write a resume [REH-zoo-may].

QUIZY: Is that when your friend, Ray, goes very fast?

NICOLE: Resume. It's a French word, Quizy.

DOUG: A resume is a piece of paper that lists what you can offer an employer.

JACOB: Then I'll make a resume right now.

Scene 4: The Resume

NARRATOR 1: [laughing] "Ray zooms"! Ha! Quizy is funny.

NARRATOR 2: But it looks like Jacob is getting some good advice.

NARRATOR 1: I've never made a resume before, have you?

NARRATOR 2: No. Let's find out how to make one.

JACOB: I have a piece of paper for my resume.

CHANDRA: What kind of paper is that?

DOUG: It has spaceships on it.

JACOB: Yes, it's cool, isn't it?

QUIZY: I love it.

DOUG: The paper is good for writing to a friend but not to get a job.

JACOB: Wouldn't it show that I'm an interesting person?

QUIZY: I think you're VERY interesting.

NICOLE: Maybe, but it wouldn't show that you're businesslike.

JACOB: Why would I want to do that?

DOUG: Because you want to get a job with a business, right?

JACOB: I was thinking about applying at Harry's Hardware.

CHANDRA: Harry's Hardware is a business.

JACOB: Oh, that's right. So I need to be businesslike.

NICOLE: That means no spaceship paper.

DOUG: But for now, you can write on it.

JACOB: But you said . . .

DOUG: Later you can type it up on the computer.

QUIZY: And print it out on spaceship paper?

CHANDRA: No spaceships.

JACOB: OK. What do I need on my resume?

DOUG: Your name first.

JACOB: My first name?

DOUG: Your first name AND your last name.

JACOB: First and last names. Got it.

DOUG: And your address and phone number.

CHANDRA: Why does Jacob need that?

NICOLE: Probably so they know how to get a hold of him.

QUIZY: When they want to tell him he's hired?

DOUG: Right.

CHANDRA: Now what?

JACOB: Oh, I know. I write down how much they should pay me.

DOUG: No.

NICOLE: Why not? That's why he wants a job.

JACOB: Yes, but a resume is used to sell them on why THEY should want you.

CHANDRA: You already know YOU want a job.

DOUG: Think of a resume as like a TV commercial.

NICOLE: What do you mean?

JACOB: When you see a commercial, they tell you what's great about the product.

QUIZY:	And that makes you want to buy it.
CHANDRA:	So when you give an employer a resume . . .
QUIZY:	It makes them see why they should buy you.
NICOLE:	Or hire you.
JACOB:	So I list those things we talked about. The things I've done.
DOUG:	Write a title: Skills. List what you're good at.
CHANDRA:	Math. Spelling.
NICOLE:	Strength. Friendliness.
DOUG:	Then write a title: Experience.
CHANDRA:	And list the things you do, Jacob, as regular chores.
NICOLE:	And projects you've worked on.
JACOB:	Then describe how each of those skills or experiences can help Harry's Hardware.
JACOB:	[writing] OK.
DOUG:	Now go and type it up.
CHANDRA:	We'll wait here.
QUIZY:	Jacob, can I borrow a sheet of your spaceship paper?
JACOB:	Why, Quizy?
QUIZY:	For MY resume.
NICOLE:	But it's not businesslike.
QUIZY:	It is for ME.
DOUG:	Quizy is right.
CHANDRA:	It's perfect for him!

Scene 5: The Next Step

NARRATOR 1: I think I see how the resume works.

NARRATOR 2: It's not to tell the employer what YOU want.

NARRATOR 1: It's to show the employer what you can do for HIM.

NARRATOR 2: I think if I were an employer I'd want to hire someone who was looking at how he could help me.

NARRATOR 1: Instead of what he can get out of me.

NARRATOR 2: Let's find out what Jacob should do next.

JACOB: Here's my resume.

CHANDRA: It looks good.

NICOLE: All the words are spelled correctly.

QUIZY: Because Jacob is a good speller!

DOUG: It's very neat.

JACOB: Are you sure plain white paper is OK?

QUIZY: It looks so . . . plain.

NICOLE: It looks businesslike.

JACOB: OK. Then wish me luck.

QUIZY: Where are you going?

JACOB: I'm going to Harry's Hardware.

CHANDRA: Right now?

JACOB: Yes.

DOUG: Do you have an appointment?

JACOB: What do you mean?

DOUG: I mean did you call Harry's Hardware?

CHANDRA: Why would he do that?

JACOB: I was just going to go over there.

NICOLE: What if Harry isn't there?

JACOB: I didn't think of that.

CHANDRA: In fact, sometimes the store closes at lunchtime.

DOUG: Maybe no one is there.

JACOB: What do I do then? Just hang around outside the store?

DOUG: No, first phone the store and ask if you can speak with Harry.

NICOLE: In fact, you should ask for Mr. Miller.

CHANDRA: Who is Mr. Miller?

NICOLE: He's the owner of Harry's Hardware.

DOUG: Mr. Miller is Harry?

NICOLE: Yes, his name is Harry Miller. But you should call him Mr. Miller.

CHANDRA: Because it's more businesslike.

JACOB: Why should I phone at all? I already know they need help.

QUIZY: Yes, they have a sign saying they need part-time workers.

CHANDRA: That's a good sign.

QUIZY: Yes, I just said they had a sign.

CHANDRA: I meant the fact there is a sign saying they need help is a good sign that Jacob has a better chance of getting a job there.

QUIZY: So a sign is a good sign?

CHANDRA: Yes, Quizy.

QUIZY: Then the sign is good.

CHANDRA: Yes.

QUIZY: So the good sign is a good sign.

CHANDRA: [sighing] Yes, Quizy.

Scene 6: Going to the Interview

NARRATOR 1: There's a lot to do before you even go to the interview.

NARRATOR 2: Yes, there is!

NICOLE: You have to be businesslike when trying to get a job.

DOUG: And part of being businesslike is politely making an appointment.

JACOB: I'll go call them and then I'll go.

CHANDRA: You're not going to wear that to the interview, are you?

JACOB: What's wrong with what I'm wearing?

DOUG: That shirt you're wearing is wrong.

NICOLE: It has a picture of a spaceship on the front.

QUIZY: I love it!

CHANDRA: The spaceship isn't very businesslike.

QUIZY: It would have matched the paper, though.

JACOB: Most of my shirts have pictures on them.

DOUG: Then change into one that doesn't have catsup slopped down the front.

JACOB: [wiping his shirt] Oh.

NICOLE: And comb your hair so it isn't sticking up in back.

JACOB: [smoothing his hair] Oh.

CHANDRA: You want to make a good impression.

NICOLE: You want to show that you're neat.

CHANDRA: And that you care about yourself.

JACOB: I don't think looking good is part of the job description.

DOUG: But if Harry has two people that he likes equally . . .

JACOB: He might just decide to go with the person who has made an effort to present himself well.

DOUG: And make sure you wash your hands.

JACOB: Why?

DOUG: So that when you shake Harry's hand, he doesn't get all sticky.

JACOB: Shake his hand?

DOUG: Remember—be businesslike.

JACOB: [sighing] Right.

QUIZY: What's wrong, Jacob?

JACOB: I've never shaken anyone's hand before.

QUIZY: I'll show you how. [shaking all over]

CHANDRA: No, Quizy. You're shaking your whole body.

QUIZY: Yes, it's much better than only shaking your hand.

DOUG: Let's practice, Jacob. The handshake should be firm.

NICOLE: To show your confidence.

DOUG: But not hard.

CHANDRA: Because you want to show you're friendly.

QUIZY: But he also wants to show he's strong.

DOUG: But not too strong. He's not applying for a job as a wrestler.

EVERYONE: [Everyone practices shaking hands with each other.]

JACOB: OK. I've got a T-shirt that's clean and doesn't have any pictures on it. It's plain.

CHANDRA: Like the paper.

JACOB: I'll call Harry's Hardware and comb my hair and wash my hands.

NICOLE: To show you're businesslike.

JACOB: Then I'll be ready?

DOUG: Yes.

JACOB: Is there anything else I should know before I talk with Harry?

CHANDRA: Be polite.

NICOLE: And friendly.

DOUG: And eager.

CHANDRA: And businesslike.

NICOLE: Remember to think about what you can offer Harry if he hires you.

CHANDRA: Not what you want from him.

DOUG: Good luck!

QUIZY: Wait, Jacob. Can I borrow your shirt?

JACOB: This one?

QUIZY: Yes, the one with the spaceship.

CHANDRA: Why?

QUIZY: It matches the spaceship paper for my resume.

NICOLE: What are you going to do, Quizy?

QUIZY: I'm looking for a job.

DOUG: What kind of a job?

QUIZY: I don't know. But I already have a spaceship.

JACOB: Sure, Quizy. You can borrow my T-shirt and all the spaceship paper you want.

DOUG: In your case, Quizy, spaceship paper and spaceship T-shirts ARE businesslike!

GLOSSARY

Employee: Person hired by another person or business to perform work, who is paid a salary or wage.

Employer: Person or business that agrees to pay a person a wage for time or work done.

Gross pay: The total amount of pay due an employee before subtracting deductions such as taxes and benefits.

Interview: A meeting between an employer and a person applying for a job.

Net pay: The amount of pay due an employee after subtracting deductions.

Payroll deductions: Amounts subtracted from an employee's paycheck. Includes such things as taxes, insurance, and union dues.

Resume: A one- or two-page written summary of skills and experience a person can offer to an employer.

DOING TO UNDERSTAND

The following activities are included as handouts:

1. Payroll Deductions
2. Create an Employment Package
3. Job Interview
4. Future Careers
5. Board Game

ACTIVITY 1. PAYROLL DEDUCTIONS

When you have a job, you do not receive all of the money you have earned. The employer (your boss) is required to withhold (take out) taxes and other expenses he pays on your behalf. These items are called payroll deductions and include state and federal (U.S.) taxes, social security, insurance (for full-time employees), and union dues. Find out what your state minimum wage is. Find out what the state and federal payroll taxes are.

Compute the following: If you earned an hourly wage of $10 an hour and worked two hours a day for three days a week, how much would you have earned? That amount is your gross pay.

Now assume that federal income tax is 20 percent of your gross pay, state income tax is 9 percent, social security is 7.5 percent, and insurance costs $5 per week. Calculate each of those amounts. Then deduct them amounts from the gross pay. The remainder is the net pay you would receive in your paycheck.

If you worked the same number of hours every week for the same pay, how much would you earn in one month? In one year (based on 52 weeks)? Fill in the following chart to show how one week's payroll is calculated.

Pay Calculation (per Week)

Gross pay: ($10 x 2 hours x 3 days)	$	
Deductions:		
Federal tax (20%)	$	
State tax (9%)	$	
Social Security (7.5%)	$	
Insurance	$ 5.00	
Total deductions	$	
Net pay (Gross minus deductions)		$

ACTIVITY 2. CREATE AN EMPLOYMENT PACKAGE

Gather all the information you will need to give an employer so that you can show you are prepared. Include your social security number, address, telephone number, and the specific hours and days of the week you are able to work at a job. Jot down information about your education, work experience, cocurricular activities (school leadership, classroom duties, school honors), and extracurricular activities (club memberships, church, hobbies). This is the information you would take with you to an interview in case you need to complete an employment application.

Create a resume using the template on page 51. As a class, brainstorm ideas to make your resume appealing, such as using a neat computer typeface; leaving enough white space in the margins and between paragraph; and not including things like gender, height, weight, eye color, etc. Use plain white paper.

Then prepare a typed cover letter using a business style similar to the example on page 52. Use your personal information. This letter would be handed or mailed to the employer along with the resume. Use the example to help you create your own letter. In the first paragraph, mention the job you are applying for, how you learned about it, and if someone the employer knows told you about the job.

In the second paragraph, acknowledge the skills required for the job and what skills and experience you have that will meet those needs.

In the final paragraph, refer to your resume, which you will enclose, and say you'll call to set up an interview.

RESUME

Quizy Quasar
42 Grindon Grove
Planet Zirtron   Phone: (999) 999-9999

I am seeking employment as a spaceship operator to transport cargo or humans between Earth and Planet Zirtron.

SKILLS

Honesty   Quick learner
Leadership   Curiosity

WORK EXPERIENCE

2001–Present (Earth time)   Multiple space flights between Planet Zirtron and Earth
1999–2001 (Earth time)   Starliner captain for Galaxy Getaways touring the Norlac Nebula

EDUCATION

1999 (Earth time)   Certificate of Completion, Zirtron Flight School
1995 (Earth time)   Graduated, Zirtron Space Academy
1990 (Earth time)   Graduated, Zirtron Middle School

HOBBIES

Founding member, Tissue Box Treasure Club (Earth Chapter)
Collecting empty tissue boxes
Exploring Earth and neighboring planets

COVER LETTER

YOUR NAME
Your street address
Your city, state, zip code
Your phone number

Today's date

First and last name of the person in charge of hiring
Business name
Business street address
Business city address, state, and zip code

Application for Employment

Dear Mr. [or Ms.] [insert last name]:

    I am looking for a job as [insert description or title]. I am a hard worker, honest, and eager to help your business.

    Enclosed is my resume. My skills of [list them] and experience doing [list them] would make me a valuable employee.

    I will phone you in a few days to arrange an interview to see how I can be part of your team.

    Thank you for your consideration.

                                        Very truly yours,

                                        [Your Name]

ACTIVITY 3. JOB INTERVIEW

Form teams of two people and practice interviews. Have one person be the employer who wants to hire someone and the other person be the applicant hoping to get the job. Then switch places. Set up the format ahead of time using a real company that students can learn about.

Here are some tips for the person looking for a job:

- Learn as much as possible about the company before the interview (including anyone you know who works there). This will help you look knowledgeable and enthusiastic.
- Pay attention to grooming and appearance. Be neat and clean.
- Be on time or a little early.
- Bring a copy of your resume even if you have already given it to the employer.
- Prepare a list of any questions you have about the company, but don't ask them until the end of the interview, when the employer asks if you have any questions.
- Remain enthusiastic and polite.
- Always thank the person interviewing you for his time.
- Follow up in a few days with a personal thank-you note.

The employer will be asking himself these questions:

- How alert is the person?
- Did he or she respond simply, or ramble?
- Did he or she show depth when communicating?
- Has he or she shown good judgment or common sense?
- Was he or she enthusiastic?
- Was he or she respectful?
- Did he or she make good eye contact?

Think through the following typical questions an employer may ask so you can be prepared and appear confident during an interview.

- What are your long-term and short-term goals?
- How are you preparing yourself to achieve your goals?
- What do you want to do in life?
- How would you describe your strengths and weaknesses?
- What skills do you have that you think will make you successful?
- How do you think you can contribute to this business?
- Why should I hire you?

ACTIVITY 3. JOB INTERVIEW (CONT.)

Here is a sample of a thank-you letter that you would send to the employer after being interviewed.

> YOUR NAME
> Your street address
> Your city, state, and zip code
> Your phone number
>
> Date
>
> First and last name of person who interviewed you
> Business name
> Business street address
> Business city, state, and zip code
>
> Regarding [Job title]
>
> Dear Mr. [or Ms.] [insert last name]:
>
> Thank you for meeting with me on [insert date]. I enjoyed talking with you about how I could help [insert name of business].
>
> Please let me know if you have any more questions.
>
> I look forward to hearing from you.
>
> Sincerely,
>
> [Your Name]

ACTIVITY 4. FUTURE CAREERS

Read through the "help wanted" ads in the newspaper. Create a chart showing jobs you might be interested in one day, what skills are required, and how much those jobs pay.

Think about how you would work toward getting the education, skills, and experience so that one day you might be hired for a similar job. Find someone who has the job that you might want one day. Interview that person to find out how he prepared for that job and ask his advice on what you should do to prepare for a similar job in the future. Use this interview experience as practice for your own job interview.

Report what you learned to the class.

ACTIVITY 5. BOARD GAME

Work Wise

The object of the Work Wise board game is to have the most money at the end of the game. This game can be played in small groups of two to four. To play you need:

- a calculator
- a pencil and paper
- small game pieces for each player
- 1 die
- 1 game board (see appendix 1) for each player
- 1 center board (see appendix 1)
- 1 bank board (see appendix 1)
- the Star, Moon, Sun, and Flash cards from the handouts (pp. 57–60)
- paper money (see appendix 1)

Set Up

Provide one game board for each player. Photocopy the cards. For the Work Wise Game, a group of four players will need one set of Star cards, one set of Moon cards, one set of Sun cards, and one set of Flash cards. Cut all cards and money along the lines.

Place the piles of cards facedown in their boxes on the center board. When players have drawn all the cards in one pile, they should be shuffled and replaced, facedown on the center board, to reuse.

☆ STAR CARDS move the game forward

☾ MOON CARDS move the game back

☼ SUN CARDS help all players

⚡ FLASH CARDS speed a player ahead

Play

Each player rolls the die to find out who plays first; whoever gets the largest number on the die plays first. Play then rotates counterclockwise.

Players travel around the board, moving forward the number of spaces on the die. If a player lands on a space with a symbol on it, that player takes a card from the pile with that symbol and follows the instructions on that card.

If a player lands on a "Flash" space and draws a card that sends him or her across the speed zone, that player moves through the center bar of the dollar sign to the next nearest shaded space at the end of the speed zone.

A player who does not have enough to pay the total owed must pay all he or she has to the bank and then skip one turn.

The game ends when the first person finishes a trip around the board and lands on "Finish." The player does not have to have an exact roll of the die to land on "Finish."

All players then count their money. The person with the most money (NOT the first player to finish) wins the game.

STAR CARDS FOR WORK WISE GAME

(Photocopy, cut, and place facedown on center board.)

If you didn't have a job before, now you do! You earn $10 an hour at Harry's Hardware. Receive $25 from the bank right now. If this job pays more than your old job, from now on you work for Harry! 	If you didn't have a job before, now you do! You earn $8 an hour at Sporty's Sport Shop. Receive $15 from the bank right now. If this job pays more than your old job, from now on you work for Sporty's! 	If you didn't have a job before, now you do! You earn $7 an hour at Walt's Warehouse. Receive $18 from the bank right now. If this job pays more than your old job, from now on you work for Walt's! 
If you didn't have a job before, now you do, cleaning up after your neighbor's dog. You will be paid $10 a week. If you land on a MOON space, you don't have to deduct taxes or move backward—just receive $10. And also receive $10 from the bank right now. 	If you didn't have a job before, now you do! You babysit the neighbors. You will be paid $20 a week. If you land on a MOON space, you don't have to deduct taxes or move backward—just receive $20 each time. And also receive $20 from the bank right now. 	If you didn't have a job before, now you do! You earn $10 an hour at Meal Mart. Receive $20 from the bank right now. If this job pays more than your old job, from now on you work for Meal Mart! 
If you didn't have a job before, now you do! You earn $20 an hour at Busy Business. Receive $50 from the bank right now. If this job pays more than your old job, from now on you work for Busy Business! 	You have an interview! Move ahead 3 spaces.	You have an interview! Move ahead 3 spaces.

MOON CARDS FOR WORK WISE GAME

(Photocopy, cut, and place facedown on center board.)

Payday! You've earned $50 but have to pay 4% of that in taxes. What is your net pay? Figure out what your paycheck is and receive that amount from the bank. If you don't have a job yet, move back 1 space.	Payday! You've earned $50 but have to pay 4% of that in taxes. What is your net pay? Figure out what your paycheck is and receive that amount from the bank. If you don't have a job yet, move back 1 space.	Payday! You earned $100 this week but you have to pay 4% in taxes. What is your net pay? Figure out what your paycheck is and receive that amount from the bank. If you don't have a job yet, move back 1 space.
Payday! You earned $100 this week but you have to pay 4% in taxes. What is your net pay? Figure out what your paycheck is and receive that amount from the bank. If you don't have a job yet, move back 1 space.	Payday! You earned $200 this week but you have to pay 4% in taxes. What is your net pay? Figure out what your paycheck is and receive that amount from the bank. If you don't have a job yet, move back 1 space.	Payday! You earned $200 this week but you have to pay 4% in taxes. What is your net pay? Figure out what your paycheck is and receive that amount from the bank. If you don't have a job yet, move back 1 space.
If you don't have a job yet, move BACK to the nearest STAR space.	If you don't have a job yet, move BACK to the nearest STAR space.	If you don't have a job yet, move BACK to the nearest STAR space.

SUN CARDS FOR THE WORK WISE GAME

(Photocopy, cut, and place facedown on center board.)

Everybody gets a bonus! All players receive $20.	Everybody gets a bonus! All players receive $20.	Everybody gets a bonus! All players receive $20.
Everyone moves ahead 2 spaces and takes a card for the space they land on.	Everyone moves ahead 2 spaces and takes a card for the space they land on.	Everyone moves ahead 2 spaces and takes a card for the space they land on.
Your employer needs extra help and hires all players for one week. All players receive $50 this turn.	Your employer needs extra help and hires all players for one week. All players receive $50 this turn.	Your employer needs extra help and hires all players for one week. All players receive $50 this turn.

From *Fun with Finance: Math + Literacy = Success* by Carol Peterson. Santa Barbara, CA: Libraries Unlimited. Copyright © 2009.

FLASH CARDS FOR WORK WISE GAME

(Photocopy, cut, and place facedown on center board.)

Advance to nearest speed zone. Cross zone and land on next STAR space after zone. Take a Star card AND receive $100 from the bank.	Advance to nearest speed zone. Cross zone and land on next STAR space after zone. Take a Star card AND receive $100 from the bank.	You have an interview! Advance to nearest STAR space and receive $50 plus what the Star card says.
You have an interview! Advance to nearest STAR space and receive $50 plus what the Star card says.	You have an interview! Advance to nearest STAR space and receive $50 plus what the Star card says.	You have an interview! Advance to nearest STAR space and receive $20 plus what the Star card says.
You have an interview! Advance to nearest STAR space and receive $20 plus what the Star card says.	Take an extra turn.	Take an extra turn.

60   From *Fun with Finance: Math + Literacy = Success* by Carol Peterson. Santa Barbara, CA: Libraries Unlimited. Copyright © 2009.

THINK ABOUT

Employment means working for another person or business in exchange for pay. The employee (the worker) trades his or her time and skills for something of value (usually money). The employer (the person or business that hires the worker) is responsible for paying the employee's wages and for depositing taxes and other benefit payments on behalf of the worker with the appropriate governmental and private entities. The employer is also responsible for making sure the workplace is safe and for obeying all laws relating to employment and business operations.

An employee also has responsibilities to the employer. In addition to doing the job he or she is hired to do, an employee has the responsibility to be honest, to work hard, and to be respectful of other workers and the employer.

FIND OUT MORE

Resources in Your Community

Find out whether a parent or family friend of a student works in the field of human resources, employment taxes, or benefits. Ask that person to visit the class to share experiences or answer questions. Or invite a business owner to share what he or she looks for when hiring an employee.

Web Sites

- For an alphabetical list of jobs, pay, and skills needed for various jobs, go to the U.S. Department of Labor Statistics Web site at http://www.bls.gov/OCO/.
- Search the Web for the keywords "resume," "job search tips," and "interview tips."

Careers

Possible careers are unlimited. Think about what you would like to do. Learn about what you need to do to qualify for that career. Spend time making a plan to gain the necessary education, skill, and experience.

CHAPTER 3

Booming Businesses

Subject Matter: Legal entities; jobs from the point of view of employer

Math Standards Addressed:

Number Sense: computing numbers; multiplication; decimals; fractions

Data Analysis: tables; charts; graphs

Percentages

Literacy Standards Addressed:

Vocabulary and Concept Development

Reading Comprehension

Spelling

Written and Oral English Standards Addressed:

Listening and Speaking Applications

Verbal Communication

Research and Technology

WHAT IS A BUSINESS?

A *business* is an entity that produces a product or provides a service to others for profit. One type of business is simply a person doing business under a business name. That is called a "fictitious" (made up) business. Or a business could be a partnership of two or more people. Or a business could be a corporation (often called a company). Each of these types of business entities has very specific legal requirements.

64   Chapter 3: Booming Businesses

Most businesses hire people to work for them, which makes them *employers*. An employer has many specific legal responsibilities on behalf of and for its employees, including payroll; collecting and paying employment taxes for the employees; and deducting and paying medical, life, and workers' compensation insurance (in case of injury to an employee on the job) for employees.

SETTING/PROPS/COSTUMES

This play has three scenes for seven readers. Several friends—Doug, Nicole, Jacob, and Chandra—are together. Quizy (a friendly alien from another planet) is with them. They're discussing Doug's business. Props could include calculators, paper, and pencils Costumes are not needed. Quizy's clothing and appearance is limited only by students' imagination!

Pronunciation guides may be provided in the script in square brackets. The words are divided into syllables. The syllable to be stressed is in capital letters. For example, the pronunciation guide for Quizy's name would be [QUIZ-ee]. The reader should use the pronunciation guide but not read it aloud.

CHARACTERS

NARRATOR 1

NARRATOR 2

DOUG

NICOLE

JACOB

CHANDRA

QUIZY (a friendly alien visitor who collects empty tissue boxes)

Monkey Business

Scene 1: The Business

NARRATOR 1: Doug, Nicole, Jacob, and Chandra are looking at something.

NARRATOR 2: Quizy is here, too.

NARRATOR 1: I wonder what's going on.

NARRATOR 2: Let's find out.

DOUG: Here's a flyer about my new business.

NICOLE: You have a business?

JACOB: What is it?

DOUG: I take care of pets for people.

CHANDRA: You're a pet sitter?

QUIZY: That can't be good.

DOUG: Why not?

QUIZY: It must hurt.

NICOLE: Why would it hurt?

QUIZY: When you sit on the pets.

JACOB: He doesn't SIT on the pets.

CHANDRA: No, it's like a baby sitter.

DOUG: I take care of pets when people are gone.

QUIZY: Doesn't your mom object?

NICOLE: What would she object to?

QUIZY: All those animals in your house.

JACOB:	No, Quizy, the pets don't come to HIS house.
CHANDRA:	Doug goes to THEIR house.
DOUG:	Sometimes the pets come to my house.
NICOLE:	Really? When?
DOUG:	When I'm taking care of a turtle or a hamster.
JACOB:	What about a dog or a cat?
DOUG:	Then I would go to their house to take care of them.
QUIZY:	Your dad would let you stay there while the people are gone?
DOUG:	No, I'd just go feed the pets and check on them every day.
NICOLE:	And play with them?
DOUG:	Of course! That's part of my job, too.
JACOB:	Mr. Jamison has a pet monkey.
CHANDRA:	Yes, its name is Mikey.
NICOLE:	Mikey the monkey?
JACOB:	Yes. Maybe Mr. Jamison will need a pet sitter.
DOUG:	I'm not sure I would know how to take care of a monkey.
CHANDRA:	Would your mother let you bring the monkey home?
QUIZY:	She shouldn't!
NICOLE:	Why not?
QUIZY:	Monkeys are too businesslike.
JACOB:	Too businesslike?
CHANDRA:	What do you mean, Quizy?
QUIZY:	Haven't you ever heard of monkey business?
NICOLE:	I think monkey business just means something is silly.

QUIZY:	Monkeys sure are silly.
JACOB:	Well, Doug's business isn't silly.
DOUG:	In fact, I have so many pets to take care of that I'm almost too busy.
CHANDRA:	Do you need any help in your business?
DOUG:	I could always use help. Would you like to join my business?
CHANDRA:	Yes, I would.
NICOLE:	I would, too.
JACOB:	We could go together to take care of the pets.
NICOLE:	I could feed them.
JACOB:	I could play with them.
CHANDRA:	What else needs to be done?
DOUG:	Clean up the poop.
CHANDRA:	Oh. I'm not sure I want that job.
NICOLE:	Then let's alternate.
JACOB:	Yes, we can switch jobs each day.
QUIZY:	I'll take care of the monkey business.
DOUG:	Quizy, I think you already do take care of the monkey business.
NICOLE:	Yes, you silly alien!

Scene 2: Setting up the Business

NARRATOR 1:	A pet sitting business is a great idea.
NARRATOR 2:	I love animals.
NARRATOR 1:	So do I. And I worry about my pets when we go on vacation.

NARRATOR 2: It would be nice to know someone is taking care of them.

NARRATOR 1: I wonder what else Doug can tell us about his business.

NARRATOR 2: Let's find out.

QUIZY: I'm not so silly that I don't know you need an attorney.

DOUG: Why do we need an attorney, Quizy?

QUIZY: To set up your business.

NICOLE: Why do we need help?

QUIZY: Well, are you going to have a corporation?

DOUG: What's that?

JACOB: Oh, I know. It's a legal entity—almost like a person. Sometimes it's called a company.

CHANDRA: You have to file papers with your state to be an official corporation.

DOUG: That sounds too complicated.

NICOLE: We just want to take care of pets.

QUIZY: Or maybe you want to be a sole proprietor.

DOUG: What's that?

JACOB: Just one person running a business.

CHANDRA: But we have five of us.

QUIZY: Then maybe you need to be a partnership.

DOUG: Well, we would be partners, I guess.

QUIZY: But are you a limited partnership or a general partnership?

NICOLE: What's the difference?

JACOB: It has to do with who has the right to make decisions.

CHANDRA: I think we should all have the right.

DOUG: After all, the only decision we'll be making is whose turn it is to clean up the poop.

JACOB: Then we could be a general partnership.

NICOLE: General? Like in the army?

CHANDRA: No, general, like "in general." As opposed to "specific."

QUIZY: Except that it is specifically a war against poop.

JACOB: Then we need to make sure you know who will collect the money.

CHANDRA: That's called accounts receivable.

DOUG: Why is it called that?

JACOB: Because each person you take care of their pets for will be an account.

CHANDRA: And the money you receive is a "receivable."

JACOB: And then you have accounts payable.

NICOLE: What's that?

CHANDRA: Things like if you buy any pet food.

DOUG: The owners will have that.

JACOB: Or a pet toy.

NICOLE: We might buy a toy.

QUIZY: Or if the monkey gets loose.

JACOB: Why would that cost anything?

QUIZY: Because it might practice karate in your mother's living room.

CHANDRA: What?

QUIZY: And knock over her vase.

DOUG: Quizy.

QUIZY: And you have to buy a new vase.

NICOLE: OK, Quizy. We get the idea.

JACOB: Accounts payable are just things you might have to buy.

CHANDRA: And then you need a HR person.

DOUG: HR? What does that mean?

JACOB: HR stands for human resources.

NICOLE: What is that?

CHANDRA: Employees.

DOUG: Are we employees?

JACOB: We would be employees if our business was a corporation.

NICOLE: But it's not.

CHANDRA: Or three of us would be employees if the business was a sole proprietorship of the fourth person.

DOUG: But we've already decided to be partners.

JACOB: Then we won't need to deduct payroll taxes.

NICOLE: Payroll taxes?

QUIZY: Or have workers' compensation insurance.

DOUG: What's that?

QUIZY: In case the monkey bites your finger off.

CHANDRA: Ouch!

QUIZY: And we won't have to have health insurance.

NICOLE: What?

QUIZY: Or vacations or timecards or sick days or . . .

JACOB: Quizy, stop!

Scene 3: Just a Little Business

NARRATOR 1: I didn't know there were so many kinds of businesses.

NARRATOR 2: Or so many legal things an employer has to do.

NARRATOR 1: I'm not sure I still want to have a business.

NARRATOR 2: Me either. Maybe the kids have another idea.

DOUG: We just want to have a business to take care of pets.

NICOLE: We're just kids.

JACOB: We're not going to move away from home and support ourselves.

CHANDRA: We just want to help people

DOUG: And get some spending money. Do we really need to know all that legal stuff?

QUIZY: You'll probably be OK for now.

NICOLE: Without a corporation?

JACOB: Without a sole proprietorship?

CHANDRA: Without a partnership?

DOUG: Without payroll taxes?

NICOLE: Without human resources?

JACOB: Without workers' compensation?

CHANDRA: Without health insurance?

DOUG: Without vacations?

NICOLE: Without timecards?

JACOB: Without sick days?

QUIZY: Yes. For now.

CHANDRA: Maybe when we're older, we'll want to have a real business.

DOUG: Then we'll have to pay attention to all those legal things.

NICOLE: I never knew you had to even do anything like that.

JACOB: There sure are a lot of laws.

CHANDRA: Just to have a business.

DOUG: But I suppose it is a way to protect people.

NICOLE: To make sure employees are taken care of.

JACOB: And to make sure the business taxes are paid.

DOUG: The business has to pay taxes, too?

NICOLE: On the money it brings in?

JACOB: Yes, on the accounts receivable.

DOUG: Then for now, I'm glad we're still kids.

NICOLE: And all we're doing is taking care of dogs and cats.

JACOB: And turtles and hamsters.

CHANDRA: And monkeys.

DOUG: All that other stuff would be silly for our little business.

NICOLE: Right, I'm glad we don't need an attorney for a dog/cat/turtle/hamster/monkey business.

QUIZY: That's it!

JACOB: What's it?

QUIZY: I've been trying to figure out a good name for your business. It's perfect!

CHANDRA: What's perfect?

QUIZY: The name—Monkey Business!

DOUG: I like it.

NICOLE: Me, too.

JACOB: It's the perfect name.

QUIZY: Here's the new rule: the alien who names the business doesn't have to pick up the poop.

GLOSSARY

Accounts payable: Moneys that must be paid out by a business.

Accounts receivable: Moneys that are received by a business.

Business: A legal entity set up to provide products or services for profit.

Corporation: An entity set up with the legal rights and duties of an individual.

Employee: A person who works for another person or business for wages.

Employer: A person or business that pays wages to another person or business for work performed.

Gross: The total before subtracting costs.

Net: The total after subtracting costs.

Partnership: A legal relationship between two or more people for the purpose of conducting business.

General partnership: A specific legal form of partnership in which all partners have equal rights and liabilities.

Limited partnership: A specific legal form of partnership in which one partner has authority for decisions and the other partners have limited rights and liabilities.

DOING TO UNDERSTAND

The following activities are included as handouts:

1. Gross Wage
2. Employee Taxes
3. Insurance Deductions
4. The Check Stub and Paycheck
5. Starting a Business
6. Board Game

ACTIVITY 1. GROSS WAGE

Find out what the current minimum wage is for your state. Find out what the rate is for the entire country. How do they compare? The higher of the two rates is the one the employer must use.

Calculate how much a person would earn at that rate working eight hours a day for five days a week. Multiply that by four to estimate the amount a person would be paid in one month. Multiply that by 12. How much would the person make in a year?

These figures are the employee's GROSS WAGE. That means it is the amount the employee made; but it will usually not be the amount the employee receives, because taxes and other items must first be subtracted.

ACTIVITY 2. EMPLOYEE TAXES

Now that you have a figure from Activity 1 for the employee's gross wage, let's calculate employee taxes. Find out how much the federal income tax rate is. You can find this out by going online at www.irs.gov. Then find out what the personal income tax rate is in your state. Assume that the employee takes ZERO deductions. That means she has no one she must take care of and therefore expects not to lessen her tax payments by any amount based on her taking care of other people.

If the tax is in the form of a percentage, multiply the WEEKLY GROSS WAGE times each of those tax rates. If the tax is listed on a table, locate those numbers.

Another type of tax is FICA. This stands for Federal Insurance Contributions Act. It is usually just called Social Security and refers to money set aside into a U.S. government account for the employee's old age. The FICA rate may change slightly each year, but for this activity, assume it is 8 percent. Multiply the gross wages by 8 percent.

There may be local taxes also. But for this activity, we will assume only these three taxes.

ACTIVITY 3. INSURANCE DEDUCTIONS

In addition to taxes, there may be other items the employer is required to deduct from an employee's wages. Unemployment insurance is one such item. This amount is deposited by the employer into a state account in the event the employer is forced to cut back the employee's job. This account then pays the employee unemployment wages while she looks for a new job. For this activity, assume a rate of 1 percent. Multiply the GROSS WAGE amount from Activity 1 by 1 percent.

In addition, full-time employees are often able to pay for less expensive health insurance through their employer. That amount would also be deducted from the gross wages in Activity 1 and paid directly by the employer to the health insurance provider. We will assume that there is no health insurance in this case.

There may also be retirement plans, union dues, or other accounts for the employee's benefit that are deducted and paid by the employer. We will not assume any of those for this activity.

ACTIVITY 4. THE CHECK STUB AND PAYCHECK

An employee's "check stub" is the part of the paycheck that has information about how much an employee is being paid. Now that you have the deductions figured out for the wages, fill in the check stub. Indicate the number of hours, the rate of pay, and the gross wages from Activity 1. Then list the amounts of the taxes and other deductions from Activities 2 and 3. Subtract them from the total and fill in the amount of the NET WAGE. The net wage is the amount the employee would receive.

An employer might want to include other information, such as the employee's social security number and the amounts of taxes and wages paid so far that year.

Then fill out the payroll check.

"Pay to the order of" means whom you are paying. On that line the employer would fill in the name of the employee (both first and last names).

Write in the dollar amount next to the dollar sign, like this: $156.37.

Then on the long line underneath the name of the person you are writing the check to, write the amount again, using words instead of just numbers. So you would write $156.37 like this:

ONE HUNDRED FIFTY-SIX AND 37/100

The word "dollars" is usually already printed on the check at the end of that line.

Then the employer would sign the check on the line at the bottom right-hand corner of the check.

That is also how you would fill out checks when you have your own checking account. When a person receives a check, she may either deposit the check into a bank account or exchange it for cash. To do either, she has to turn the check over and turn it vertically. On the back side of the check, near the top, she signs her name in cursive, exactly as it was written out on the front. Have you ever received a check as a gift and done this at the bank?

# HOURS WORKED:	_____
PAY RATE:	_____
TOTAL GROSS WAGES:	_____
Federal tax:	_____
State tax:	_____
FICA:	_____
Unemployment:	_____
Total deductions:	_____
NET PAY: _____	

MONKEY BUSINESS
1234 Main Street
Hometown, IA   Date _____

Pay to the order of _____ $_____

_____ DOLLARS

_____

From Fun with Finance: Math + Literacy = Success by Carol Peterson. Santa Barbara, CA: Libraries Unlimited. Copyright © 2009.

ACTIVITY 5. STARTING A BUSINESS

As a class, discuss the different types of business entities. Why would a business want to be each one? What types of businesses might work best for each legal entity? Talk about the steps you would have to take to set up a business:

- Decide on a legal entity.

- File paperwork, applications, notices required to set up the business; pay all fees to get started.

- Apply for an Employer Identification Number (like a social security number that people have) if the business will have employees.

- If a business will have employees, the employees must each fill out a Form W-4 to let the business know how much in taxes the employer should withhold and pay on their behalf.

- Choose a tax year. People pay taxes based on a calendar year from January 1 through December 31. The taxes they owe and pay are based on the money they earned during that time. A business, however, can decide to pay taxes based on a different time period. For example, a common business tax year is from July 1 through June 30. For what reasons might a business choose a different tax year?

- Set up a schedule with banks and tax agencies to pay business and employment taxes and complete and file tax returns weekly, monthly, quarterly, and yearly.

ACTIVITY 6. BOARD GAME

Booming Business

The object of the Booming Business board game is to still be in business at the end of the game. This game can be played in small groups of two to six. To play you need:

- small game pieces for each player
- 1 die
- 1 game board (see appendix 1) for each player
- 1 center board (see appendix 1)
- 1 bank board (see appendix 1)
- the Star, Moon, Sun, and Flash cards from the handouts (pp. 80–83)
- paper money (Appendix 1)

Set Up

Photocopy one set of cards for each game played. For example, a group of four players will need one set of Star cards, one set of Moon cards, one set of Sun cards, and one set of Flash cards. Place the piles of cards facedown in their boxes on the center board. When players have drawn all the cards in one pile, they should be shuffled and replaced, facedown on the center board, to reuse.

☆ STAR CARDS move the game forward

☾ MOON CARDS move the game back

☀ SUN CARDS help all players

⚡ FLASH CARDS speed a player ahead

Cut all cards and money along the lines. Provide one game board for each player.

Photocopy enough money so there are four pages' worth for each player. At the beginning of the game, each player receives one of each of the following bills: $10, $20, $50, $100. The rest of the money is placed on the bank board for use during play.

Play

Each player rolls the die to find out who plays first; whoever gets the largest number on the die plays first. Play then rotates counterclockwise.

Players travel around the board, moving forward the number of spaces on the die. If a player lands on a space with a symbol on it, that player takes a card from the pile with that symbol and follows the instructions on that card.

If a player lands on a "Flash" space and draws a card that sends him or her across the speed zone, the player moves through the center bar of the dollar sign to the next nearest shaded space at the end of the speed zone.

A player who does not have enough to pay the total owed must pay all he or she has to the bank and then skip one turn.

The game ends when the first person finishes a trip around the board and lands on "Finish." The player does not have to have an exact roll of the die to land on "Finish."

ANY player who has money left at the end of the game wins!

STAR CARDS FOR BOOMING BUSINESS GAME

(Photocopy, cut, and place facedown on center board.)

You make a profit this month! Receive $50 from the bank. ☆	You make a profit this month! Receive $50 from the bank. ☆	You make a profit this month! Receive $50 from the bank. ☆
You have a successful sale. Receive $100 from the bank. ☆	Your city buys all its toilet paper from your company. Receive $100 from the bank. ☆	Your company stock goes up. Receive $50 from the bank. ☆
Your employees work really hard this month and bring in more money to the business. Receive $100 from the bank. ☆	Your new chef gets a good review from the newspaper. More people come to eat at your café. Receive $50 from the bank. ☆	You pay all your bills on time and receive a 5% discount. Receive $50 from the bank. ☆

MOON CARDS FOR BOOMING BUSINESS GAME

(Photocopy, cut, and place facedown on center board.)

Your biggest accounts receivable is late on its payment to you. You have to borrow money to pay your bills. Pay the bank $200	Your biggest accounts receivable is late on its payment to you. You have to borrow money to pay your bills. Pay the bank $200	Your biggest accounts receivable is late on its payment to you. You have to borrow money to pay your bills. Pay the bank $200
Your computer crashed. You have to buy a new one. Pay the bank $100.	Your machinery broke. You have to have it repaired. Pay the bank $100.	Your car breaks down on the way to the bank so your payroll tax deposit is late. Pay the bank a $100 penalty to the IRS.
Move back 1 space.	Move back 1 space.	Move back 1 space.

SUN CARDS FOR BOOMING BUSINESS GAME

(Photocopy, cut, and place facedown on center board.)

Business is good. Everyone receives $50 from the bank.	Business is good. Everyone receives $50 from the bank.	Business is good. Everyone receives $50 from the bank.
Payroll tax rates go down. Everyone receives $50 from the bank.	Workers' compensation insurance rates go down. Everyone receives $50 from the bank.	Electricity costs go down. Everyone receives $50 from the bank.
The landlord made an error on the property tax she charged. Everyone receives $20 from the bank.	The stock market is up. Everyone's stock is rising. Everyone receives $20 from the bank.	Your suppliers lower their costs. Everyone receives $10 from the bank.

FLASH CARDS FOR BOOMING BUSINESS GAME

(Photocopy, cut, and place facedown on center board.)

Advance to nearest speed zone. Cross zone and land on next STAR space after zone. Take a Star card.	Advance to nearest speed zone. Cross zone and land on next STAR space after zone. Take a Star card.	Your business has record earnings. Receive $200 from the bank.
Your business has record earnings. Receive $200 from the bank.	Your payroll taxes were more than expected! Pay the bank $200.	Your workers' compensation insurance rate went up. Pay the bank $200.
Business taxes are due. Pay the bank $300.	You have to buy new equipment and supplies. Pay the bank $100.	You have a fast food restaurant, but your employees eat up all your profits. Pay the bank $100.

84 Chapter 3: Booming Businesses

THINK ABOUT

After an employer has computed the gross and net wages for all of its employees, it must calculate and pay the taxes, insurance, and other items to various agencies. For example, the employer must deposit the employee's federal income taxes with the U.S. government; must deposit the employee's state income taxes with the state, and so on. In addition, all insurance payments and union dues must also be paid for the employee by the employer.

The employer also has many other costs related to its employees. For example, the employer must pay an amount equal to the amount of social security tax (FICA) paid by the employee. That means it deducts and pays taxes so that the employee doesn't have to do it herself and must ALSO pay an equal amount of social security tax for the employee out of the business's other money. The employer must also usually provide workers' compensation insurance, which means it pays an insurance company money to cover any injury to employees while they are working.

All of these taxes and insurance paid on behalf of the employees are in addition to the costs of doing business—rent for a building, electricity, advertising, office equipment, vacation or sick pay and the cost of hiring temporary workers to do the work of vacationing or sick employees, and the cost of materials it must buy to produce products it sells. Although it is part of "the American dream" to own a business, there are lots of lumpy pillows you have to plump up before you can fall asleep and start that dream.

As a class, discuss several businesses you might like to own. What specific problems or costs might each business have? What benefits? Would any one of the business entities (sole proprietorship, partnership, corporation) be a better choice than another?

FIND OUT MORE

Resources in Your Community

Find out whether a parent or family friend of a student has a business of her own. Ask that person to visit the class to share experiences or answer questions.

Web Sites

- For things you should know if you want to set up a business, go to the Internal Revenue Service Web site at www.irs.gov/businesses.
- Also check your state tax authority for information on what your state requires.

Careers

Related jobs include business owner, business manager, human resource manager, insurance broker, tax advisor, bookkeeper, accountant, and marketer.

CHAPTER 4

Savings Savvy

Subject Matter: Financial institutions; savings; simple and compound interest

Math Standards Addressed:

   Number Sense: computing numbers; multiplication; decimals

   Data Analysis: tables; charts; graphs

   Percentages

Literacy Standards Addressed:

   Vocabulary and Concept Development

   Reading Comprehension

   Spelling

Written and Oral English Standards Addressed:

   Listening and Speaking Applications

   Verbal Communication

   Research and Technology

WHAT IS SAVING?

Saving is setting aside money as a way to provide for tomorrow. A good rule is to save 10 percent of all the money you receive. Many of the wealthiest people in the world work hard to save the first 10 percent of what they take in. They know they have expenses to pay, but they make sure to also pay themselves, by depositing 10 percent into a savings account or other investment regularly. That money then works to make more money for them.

One way to make regular saving easy is to create an automatic savings program. Many banks will transfer (move) a certain amount of money that you decide from your general bank account into a savings account each month without you ever having to think about it. You can grow your money each month without having to take any action.

Another idea is to increase the amount of automatic savings when you receive additional income, such as when your employer increases your salary. Because you were not used to having more money before, you won't miss it by putting it into savings.

SETTING/PROPS/COSTUMES

This play has five scenes for seven readers. Several friends—Doug, Nicole, Jacob, and Chandra—are together. Quizy (a friendly alien from another planet) is with them. They're discussing savings. Props could include calculators, paper, and pencils Costumes are not needed. Quizy's clothing and appearance is limited only by students' imagination!

Pronunciation guides may be provided in the script in square brackets. The words are divided into syllables. The syllable to be stressed is in capital letters. For example, the pronunciation guide for Quizy's name would be [QUIZ-ee]. The reader should use the pronunciation guide but not read it aloud.

CHARACTERS

NARRATOR 1

NARRATOR 2

DOUG

NICOLE

JACOB

CHANDRA

QUIZY (a friendly alien visitor who collects empty tissue boxes)

Something Interest-ing

Scene 1: Quizy's Bank

NARRATOR 1: Have you ever heard the saying, "Save for a rainy day"?

NARRATOR 2: Yes, but I don't know what it means.

NARRATOR 1: I think it means you should save your money so that when it rains you have enough money to buy an umbrella.

NARRATOR 2: I don't think that's what it means.

NARRATOR 1: Maybe those kids know about saving.

NARRATOR 2: Let's listen.

NICOLE: Quizy, why do you collect empty tissue boxes?

QUIZY: I can't tell you.

CHANDRA: Why not?

QUIZY: It's a secret.

DOUG: What kind of secret?

QUIZY: A big secret.

JACOB: What would happen if anyone found out your secret?

QUIZY: I'd have too many friends.

NICOLE: How can you have too many friends?

CHANDRA: Isn't having friends a good thing?

QUIZY: Not this way.

DOUG: Why?

QUIZY: Everyone is going to want to be my friend.

JACOB: Because you have empty tissue boxes?

QUIZY: No, because one day they'll be full.

NICOLE: They'll be full of tissues?

QUIZY: No.

CHANDRA: Full of what?

QUIZY: That's my secret.

Scene 2: A Better Bank

NARRATOR 1: I wonder what Quizy puts in his empty tissue boxes.

NARRATOR 2: I can't guess.

NARRATOR 1: Maybe Quizy will tell us.

DOUG: Quizy, what do you keep in your empty tissue boxes?

JACOB: We promise not to tell anyone.

[Everyone nods.]

QUIZY: OK. They'll be full of money.

CHANDRA: Why will they be full of money?

QUIZY: Because that's where I put my money.

NICOLE: What money?

QUIZY: The tenth.

CHANDRA: The tenth of what?

QUIZY: The tenth of everything.

DOUG: Everything?

QUIZY:	One-tenth of all the money I ever get.
JACOB:	You save one-tenth of all the money you get?
QUIZY:	Yes. And then I put it in my empty tissue boxes.
NICOLE:	That's great that you save so much.
DOUG:	But why do you put your money in empty tissue boxes?
QUIZY:	To keep it safe.
CHANDRA:	That doesn't sound very safe.
DOUG:	Why don't you put the money in the bank?
QUIZY:	What's a bank?
JACOB:	It's where people on Earth keep their money.
NICOLE:	You've been to the bank downtown with us.
QUIZY:	I'd never put my money there.
CHANDRA:	Why not?
QUIZY:	There are always other people at the bank.
DOUG:	So?
QUIZY:	So my money wouldn't be secret.
JACOB:	But you would get extra money by keeping it at the bank.
QUIZY:	Really?
NICOLE:	Yes. The bank would give you interest.
QUIZY:	What does that mean?
CHANDRA:	The bank would pay you a percentage of your money.
DOUG:	It's called interest.
QUIZY:	Why would the bank do that?
JACOB:	They pay you interest to encourage you to keep your money there.
QUIZY:	Why do they want me to keep my money there?

Scene 3: What Is Interest?

NARRATOR 1: Quizy doesn't understand why banks want to pay him money.

NARRATOR 2: I'm not sure either.

NARRATOR 1: Let's find out what the kids tell him.

NICOLE: The banks pay you interest so they can use your money.

QUIZY: I knew there was a catch. Does the bank go shopping with my money?

CHANDRA: No, the bank lends your money to other people.

QUIZY: Why?

DOUG: Because the people they lend the money to pay the bank interest.

QUIZY: That's silly. The bank pays me interest; other people pay the bank interest.

JACOB: It's not silly at all.

NICOLE: The people who borrow money pay the bank more interest than the bank pays you.

QUIZY: Oh, it's a scam!

CHANDRA: No, it's a way for money to work for lots of people at once.

DOUG: You get interest.

JACOB: The bank gets interest.

NICOLE: The people who borrow can use the money for what they need.

CHANDRA: And it's all the same money.

DOUG: Being used again and again.

QUIZY: Money can sure get around better if I don't keep it in my tissue box.

JACOB:	Yes it can.
QUIZY:	How much interest will the bank pay me?
NICOLE:	Each bank may pay a different amount.
CHANDRA:	It's called the "interest rate."
DOUG:	I saw that the bank on the corner pays 10 percent for a long-term savings account.
QUIZY:	Is that a lot?
JACOB:	It's better than keeping it in a tissue box.
QUIZY:	So the bank will pay me 10 percent every day?
NICOLE:	No, it will pay you 10 percent a year.
CHANDRA:	But it pays that 10 percent over all 12 months.
DOUG:	A little bit of the 10 percent each month.
QUIZY:	So I get less than a whole 1 percent each month?
JACOB:	Yes.
QUIZY:	That's not much.
NICOLE:	If you had $100 that would be 83 cents a month.
QUIZY:	How do you know that?
CHANDRA:	You multiply $100 times 10 percent.
DOUG:	Or times .10.
JACOB:	Right. And that equals $10.00
NICOLE:	Then you divide the $10.00 by the 12 months.
CHANDRA:	So 83 cents a month on $100 isn't bad.
DOUG:	It's like free money.
QUIZY:	It's not bad at all, because I have more than $100.
JACOB:	Quizy, that's great.
NICOLE:	How much do you have?
QUIZY:	It's a secret.
CHANDRA:	We remember.

Scene 4: Compounding the Interest

NARRATOR 1: Interest sounds great.

NARRATOR 2: Just wait. It gets better.

NARRATOR 1: It gets better?

NARRATOR 2: Yes, let's listen.

QUIZY: So that means I could have an extra $10.00 a year for every $100 I have.

DOUG: No.

QUIZY: No? You said . . .

JACOB: We were just giving you an example of how interest works.

NICOLE: That example was "simple interest."

QUIZY: What was simple about it? It sounded like hard math to me.

DOUG: It was simple instead of "compound."

QUIZY: What's compound interest?

JACOB: It's another type of interest.

NICOLE: It's better interest.

DOUG: It's the type of interest the bank actually pays you.

QUIZY: I knew there was a catch. It's a scam, right? Those compounded banks!

JACOB: No, Quizy. Compound interest is a good thing.

QUIZY: What is compound interest?

NICOLE: It's when you are paid interest on the interest.

QUIZY: That's very interesting.

CHANDRA: Here's how it works.

DOUG: Let's say you have $100.

QUIZY: I have more than $100.

JACOB: OK. Let's say you have $1,000.

QUIZY: I have more than . . .

NICOLE: OK, but we'll just SAY you have $1,000 for now.

CHANDRA: The bank pays you 10 percent the first month.

DOUG: The 10 percent is for a year.

JACOB: Right. So you divide the 10 percent amount on $1,000 by 12 months.

NICOLE: That means the first month the bank pays you $8.33.

QUIZY: Cool.

DOUG: So Quizy, how much would you then have?

JACOB: Remember it would be your original $1,000 plus $8.33 in interest.

QUIZY: I would have $1,008.33.

NICOLE: Right. Then the next month, the bank pays you 10 percent on your $1,008.33.

CHANDRA: Divided by 12 months.

DOUG: So that next month the bank pays you $8.40.

QUIZY: After that second month I'd have $1,008.33 plus $8.40.

JACOB: Yes. Then the next month the bank pays you 10 percent on your $1,016.73.

NICOLE: Divided by 12.

DOUG: That's $8.47.

JACOB: Then the next month the bank pays you 10 percent on your $1,025.20.

NICOLE: Divided by 12.

DOUG: That's $8.54.

JACOB:	Then the next month the bank pays you 10 percent on your $1,033.74.
NICOLE:	Divided by 12.
CHANDRA:	That's $8.61.
QUIZY:	I get the idea.
DOUG:	The amount of interest gets larger each month.
JACOB:	Because it includes interest paid on interest.
NICOLE:	By the end of the year you'd have $1,104.69.
CHANDRA:	Compare that to simple interest of 10 percent.
DOUG:	That was $1,100.
QUIZY:	Big deal. It's only an extra $4.69 for the whole year. I might as well keep it in my tissue box where it's safe.
JACOB:	You're not getting it, Quizy.

Scene 5: The Best Is Yet to Come

NARRATOR 1:	I thought I understood interest.
NARRATOR 2:	But Jacob said Quizy is not getting it.
NARRATOR 1:	I wonder what he means.
NARRATOR 2:	Could it get even better?
QUIZY:	What do you mean, I'm not getting it?
NICOLE:	Time.
QUIZY:	Time for what?
CHANDRA:	For your money.
QUIZY:	What do you mean?
DOUG:	Quizy, what if you put $1,000 into a savings account at 10 percent for eight years in a row?
QUIZY:	I could do that.

JACOB: Then after those eight years, you never put another penny into it.

QUIZY: I could do that, too.

NICOLE: You would have put away a total of $8,000.

DOUG: Because you saved $1,000 a year multiplied by eight years.

JACOB: If you only got SIMPLE interest, Quizy, how much would you have at the end of eight years?

QUIZY: I would have $8,000 multiplied by 10 percent.

NICOLE: That's $800 in interest plus the $8,000 you put in.

CHANDRA: So you'd have a total of $8,800.

QUIZY: That's better than keeping it in a tissue box.

DOUG: Yes, but if the bank paid you compound interest . . .

JACOB: Interest on the principal and interest on the interest . . .

QUIZY: Why would the bank pay HIM interest if it's my money?

NICOLE: Quizy, what are you talking about?

QUIZY: Why would the bank pay Principal Brown?

CHANDRA: We weren't talking about Principal Brown at school.

DOUG: We meant principal. With a small "p".

JACOB: It means the amount that you saved, not including the interest.

QUIZY: Oh, that's good, because Principal Brown is not very interesting.

NICOLE: So, if the bank paid you compound interest . . .

CHANDRA: Interest on the principal and interest on the interest—you'd have . . .

QUIZY: A lot more money.

DOUG: A lot more.

JACOB: And if you left the money in the bank . . .

NICOLE: And never took any out . . .

CHANDRA: And never saved any more than the first $8,000 . . .

QUIZY: Then I'd have an even lot more?

DOUG: After 37 years, you'd have $427,736.

QUIZY: What?

JACOB: That's almost half a million dollars.

QUIZY: That's practically a gazillion dollars!

NICOLE: And you only put in $8,000.

QUIZY: That's a lot of lots.

CHANDRA: What are you thinking, Quizy?

QUIZY: Compound interest is very interesting.

DOUG: It is a better investment than sticking your money in a tissue box!

JACOB: Yes, it is.

QUIZY: But 37 years is a long time.

NICOLE: But you only have to put money in for eight years.

QUIZY: Well, I have to say, it's about time.

CHANDRA: It's about time for what?

QUIZY: Interest.

DOUG: What do you mean?

QUIZY: Time. Interest. Compounded interest.

JACOB: What are you talking about, Quizy?

QUIZY: Compounded interest is all about time.

NICOLE: Yes. The longer you leave your money alone, the more interest you will be paid.

QUIZY: So the sooner I get started . . .

CHANDRA: The more interest you'll get.

QUIZY: Yes, it is.

DOUG: It is what?

QUIZY: VERY INTERESTING!

NICOLE: Quizy, now that you know about compound interest, we have a question for you.

QUIZY: What is it?

CHANDRA: Are you going to stop collecting empty tissue boxes?

QUIZY: Oh, no!

DOUG: What are you going to do with them?

QUIZY: I have a new plan.

JACOB: Let me guess. The plan is a secret, right?

QUIZY: A really big secret!

GLOSSARY

Annual percentage: The percentage computed over one year's time.

Compound interest: The percentage amount paid on both the principal and interest.

Percentage: A part of a whole expressed in hundredths.

Principal: The amount of money upon which the interest is paid.

Save: To put aside.

Simple interest: A percentage amount paid on the principal.

DOING TO UNDERSTAND

The following activities are included as handouts:

1. Calculate Simple Interest
2. Calculate Compound Interest and Principal
3. Compare Simple and Compound Interest
4. Think about and Discuss
5. Interest Rates
6. Board Game

The amount of interest paid is based on the amount you save, the interest rate you earn, and the length of time you save it for. Compound interest is paid on both the amount you save and the interest you have earned on that initial amount.

ACTIVITY 1. CALCULATE SIMPLE INTEREST

Create a graph with five columns. Find an interest chart or online calculator. Chart how much money you would end up with if you STARTED saving at age 12, age 20, age 30, and age 40 and saved UNTIL age 60. How much would you have if you saved $1,000 a year until age 60? Calculate the amounts for simple interest at the different interest rates on the following chart. What kind of chart or graph could you create to show the information from this table?

Simple Interest and Principal

Starting Age	No. Years to Age 60	2% per Year	5% per Year	10% per Year
12				
20				
30				
40				
50				

1. Multiply the number of years by the $1,000 saved per year to get the total principal.
2. Multiply the percentage by the $1,000 to get the amount of interest per year.
3. Multiply the interest per year by the number of years to get the total interest earned.
4. Add the total principal saved and the total interest earned to get the total amount you would have at age 60.

From *Fun with Finance: Math + Literacy = Success* by Carol Peterson. Santa Barbara, CA: Libraries Unlimited. Copyright © 2009.

ACTIVITY 2. CALCULATE COMPOUND INTEREST AND PRINCIPAL

Create a graph with five columns. Find an interest chart or online calculator. Chart how much money you would end up with if you STARTED saving at age 12, age 20, age 30, and age 40 and saved UNTIL age 60. How much would you have if you saved $1,000/year until age 60? Calculate the amounts for compound interest at the different interest rates on the following chart. What kind of chart or graph could you create to show the information from this table?

The calculations for this chart are for interest compounded once a year. Many savings plans compound interest monthly or quarterly (four times a year). When interest is compounded more often, the result is even more savings!

Compound Interest and Principal

Starting Age	No. Years to Age 60	2% per Year	5% per Year	10% per Year
12				
20				
30				
40				
50				

1. Multiply the $1,000 principal by the percentage to get the interest for the first year.
2. Add the $1,000 principal for the first year to the interest for the first year to get the total for the first year.
3. Add the $1,000 principal for the second year to the total for the first year to get the principal for the second year.
4. Multiply the principal for the second year by the percentage to get the interest for the second year.
5. Add the principal for the second year to the interest for the second year to get the total for the second year.
6. Add the $1,000 principal for the third year to the total for the second year to get the principal for the third year.
7. Multiply the principal for the third year by the percentage to get the interest for the third year.
8. Add the principal for the third year to the interest for the third year to get the total for the third year.
9. Continue adding the principal and calculating the interest on the yearly totals for the total number of years until age 60.

ACTIVITY 3. COMPARE SIMPLE AND COMPOUND INTEREST

Compare the charts from Activities 1 and 2.
    What can you understand about the relationship among the time you have to save, the interest rate, and whether interest is simple or compound? How would you use this information to develop your own savings plan?

ACTIVITY 4. THINK ABOUT AND DISCUSS

If you saved $1,000 a year and just put it in a bucket, at the end of 40 years you'd have $40,000. That's nice, but wouldn't it be nicer to have more?

If you made simple interest on the $1,000 a year at 12 percent, you'd get $120 in interest each year on your $1,000. Over 40 years, that 12 percent SIMPLE interest would mean:

$40,000 saved ($1,000 x 40 years)
+ 4,800 interest ($120 a year simple interest x 40 years)
$44,800 in your bucket because of simple interest

Now let's look at how much you would make if you saved the same $1,000 a year for 40 years but earned 12 percent COMPOUND interest.

$40,000 saved ($1,000 x 40 years)
+ $809,142 interest compounded for 40 years
$849,142 in your bucket because of compound interest.

The difference between 12 percent simple interest and 12 percent compound interest (interest on the interest) is:

$849,142 savings plus compound interest
− $44,800 savings plus simple interest
$804,342

The difference between simple and compound interest at the same 12 percent interest rate is more than three-quarters of a million dollars!

Now look at the chart on page 103.
The big secret to compound interest is to start saving early. The second part is to not take the savings out. Time is important. So let time work for you by leaving your money in your savings account so it keeps getting compound interest. What kind of chart or graph could you create to show the information from this table?

COMPARE SIMPLE AND COMPOUND INTEREST

Compare how the number of years, the interest rate, and whether it is simple or compound interest affects the amount of money you will have at the end of each time period.

Start Saving at Age:	No. of Years until Age 60	Total Amount Saved (Principal)/ No. of Years x $1,000 per Year
12	48	$48,000
20	40	$40,000
30	30	$30,000
40	20	$20,000

Starting Age	Simple Interest Earned	Total Amount Saved	Compound Interest Earned	Total Amount Saved
	2% SIMPLE INTEREST		2% COMPOUND INTEREST	
12	906	48,906	35,224.26	83,224.26
20	800	40,800	20,529.03	63,529.03
30	600	30,600	12,950.03	42,950.09
40	400	20,400	6,098.67	26,098.67
	5% SIMPLE INTEREST		5% COMPOUND INTEREStT	
12	2,400	50,400	163,166.04	211,166.04
20	2,000	50,000	95,056.63	135,056.63
30	1,500	31,500	44,111.61	74,111.61
40	1,000	21,000	17,108.61	37,108.17
	10% SIMPLE INTEREST		10% COMPOUND INTEREStT	
12	4,800	52,800	1,262,135.65	1,310,135.65
20	4,000	52,000	545,099.02	585,099.02
30	3,000	33,000	179,781.18	209,781.18
40	2,000	22,000	51,135.15	71,136.15

ACTIVITY 5. INTEREST RATES

Using the newspaper or Internet, find out what interest rates your local banks are paying. Which bank has the highest interest rate? What is it?

ACTIVITY 6. BOARD GAME

Savings Savvy

The object of the Savings Savvy board game is to have the most money at the end of the game. This game can be played in small groups of two to four. To play you need:

    a calculator

    a pencil and paper

    small game pieces for each player

    1 die

    1 game board (see appendix 1) for each player

    1 center board (see appendix 1)

    1 bank board (see appendix 1)

    the Star, Moon, Sun, and Flash cards from the handouts (pp. 107–110)

    paper money (see appendix 1)

Set Up

Photocopy one set of cards for each game played. For example, a group of four players will need one set of Star cards, one set of Moon cards, one set of Sun cards, and one set of Flash cards. Place the piles of cards facedown in their boxes on the center board. When players have drawn all the cards in one pile, they should be shuffled and replaced, facedown on the center board, to reuse.

    ☆ STAR CARDS move the game forward

    ☾ MOON CARDS move the game back

    ☼ SUN CARDS help all players

    ⚡ FLASH CARDS speed a player ahead

Cut all cards and money along the lines.
Provide one game board for each player.
Photocopy enough money so there are four pages' worth for each player. At the beginning of the game, each player receives one of each of the following bills: $10, $20, $50, $100. The rest of the money is placed on the bank board for use during play.

Play

Each player rolls the die to find out who plays first; whoever gets the largest number on the die plays first. Play then rotates counterclockwise.

Players travel around the board, moving forward the number of spaces on the die. If a player lands on a space with a symbol on it, that player takes a card from the pile with that symbol and follows the instructions on that card.

ACTIVITY 6. BOARD GAME (CONT.)

A player who does not have enough to pay the total owed must pay all he or she has to the bank and then skip one turn.

The game ends when the first person finishes a trip around the board and lands on "Finish." The player does not have to have an exact roll of the die to land on "Finish."

Each player then counts his money. Each player then rolls the die. If he rolls a 1, 2, or 3, he has received simple interest. He multiplies the money he has by 2 percent and receives that much money from the bank. If he rolls a 4, 5, or 6, he has received compound interest. He multiplies the money he has by 10 percent and receives that much money from the bank.

All players then count their money again. The person with the most money (NOT the first player to finish) wins the game.

STAR CARDS FOR SAVINGS SAVVY GAME

(Photocopy, cut, and place facedown on center board.)

Receive $100 from the bank. ☆	Receive $100 from the bank. ☆	Receive $100 from the bank. ☆
Receive $200 from the bank. ☆	Receive $200 from the bank. ☆	Receive $200 from the bank. ☆
Receive $200 from the bank. ☆	Receive $500 from the bank. ☆	Receive $500 from the bank. ☆

From *Fun with Finance: Math + Literacy = Success* by Carol Peterson. Santa Barbara, CA: Libraries Unlimited. Copyright © 2009.

MOON CARDS FOR SAVINGS SAVVY GAME

(Photocopy, cut, and place facedown on center board.)

EMERGENCY! Pay bank $50 for Woofy's dog license.	EMERGENCY! Woofy chewed up your shoes. Pay bank $100 for new shoes.	Pay bank $100 for birthday present for your best friend.
Your bank balance went below zero. Pay bank $100 in fees.	Pay bank $100 for holiday gifts.	EMERGENCY! Your car needs new tires. Pay bank $300.
Your bank balance went to zero. Pay bank $100 in fees.	Move back 1 space.	Move back 1 space.

SUN CARDS FOR SAVINGS SAVVY GAME

(Photocopy, cut, and place facedown on center board.)

Everyone receives $50 from the bank.	Everyone receives $50 from the bank.	Everyone receives $50 from the bank.
Everyone receives $20 from the bank.	Everyone receives $20 from the bank.	Everyone receives $20 from the bank.
Everyone receives $10 from the bank.	Everyone receives $10 from the bank.	Everyone receives $10 from the bank.

FLASH CARDS FOR SAVINGS SAVVY GAME

(Photocopy, cut, and place facedown on center board.)

Receive year end bank statement. Roll die. All players are paid that amount of interest on the money they have.	Receive year end bank statement. All players are 1% interest on the money they have.	Receive year end bank statement. Roll die. All players are paid 2% interest on the money they have.
Receive year end bank statement. Roll die. All players are paid 3% interest on the money they have.	Receive year end bank statement. Roll die. All players are paid 4% interest on the money they have.	Receive year end bank statement. Roll die. All players are paid 5% interest on the money they have.
Receive year end bank statement. Roll die. All players are paid 6% interest on the money they have.	Take an extra turn.	Take an extra turn.

THINK ABOUT

When planning for the future, people may want to establish more than one type of savings. They will often have long-term savings for retirement. At your age, retirement may seem like a long time from now. That's true. However, Quizy saw that if he saved $1,000 for eight years, he might never have to save another nickel, thanks to compound interest. Time, not the amount of money itself, is often the most important part of a savings plan. Most people invest the money that they will not need for a long time into a type of savings that pays higher interest but discourages you from taking the money out early, such as a long-term certificate of deposit or bond.

Some people also establish short-term savings. In this case, people want the money to be accessible. They may want to be able to use the money for a car, education, an emergency, or if they become unemployed (lose their source of income). So that they can get to their money easily, many people have short-term savings in a savings account or money market account.

The best advice is to spend less than you earn over a long period of time and save and/or invest that extra amount.

FIND OUT MORE

Resources in Your Community

Find out whether a parent or family friend of a student works for a bank, savings and loan, or credit union. Ask that person to visit the class to share experiences or answer questions, or to share some blank forms or other information packets with the class.

Web Sites

- For an online simple interest calculator, go to www.webmath.com.simpinterest.com.
- For an online compound interest calculator, go to www.webmath.com.compinterest.com.
- Search the Web for the keywords "finance," "banking," and "savings."

Careers

Related jobs include bank teller, bank savings advisor, savings and loan or credit union employee, and financial advisor.

CHAPTER 5

෨ $ ෫

Credit Chaos

Subject Matter: Debt; loans; credit cards; credit bureau; credit score

Math Standards Addressed:

    Number Sense: computing numbers; decimals; multiplication; fractions

    Data Analysis: tables; charts; graphs

    Percentages

Literacy Standards Addressed:

    Vocabulary and Concept Development

    Reading Comprehension

    Spelling

Written and Oral English Standards Addressed:

    Research and Technology

    Writing Applications

    Listening and Speaking Applications

    Verbal Communication

114   Chapter 5: Credit Chaos

WHAT IS CREDIT?

Credit is the providing of money to one person by another person or company with the expectation that it will be repaid. The amount of credit given is usually based on the lender's faith in the borrower's ability and honor to repay the debt.

Debt is money owed to someone else. It includes bank loans, money owed to credit card companies, money borrowed from friends or family, home mortgages, and bills that come due if not paid on time.

From the borrower's point of view, it can be helpful to be able to use other people's money to purchase large items, such as a house or car, that she needs. The borrower can pay for the item over time by making smaller, affordable payments. From the lender's point of view, giving credit to another person can bring in income, because the lender receives interest on the money lent.

Problems occur when a borrower owes more money to lenders than she can repay.

SETTING/PROPS/COSTUMES

This play has four scenes for seven readers. Doug and Nicole are with their parents. Quizy (a friendly alien visiting from another planet) is with them. The setting is the kitchen table. Props could include paper, pencils, and calculators. Costumes for Doug, Nicole, and their parents are not needed. Quizy's clothing and appearance is limited only by students' imagination!

Pronunciation guides may be provided in the script in square brackets. The words are divided into syllables. The syllable to be stressed is in capital letters. For example, the pronunciation guide for Quizy's name would be [QUIZ-ee]. The reader should use the pronunciation guide but not read it aloud.

CHARACTERS

NARRATOR 1

NARRATOR 2

MOM

DAD

DOUG

NICOLE

QUIZY (a friendly alien visitor who collects empty tissue boxes)

Credit Chaos

Scene 1: Family Finances

NARRATOR 1: The family is in the kitchen.

NARRATOR 2: Mom is paying bills.

NARRATOR 1: She doesn't look happy.

NARRATOR 2: Let's find out why.

MOM: We need to do something about all these bills!

DAD: What do you mean?

MOM: We're so far in debt, I don't think we'll ever be able to pay our bills.

DAD: I'm working two jobs.

MOM: I am, too.

QUIZY: I'm allergic to jobs.

MOM: I'm worried that we might have to declare bankruptcy.

DAD: I don't want to do that. I'd feel horrible.

MOM: I'd feel like we failed.

DAD: But at least we could start over financially.

DOUG: Not really.

MOM: What do you mean?

NICOLE: He means that if you declare bankruptcy, your credit is never the same again.

DOUG: We learned about bankruptcy at school.

NICOLE: There are two types of bankruptcy: Chapter 7 and Chapter 11.

QUIZY: Chapters? Are they in some kind of book?

DOUG: The chapters refer to the laws they're written in.

QUIZY: Are the laws in a book?

NICOLE: Sort of.

DAD: What is the difference between the two types of bankruptcy?

QUIZY: And what happened to chapters 8, 9, and 10?

DOUG: Chapter 7 bankruptcy is total bankruptcy.

NICOLE: It means all of your debts are wiped off, and you have to sell everything you own to pay as much of what you owe as you can.

DOUG: But under Chapter 7 bankruptcy, you still don't start out clean again.

MOM: Why not?

NICOLE: Total bankruptcy stays on your credit report for 10 years.

QUIZY: What is a credit report?

DAD: A credit report is a list of information that tells lenders how risky it might be to lend money to you.

DOUG: So if your credit report is good, then lenders will be willing to lend money to you.

NICOLE: And if the credit report is bad, then they won't want to lend you money.

QUIZY: If you couldn't pay your bills and went bankrupt, though, you'd never WANT to borrow money again, right?

MOM: Sometimes borrowing money can be helpful.

DAD: Like when you don't have enough money to buy something big that you really need.

DOUG: Like a house.

NICOLE: Or a car to get you to work.

QUIZY: Or a spaceship.

MOM: Then your credit rating would be really important.

DAD: But I thought your credit went back to being OK after a bankruptcy.

DOUG: The bankruptcy stays on your credit report for 10 years.

NICOLE: And every lender will see it.

MOM: What about Chapter 11 bankruptcy?

DOUG: Chapter 11 is like a payment plan.

NICOLE: Everyone to whom you owe money tells the court how much you owe them.

DOUG: And the court decides how much money you will pay to each of them.

NICOLE: And the court decides when you'll pay them.

DAD: What about your credit report then?

DOUG: Chapter 11 is still a bankruptcy.

NICOLE: The Chapter 11 bankruptcy information stays on your credit report for 7 years.

QUIZY: So after 7 or 10 years, your credit report is good after a bankruptcy?

DOUG: Only if you have consistently paid your bills and don't get into trouble.

NICOLE: But loan applications ask if you have EVER filed bankruptcy.

QUIZY: Forever!

MOM: So once you get into financial trouble, it stays with you.

DAD: It's a better idea never to get into credit trouble in the first place.

QUIZY: Or you may end up in Chapter 100 gazillion!

Scene 2: Creating a Budget

NARRATOR 1: I didn't know bankruptcy affects you forever.

NARRATOR 2: No wonder Mom looks so unhappy.

NARRATOR 2: It must feel terrible not to have enough money to pay all your bills.

NARRATOR 1: And the bills just keep getting bigger if you don't pay them.

NARRATOR 2: I never want to go bankrupt.

NARRATOR 1: Me either. But what will the family do?

NARRATOR 2: Let's find out.

DOUG: At school we learned about budgets.

NICOLE: Yes, a budget helps you know where your money is going.

DOUG: And where it NEEDS to go.

QUIZY: Our money has already left.

MOM: Do you think we should do a budget?

DAD: Maybe we won't feel like it's hopeless.

DOUG: First we need to know what bills we have.

NICOLE: How much money does it take for our housing?

DOUG: How much for utilities—electricity, water, telephone?

NICOLE: How much for car payments?

DOUG: How much for insurance?

QUIZY:	Don't forget boxes of tissues.
MOM:	Write down groceries.
DAD:	And gasoline.
QUIZY:	And extra tissues.
DOUG:	OK, I'll add up all those amounts.
NARRATOR 1:	Doug added all the bills.
NARRATOR 2:	Then Doug showed everyone the total.
NICOLE:	That's how much money we need to have to live on each month.
DAD:	Don't forget the credit card bills.
MOM:	How can I forget them? I dream about them!
QUIZY:	Sounds like a nightmare to me.
DOUG:	Let's list all of the credit card bills, too.
NICOLE:	Both the amount you have to pay each month . . .
DOUG:	And the total amount you owe.
QUIZY:	Aren't they the same?
DOUG:	Usually each month you have to pay a part of what you owe.
MOM:	The problem is that the credit card companies also charge interest each month if you don't pay the total amount you owe.
QUIZY:	Pay interest? That's not very interesting at all!
NICOLE:	It's how the credit card companies make money.
DOUG:	Buying things on credit is like a loan.
DAD:	But it makes it hard to ever get out of debt if you're only paying the interest each month.
MOM:	That's the reason for my nightmares.
QUIZY:	Why not just toss the bills in the trash and skip it?

DOUG: Not paying what you owe is wrong.

NICOLE: It's like stealing.

DAD: How will we ever get out of debt?

Scene 3: A Plan to Get Out of Debt

NARRATOR 1: So the family now has a budget.

NARRATOR 2: They now know what bills they have each month.

NARRATOR 1: But it doesn't sound like they'll ever get out of debt.

NARRATOR 2: Maybe they can think of something. Let's listen.

MOM: We could borrow more money from our house to pay off the small bills.

DOUG: That would only get us in more debt.

NICOLE: And just rearrange what we owe.

DAD: Can we cut back on what we spend?

MOM: That would mean more money to pay our debts.

NARRATOR 1: The family thought about what they could do to spend less.

NARRATOR 2: They made a list.

DOUG: We could turn off the lights when we're not using them.

MOM: That would save money.

NICOLE: And we could use less water.

QUIZY: I volunteer to stop taking showers.

DAD: I could BBQ hamburgers every Saturday.

MOM: Instead of going out to eat at a restaurant.

DOUG: We could BBQ all winter!

NICOLE: And have indoor picnics!

DOUG: Picnics in the winter? Cool.

QUIZY:	Winter picnics aren't just cool; they're cold!
DAD:	I could put off buying a new suit for now.
MOM:	And I don't have to have my nails done every week.
DOUG:	I'll mow the lawn so you don't have to pay the lawn service
NICOLE:	And I'll help you clean the house, Mom, so we don't have to have a housekeeper.
MOM:	But is there any way we could get EXTRA money?
QUIZY:	How about a yard sale?
DOUG:	In the winter?
QUIZY:	There'd be less competition.
NICOLE:	Let's guess we make $250 from the yard sale.
DAD:	That still won't pay off all our debt.
MOM:	The car payment is huge!
DAD:	What we get from a yard sale will hardly make a dent on the car.
QUIZY:	Isn't not having a dent on the car a good thing?
MOM:	It all just feels hopeless.
QUIZY:	There is a way . . .
DAD:	I guess we just keep paying the minimum amount and do our best.
QUIZY:	There is a way . . .
DOUG:	We'll keep thinking.
QUIZY:	There is a way . . .
NICOLE:	We'll think of something.
QUIZY:	[loudly] THERE IS A WAY!

Scene 4: Quizy's Plan

NARRATOR 1: I love yard sales.

NARRATOR 2: Me, too. My family made lots of money at ours.

NARRATOR 1: And other people can get good bargains, too.

NARRATOR 2: But it doesn't sound like it'll solve the family problems.

NARRATOR 1: Maybe they can think of something else to do.

NARRATOR 2: Quizy seems to have an idea.

DOUG: Shh, Quizy. We're trying to think.

QUIZY: I already did the thinking.

NICOLE: Your ideas are usually bad.

QUIZY: You'll like this one.

MOM: OK, Quizy. What is it?

QUIZY: Pay the littlest debt off first.

DAD: Does anyone have any GOOD ideas?

DOUG: See, Quizy. That didn't help.

NICOLE: It's not the littlest debt that hurts the most, Quizy. It's the biggest one.

QUIZY: Exactly.

DOUG: What do you mean?

QUIZY: We owe about a gazillion bucks, right?

MOM: It feels like it.

QUIZY: Out of the gazillion bucks we owe, which debt is the smallest?

DAD: We owe Harry's Hardware Store $300.

QUIZY: What have you been paying Harry every month?

MOM: We've been paying the minimum payment of $40.

QUIZY: So if you get $250 from the yard sale and save $10 next month by me not taking showers . . .

DOUG: That's $260.

QUIZY: Your budget already says you were going to pay Harry's Hardware Store $40.

MOM: Right.

QUIZY: So instead of paying Harry's Hardware $40 next month, pay Harry the money from the yard sale plus the money saved on water plus the minimum payment.

NICOLE: That'd pay off the whole thing.

DOUG: All $300.

MOM: We'd still be really big in debt.

QUIZY: But, Mother-Doom-and-Gloom, how would you feel if you owed Harry's Hardware Store zero?

MOM: That'd feel great!

DOUG: That's a really good idea, Quizy.

NICOLE: But next month we won't have anything left for another yard sale.

QUIZY: You don't need another yard sale.

DAD: Why not?

QUIZY: Because next month you'll have an extra $40.

MOM: From the $40 that we no longer have to pay Harry's Hardware Store!

QUIZY: Right. So next month you pay that extra $40 to the next largest bill.

MOM: That'd be Zapata's Shoe Shop. We owe them $500.

NICOLE: What's the minimum payment you've been paying them?

DAD: $120 a month.

QUIZY: So you pay them $160 next month.

DOUG: And the next month.

NICOLE: And the next.

QUIZY: Before long you'll owe Zapata's a great big zero. How nice will that feel?

MOM: Better and better!

DOUG: Then after Zapata's is paid off, we have an extra $120 to pay off the next biggest debt?

QUIZY: No, then you'll have an extra $160.

NICOLE: The $120 from Zapata's plus the $40 from Harry's Hardware?

QUIZY: Right. You keep paying the debts off from smallest to the largest.

MOM: When one is paid off, we'll use that monthly amount to pay off the next biggest debt.

DAD: We could eventually be out of debt?

QUIZY: I figure in nine years, you'll be completely debt free.

MOM: Nine years? That's so long! I WAS starting to feel better.

DAD: Quizy, surely we'll be out of debt before then.

QUIZY: Nope. About nine years. No Harry's Hardware debt. No shoe debt. No car debt. No home loan.

DAD: What? No home loan either?

MOM: You mean we could even pay off our mortgage?

QUIZY: It is debt, isn't it?

MOM: Yes, but I never imagined we could pay off the house!

DAD: What a great feeling that would be!

NICOLE:	Quizy might even start taking showers again.
QUIZY:	Maybe bubble baths.
DOUG:	We pay off the smaller debts first.
QUIZY:	In a few months.
NICOLE:	Then the car loan.
QUIZY:	A little longer.
MOM:	Then the home loan.
QUIZY:	It will work as long as you don't go back into debt.
MOM:	We have a budget to follow now.
DAD:	I'll stick my credit cards in my drawer.
DOUG:	I'll turn out the lights I'm not using.
NICOLE:	I'll make signs for the yard sale.
MOM:	No debt. It's like a dream.
QUIZY:	A good one!
NARRATOR 1:	And that's just what the family did.
NARRATOR 2:	They made a budget.
NARRATOR 1:	And followed it.
NARRATOR 2:	They cut back on spending and paid off the smallest debt.
NARRATOR 1:	Then the next smallest debt.
NARRATOR 2:	Until all the debts were paid.
NARRATOR 1:	Even the house.
NARRATOR 2:	Quizy is taking bubble baths.
NARRATOR 1:	And Mom is buying him fancy bubble bath to say thank you.
NARRATOR 2:	Bubble bath is the first item in the new budget.

GLOSSARY

Balance: The remaining amount that is owed after each payment has been deducted.

Bankruptcy: A legal process to allow a debtor to be released from debt owed to others.

Budget: Usually a monthly written plan to pay expenses; organized by categories such as housing, food, utilities.

Chapter 7: A form of bankruptcy in which all real estate, cars, boats, and other property not exempt is turned over to a court trustee, who sells it for cash to pay creditors.

Chapter 11: A form of bankruptcy in which a person's debts are paid off through court instructions over a period of three to five years.

Credit bureau: One of three companies that gather information on how people have paid money owed to others. The three companies are Equifax, Experian, and Transunion.

Credit rating: A number rating given by the credit bureaus that quickly shows how well a person has timely paid money owed to others.

Creditor: The person or company to whom a debt is owed.

Debt: The amount of money owed.

Debtor: A person or company that owes money to another person or company.

Mortgage: The loan taken to purchase a home.

DOING TO UNDERSTAND

The following activities are included as handouts:

1. Credit Reports
2. Home Mortgages
3. The Real Cost of Debt
4. Another Cost of Debt
5. Improving Your Credit Score
6. Board Game

ACTIVITY 1. CREDIT REPORTS

Suggest students discuss credit with their parents. Do they know the names of the credit reporting agencies? Do they know their credit scores? If the parents agree, have the students work with them to contact the credit bureaus and review the credit reports with them.

ACTIVITY 2. HOME MORTGAGES

When people want to buy a home, they first must decide how much they can afford to pay each month. There is no point in looking at houses that cost much more money than the person can afford to pay. But how do you know how much you can afford?

In 2008 many people lost their homes. Many of these people had been given loans that they really could not afford. Instead of having a loan with payment that stayed the same amount each month for the 30 years of the loan, many of these loan payments increased over time. The problem was that although the people might have had enough income to pay for the loan at first, they could not afford the increased monthly payments. Because they could not afford the higher payments, they did not make the loan payments, and the banks foreclosed on their homes. That means the banks took the homes instead of the money owed. Because so many people lost their homes and the banks now owned homes instead of having money coming in (from loan payments) and going back out to earn more interest, the economy of the United States was hit hard.

Most banks and lenders now have much stricter formulas to estimate how much you should pay for a house. The formula is based on the size of loan you could qualify for. This is how it might work.

First determine your monthly income. How much does the borrower (including the husband and wife if they are buying the house together) bring in from jobs, investments, and other income? How much are the borrower's monthly expenses for the family, not including present housing costs? The difference between the income and expenses is the amount of money available each month for a mortgage payment.

Based on that amount, the lender then computes what a mortgage (home loan) could be based on various percentages of interest. For example:

Total monthly income of the Weaver family: $4,000

Total monthly expenses (not including rent): $3,000

Total monthly available for mortgage payment: $1,000

Let's assume each loan pays $100 per month on the principal amount of the loan (the amount not including interest). You would compute interest on the loan by multiplying the interest rate (the percentage) times the loan amount. Then divide that amount by 12 to get the monthly interest payment.

ACTIVITY 2. HOME MORTGAGES (CONT.)

For our activity, assume that each loan payment includes $100 toward payment of the loan balance. That means to figure out the monthly mortgage payment, you will add the $100 to the monthly interest payment.

Which of the following loans could the Weavers qualify for?
- $100,000 loan based on 5% interest + $100 applied to pay off the loan = _____
- $100,000 loan based on 6% interest + $100 applied to pay off the loan = _____
- $100,000 loan based on 7% interest + $100 applied to pay off the loan = _____
- $150,000 loan based on 5% interest + $100 applied to pay off the loan = _____
- $150,000 loan based on 6% interest + $100 applied to pay off the loan = _____
- $150,000 loan based on 7% interest + $100 applied to pay off the loan = _____
- $200,000 loan based on 5% interest + $100 applied to pay off the loan = _____
- $200,000 loan based on 6% interest + $100 applied to pay off the loan = _____
- $200,000 loan based on 7% interest + $100 applied to pay off the loan = _____

Finally, the borrower must know how much of a down payment she has for a home. A down payment is the amount of money she will pay in addition to the loan. The down payment plus the loan amount is the cost of the home (including real estate costs, taxes, and title insurance) a person can afford to purchase. If the Weavers have money for a $20,000 down payment, which of the above loans could they qualify for?

ACTIVITY 3. THE REAL COST OF DEBT

When you get older you may want to buy a home. For example, if you want a loan for $100,000, you may get a 30-year mortgage. That means you promise to pay back the $100,000 over the next 30 years—one month at a time. If the interest rate you have is 5 percent, then your monthly mortgage payment (the 5 percent interest plus payment on the $100,000 owed) will be about $450. Paying $450 for 360 months (12 months x 30 years) equals a total paid of $162,000.

That means your $100,000 house will actually cost you $162,000. The $62,000 is the cost of borrowing money. The benefit is that often real estate will increase in value over time, and thus by the end of the 30 years, the house may be worth more than the $162,000 it really cost you. Also, you need a place to live anyway, and a benefit of paying interest may be paying lower income taxes. Keep in mind, however, that whatever the price of the house or other item is, once you go into debt, the cost of interest increases the real cost of that item.

Look through the newspapers and find three houses for sale. For each one, assume you will have $20,000 as a down payment. What amount will your loan have to be on each house? Based on a 5 perent interest rate, what would your monthly interest payment be? Multiply that amount by 360 months for a 30-year mortgage. What amount of interest will you have paid over 30 years? How does that compare to the price of the house? Do any of the three houses now look better to you?

Recalculate the figures based on having $30,000 as a down payment. How does this change the cost of the loan over 30 years?

What if you borrowed the same amounts of money but paid it off over 15 years instead of 30? That would mean you doubled the principal amount each month but kept the amount of interest paid the same. So for example, instead of paying $100 toward the amount of the loan, you would pay $200 plus the monthly interest. But you would be paying 15 years' LESS interest. Discuss your results as a class.

However, the cost of debt isn't just the amount that you owe. For example, perhaps you owe Z Credit Card Company $5,000 and pay off $1,000 of what you owe each year. The credit card company charges you 18 percent interest per month on the balance owed. In five years, you would pay about $2,700 in interest plus the $5,000 amount you owed.

ACTIVITY 4. ANOTHER COST OF DEBT

The cost of debt isn't just the amount that you owe. It can also include how much you lose by not investing that money elsewhere.

What if you had never had that credit card debt in Activity 3? What if you instead had put $1,000 each year into an investment that paid 12 percent a year? Instead of paying $7,700 ($5,000 plus $2,700 in interest) over five years, you could have KEPT the $7,700. Plus, if you had invested one-fifth of that amount each year ($1,540) at 12 percent compounded interest, you would have had $13,671.40! Instead of paying $7,700 for something that cost you $5,000 when you charged it, you could have HAD $13,671.40. That means you could then buy that $5,000 item and still have $8,671.40 left.

Think about buying different items. How much could you have saved and earned if you had not bought that item on credit?

1. You bought a new TV for $2,000 and paid $500 a year in interest over four years;

2. You bought a new car for $20,000 and paid $2,500 a year in interest over seven years;

3. You bought many little items (such as clothing, CDs, and dinners out) for a total of $10,000 and paid $1,500 a year in interest over four years.

ACTIVITY 5. IMPROVING YOUR CREDIT SCORE

Discuss as a class ways to improve your credit. Go through the following steps and discuss what each means and why it would be part of improving your credit score or keeping your credit good.

- Remember that bad things stay on your credit report longer than good things. So although it is important to pay your bills on time, it may take six to twelve months for good payment records to show up on your credit report. On the other hand, a single late payment may show up on your credit report the very next month.

- Get a copy of your credit report. Look through the report and see if any creditors have reported things that are not correct. Mistakes can happen. For example, other people with the same name as you may have bad credit, and the creditors may incorrectly note that person's bad credit on your credit report. If you find a mistake, contact the credit reporting agency and make sure it is removed from your credit report.

- Do not open many new accounts in a short time. Often stores will try to get people to open new accounts to get a discount on a purchase. Opening new accounts means that you have a lot of credit available to you. The more credit you have available, the more in debt you COULD become.

- Pay your bills on time.

- Try to pay your credit cards off each month or try not to use your credit cards at all. If you have credit available to you but do not use it, you are less of a "risk" to creditors. That could mean a better credit score.

- Try to pay your bills instead of declaring bankruptcy. Bankruptcy might seem the easy way out of your problems, but a bankruptcy will mean much higher interest rates on your credit in the future because you are no longer a good risk.

ACTIVITY 6. BOARD GAME

Credit Chaos

The object of the Credit Chaos board game is to have the highest credit rating at the end of the game. This game can be played in small groups of two to four. To play you need:

a calculator

a pencil and paper

small game pieces for each player

1 die

1 game board (see appendix 1) for each player

1 center board (see appendix 1)

the Star, Moon, Sun, and Flash cards from the handouts (pp. 135–138)

Set Up

Photocopy one set of cards for each game played. For example, a group of four players will need one set of Star cards, one set of Moon cards, one set of Sun cards, and one set of Flash cards. Place the piles of cards facedown in their boxes on the center board. When players have drawn all the cards in one pile, they should be shuffled and replaced, facedown on the center board, to reuse. Paper money is not required for this game.

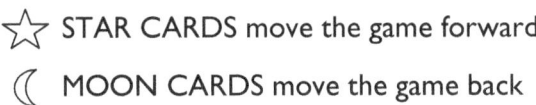 STAR CARDS move the game forward

 MOON CARDS move the game back

 SUN CARDS help all players

FLASH CARDS speed a player ahead

Cut all cards along the lines.
Provide one game board for each player.

Play

Each player rolls the die to find out who plays first; whoever gets the largest number on the die plays first. Play then rotates counterclockwise.

Players travel around the board, moving forward the number of spaces on the die. If a player lands on a space with a symbol on it, that player takes a card from the pile with that symbol and follows the instructions on that card. All players begin the game with a "good credit score" of 660. Players keep track of increases and decreases in their credit score on paper. Each player's credit score goes up or down as she travels around the board.

The game ends when the first person finishes a trip around the board and lands on "Finish." The player does not have to have an exact roll of the die to land on "Finish."

ACTIVITY 6. BOARD GAME (CONT.)

The first player to finish adds 50 points to her credit score. Players determine their credit score as follows:

    349–619 is POOR

    620–659 is FAIR

    660–749 is GOOD

    750–849 is EXCELLENT

The player with the highest credit score wins the game.

STAR CARDS FOR CREDIT CHAOS GAME

(Photocopy, cut, and place facedown on center board.)

You pay your electric bills on time. Add 10 points to your credit score. ☆	You pay your phone bills on time. Add 10 points to your credit score. ☆	You pay your water bills on time. Add 10 points to your credit score. ☆
You make your car payments on time. Add 20 points to your credit score. ☆	You make your car payments on time. Add 20 points to your credit score. ☆	You make your car payments on time. Add 20 points to your credit score. ☆
You make your house payments on time. Add 50 points to your credit score. ☆	You make your house payments on time. Add 50 points to your credit score. ☆	You pay your credit card bills on time. Add 50 points to your credit score. ☆

MOON CARDS FOR CREDIT CHAOS GAME

(Photocopy, cut, and place facedown on center board.)

Your phone bill payment is late! Take 10 points off your credit score.	Your electricity bill payment is late! Take 10 points off your credit score.	Your water bill payment is late! Take 10 points off your credit score.
Your car payment is late! Take 30 points off your credit score.	Your house payment is late! Take 40 points off your credit score.	Your house payment has been late 3 months in a row! Take 50 points off your credit score.
Your house payment has been late 3 months in a row! Take 50 points off your credit score.	Your credit card payment is late! Take 50 points off your credit score.	Your department store credit card payment is late! Take 50 points off your credit score.

SUN CARDS FOR CREDIT CHAOS GAME

(Photocopy, cut, and place facedown on center board.)

All players add 10 points to their credit score.	All players add 10 points to their credit score.	All players add 10 points to their credit score.
All players add 20 points to their credit score.	All players add 20 points to their credit score.	All players add 20 points to their credit score.
All players add 30 points to their credit score.	All players add 30 points to their credit score.	All players add 30 points to their credit score.

From *Fun with Finance: Math + Literacy = Success* by Carol Peterson. Santa Barbara, CA: Libraries Unlimited. Copyright © 2009.

FLASH CARDS FOR CREDIT CHAOS GAME

(Photocopy, cut, and place facedown on center board.)

You pay your bills on time! Your credit score increases by 20.	You pay your bills on time! Your credit score increases by 20.	You pay your bills on time! Your credit score increases by 20.
You pay your bills on time! Your credit score increases by 50.	You pay your bills on time! Your credit score increases by 50.	You pay your bills on time! Your credit score increases by 50.
You pay your bills on time! Your credit score increases by 100.	You pay your bills on time! Your credit score increases by 100.	You pay your bills on time! Your credit score increases by 100.

THINK ABOUT

Debt also causes stress by forcing us to keep paying tomorrow for what we buy today. "New stuff" may be nice now, but after awhile it's just "old stuff." Savings and investments, however, are future security and prosperity.

If you use a credit card to buy something on sale because you don't have the money now, that could be a good thing, because you can save money on the item on sale. If you don't pay the credit card bill off entirely right away, but instead carry over the balance due month after month, then you end up paying interest on the amount. By the time you have paid off the credit card bill and all of the interest, you might find that it would have been cheaper to wait until you had saved up the money to buy the item at full price!

When a person does not pay her bills on time or at all, the person or company owed the money can report that information to the three credit bureaus: Equifax, Experian, and Transunion. The credit bureaus gather information about each person's record of payments and the amounts of money owed to lenders. When a new person or company is thinking about lending money to that person, they can contact the credit bureaus and learn quickly whether it is a good or a bad idea to lend that person money, based on her past payment record and on how much money she already owes to others.

The credit bureaus assign each person a "credit rating." This quickly summarizes that person's credit record. Generally credit ratings are scored as follows:

349–619 is POOR

620–659 is FAIR

660–749 is GOOD

750–849 is EXCELLENT

It is a good idea for people to look at their own credit scores from time to time, especially when they are considering applying for a loan. That way they will know what the lender will see and can address anything on the credit report that may not look perfect.

FIND OUT MORE

Resources in Your Community

Find out whether a parent or family friend of a student works in lending or credit counseling. Ask that person to visit the class to share experiences or answer questions.

Web Sites

Visit the three credit bureaus at

- www.Equifax.com
- www.experian.com
- www.transunion.com

Careers

Related jobs include credit counselor, loan officer, banker, and mortgage broker.

CHAPTER 6

Budget Bonus

Subject Matter: Budgets—what they are, how to create them, and how to live within them

Math Standards Addressed:

    Number Sense: computing numbers; multiplication; decimals; fractions

    Data Analysis: tables; charts; graphs

    Percentages

Literacy Standards Addressed:

    Vocabulary and Concept Development

    Reading Comprehension

    Spelling

Written and Oral English Standards Addressed:

    Research and Technology

    Writing Applications

    Listening and Speaking Applications

    Verbal Communication

WHAT IS A BUDGET?

A *budget* is a written plan to assign money to pay all bills and provide for savings and investment for a specific time period. To create a budget, you first determine how much money you bring in during the period of time. Then you list each item that must be paid out of that income. The goal is to have the amount of income equal the amount of the bills, savings, and investment.

SETTING/PROPS/COSTUMES

This play has four scenes for seven readers. Doug and Nicole and their parents are together. Their friend, Quizy (an alien from another planet), is with them. They're discussing budgets. Props could include calculators, paper, and pencils. Costumes are not needed. Quizy's clothing and appearance is limited only by students' imagination!

Pronunciation guides may be provided in the script in square brackets. The words are divided into syllables. The syllable to be stressed is in capital letters. For example, the pronunciation guide for Quizy's name would be [QUIZ-ee]. The reader should use the pronunciation guide but not read it aloud.

CHARACTERS

NARRATOR 1

NARRATOR 2

DOUG

NICOLE

DAD

MOM

QUIZY (an alien visitor who collects empty tissue boxes)

Planning to Spend

Scene 1: What Is a Budget?

NARRATOR 1: It seems like I'm always running out of money.

NARRATOR 2: Me, too!

NARRATOR 1: We need a budget.

NARRATOR 2: I don't know how to make one.

NARRATOR 1: Maybe Doug and Nicole's family do.

NARRATOR 1: Let's listen.

DAD: Time to make a budget.

QUIZY: It won't.

DOUG: It won't what?

QUIZY: It won't budge. It won't move at all.

NICOLE: Not "budge." Budget.

QUIZY: What's that?

MOM: It's a way to know where your money should go.

QUIZY: I'll take the money.

DOUG: No, the money has to pay the bills.

QUIZY: Who's he?

NICOLE: He who?

QUIZY: Yes.

DOUG: Yes what?

QUIZY: Who is this guy named Bill?

NICOLE: Not Bill a person.

DAD: Bills are things we have to pay.

MOM: Money we owe to other people.

DOUG: And companies.

NICOLE: Like for electricity.

DAD: And water.

MOM: And our home loan.

DOUG: And the telephone company.

NICOLE: Those types of bills.

QUIZY: But what's a budget?

DAD: It's a way to know how much we have to pay for each bill.

DOUG: Why don't you just put them in a pile and look at them?

MOM: We don't have all the bills for the month yet.

NICOLE: Why not?

DAD: The bills come at different times.

QUIZY: Don't they come in the mail?

MOM: Yes.

QUIZY: The mail always comes at the same time.

DAD: Yes, but the electric bill comes the first week of the month.

MOM: The water bill comes the third week of the month.

DOUG: Then can't you just save all the bills and pay them at once?

DAD: No.

NICOLE: Why not?

MOM:	Because the bills should be paid when they are received.
QUIZY:	Why not just save them anyway?
DAD:	Because that's not right to do.
MOM:	We owe the companies and the people the money right then.
DAD:	If we don't pay on time, then the companies and people lose money.
MOM:	And also, if we don't pay on time the companies might charge us an extra amount of money.
DOUG:	Or stop giving us that service.
QUIZY:	What service?
NICOLE:	For example, if we didn't pay the electric company, they could turn off our electricity.
QUIZY:	I always try to turn off the electricity when I'm not using it.
DAD:	She means they might turn off the electricity to our whole house.
DOUG:	So even if we flipped the light switch on . . .
MOM:	The lights wouldn't work.
QUIZY:	I have a flashlight.
DAD:	But nothing electrical would work.
MOM:	Not even the microwave.
DOUG:	Or the refrigerator.
NICOLE:	Or the TV.
QUIZY:	Then you'd better pay the electric company first.
DAD:	We have to pay all the bills.

Scene 2: Why Do We Need a Budget?

NARRATOR 1: Budgets sound complicated.

NARRATOR 2: Yes. Maybe we don't need a budget after all.

NARRATOR 1: Doug and Nicole's family seem to think they need one.

NARRATOR 2: I'm still not sure how to make one.

NARRATOR 1: Then let's find out how they do it.

DOUG: Why do you need a budget, though?

MOM: Because Dad gets a paycheck on the first of the month and the fifteenth of the month.

DAD: And Mom gets a paycheck on the twenty-third of the month.

NICOLE: So you need to know what bills have to be paid out of each paycheck.

DOUG: And what amount of money you need to NOT spend from each paycheck

DAD: That way we'll be able to make sure we have enough money for the bills that will be coming.

MOM: Then let's make our budget.

QUIZY: I have some paper.

DOUG: I have some paper, too.

QUIZY: My paper is better. It is yellow and red striped with pink flowers.

NICOLE: Very nice, Quizy.

DAD: But we'll use this plain paper.

QUIZY: My budget will be much snazzier.

MOM: I'm sure it will, Quizy.

DAD: Let's list the budget items.

DOUG:	Those are the categories we need to pay.
NICOLE:	What's a category?
QUIZY:	It's some kind of kitty. Cat-agory.
DAD:	No, it's a group of bills that are similar.
MOM:	For example, electricity and water and telephone.
DOUG:	And garbage and sewer.
NICOLE:	Those are all different.
DAD:	But they're similar because they're all utilities.
QUIZY:	You till the what?
DOUG:	Not "you till," Quizy. Utilities.
DAD:	Utilities refer to services that are provided to make our home run.
QUIZY:	I like baseball, too.
MOM:	Baseball?
DOUG:	No, not "home run," Quizy.
DAD:	Utilities make things run—work—in the home.
QUIZY:	OK, I'll put down utilities, too.
NICOLE:	What kind of utilities do you have on your planet, Quizy?
QUIZY:	Mezathine fluid.
DOUG:	What is mezathine?
QUIZY:	I have no idea, but everyone on our planet needs it.
NICOLE:	What's another category for our budget?
DAD:	Housing.
MOM:	We have to pay a certain amount of money every month to the bank.
DAD:	To pay the loan we obtained to buy this house.

DOUG:	What if you don't own a house?
MOM:	Then the house category would be rent.
NICOLE:	What is rent?
DAD:	That's the money people pay to whoever owns the house they're living in.
MOM:	Rent is the money paid for the right to live there.
QUIZY:	We don't have rent on our planet.
MOM:	Why not?
QUIZY:	Caladrops.
DOUG:	What's a caladrop?
QUIZY:	A caladrop is like a big cave.
NICOLE:	You live in caves?
QUIZY:	Sure. That's why we all need the mezathine.
DAD:	OK.
QUIZY:	And if earthlings lived on our planet they would be . . .
MOM:	Cave men?
QUIZY:	No, they would still be earthlings; but they would definitely need electricity, too.
DOUG:	Why?
QUIZY:	Our caladrops are very dark.
NICOLE:	Another category would be food.
QUIZY:	And tissues.
DAD:	Tissues?
QUIZY:	Yes, we need lots of tissues.
MOM:	Why? Do creatures on your planet cry a lot?
QUIZY:	No.
DOUG:	Do they blow their noses?

QUIZY:	We don't have noses.
NICOLE:	What do they need the tissues for?
QUIZY:	We don't need tissues. Just the boxes.
DAD:	Why do you want the boxes?
QUIZY:	Well, look! Aren't they great?
MOM:	If you think so, Quizy.
QUIZY:	I do. In fact I have all of them.
DOUG:	You have all of what?
QUIZY:	All of the tissue boxes you've used since I came to Earth.
NICOLE:	I wondered where they went.
DAD:	What are you going to do with them?
QUIZY:	They're the perfect souvenir.
MOM:	To take back to your planet?
QUIZY:	Yes.
DOUG:	Why?
QUIZY:	We don't have anything like them on my planet.
NICOLE:	OK.
QUIZY:	So I will have a special category in my budget for tissues.

Scene 3: Working the Budget

NARRATOR 1: I have my budget categories all written out.

NARRATOR 2: I do, too.

NARRATOR 1: What do we do next?

NARRATOR 2: Let's find out.

      DAD: OK, we have listed all the categories.

MOM:	And how much we expect each bill to be.
DOUG:	And when we expect each bill to come in.
NICOLE:	So now we can add up how much income we have each month.
QUIZY:	Come in.
DAD:	What?
QUIZY:	Come in.
MOM:	We're already here.
QUIZY:	You said "income."
DOUG:	Yes, she did.
QUIZY:	I'm very good at speaking Earth-ish.
NICOLE:	Yes, you are, Quizy.
QUIZY:	You're not supposed to say income. You say come in.
DAD:	Oh, now I understand. Quizy, "income" is a word.
MOM:	It means earnings.
DOUG:	What money you bring in.
QUIZY:	Oh, the MONEY "comes in."
NICOLE:	Right. But it's called income.
QUIZY:	Because it's backward.
DAD:	Backward?
QUIZY:	Yes, all the money goes out as soon as it comes in, so you have to turn the words inside out to catch it before all the money leaves.
MOM:	Sometimes it feels that way.
DOUG:	Anyway, the money that comes in is called income.
NICOLE:	We add that up.
DAD:	We have some money left over.

MOM: Not very much, but it means . . .

QUIZY: We can go shopping!

DAD: No it means we don't quite have our budget right yet.

DOUG: Why not?

MOM: Because we should make our budget and our income equal each other.

DAD: So we also should have a category called savings.

MOM: And a category called giving.

QUIZY: Giving? You can give your money to me.

DOUG: No. Giving would be what we give to people who need our help.

NICOLE: Like the children's home.

DOUG: Or the church.

NICOLE: Or the boys' camp.

QUIZY: Not me?

DAD: You don't need our money, Quizy.

MOM: You've got all those tissue boxes.

QUIZY: You're right. I'm RICH!

DOUG: So how much should we give?

DAD: Ten percent.

QUIZY: Ten percent of all the bills?

MOM: No, 10 percent of the income.

NICOLE: Why so much?

DAD: It's just a start.

MOM: With great wealth comes great responsibility.

DOUG: I've heard that before.

DAD: It just means that it's good to help people who don't have as much as you do.

NICOLE: Even if you're not really wealthy?

MOM: You're always better off than someone.

QUIZY: Wow. Think of the last person.

DOUG: What last person?

QUIZY: If you're better than someone else.

DAD: Yes.

QUIZY: And that person is better than another person.

MOM: Yes.

QUIZY: Then keep going until you get to the last person.

DOUG: Yes.

QUIZY: He's got to be really bad off.

NICOLE: Then that's more of a reason to help others.

QUIZY: But what about saving?

Scene 4: Pay Yourself First

NARRATOR 1: This budget thing isn't that hard after all.

NARRATOR 2: It sounds like there's one more item to include in our budget.

NARRATOR 1: Savings?

NARRATOR 2: Yes, let's find out how to do that.

DAD: We already have enough money to pay the bills.

MOM: Yes, but we should still plan to save money every month.

DOUG: Why?

DAD: Many reasons.

NICOLE: Dad or Mom might lose a job.

QUIZY:	Couldn't they find it again?
DOUG:	They might not be able to work if they were sick or hurt.
QUIZY:	That'd be bad.
NICOLE:	Yes, it would.
QUIZY:	But would they still have to pay the bills?
DAD:	Yes, we would.
DOUG:	Wouldn't the companies let them not pay for awhile?
QUIZY:	Give them a recess?
MOM:	No.
QUIZY:	Those meanies.
DAD:	They're not mean.
MOM:	They have bills to pay, too.
DOUG:	The companies have bills, too?
DAD:	Yes, they rely on income from the people who pay their bills.
MOM:	So they can pay their employees who work for them.
DAD:	So those employees can pay THEIR bills.
NICOLE:	Then let's hope Mom and Dad don't lose their jobs.
MOM:	There are other reasons to save, too.
QUIZY:	Like what?
DAD:	For big things that cost a lot of money.
MOM:	Like a new car.
DOUG:	Or college for us.
NICOLE:	Or investments.
QUIZY:	I know about those!

DAD:	You do, Quizy?
QUIZY:	Yes! It's how you get your money to work for you.
MOM:	That's right!
QUIZY:	We don't have investments on our planet.
DOUG:	Why not?
QUIZY:	We don't have money.
NICOLE:	Or tissue boxes, we remember.
DAD:	What do you have on your planet, Quizy?
QUIZY:	Caladrops and mezathine.
MOM:	Right. But no noses.
DOUG:	So whatever is left over at the end of the month goes into savings?
DAD:	Not if we have a budget.
NICOLE:	What do you mean?
MOM:	Because we have a budget, we know how much money goes where.
DAD:	It's a way to pre-spend our money.
DOUG:	And if savings is on our budget . . .
NICOLE:	We know just how much money to save.
MOM:	And we pay ourselves first.
DOUG:	Pay ourselves?
DAD:	Yes, by putting money into savings first, we are doing our best to plan for our future.
QUIZY:	How can you plan for the future when you don't know what will happen in the future?
MOM:	Exactly.
DOUG:	Mom, you're starting to sound like Quizy.
MOM:	Thank you . . . I think.

NICOLE: But how CAN you plan for the future?

DOUG: You can't know what will happen in the future, so the best thing you can do is save money.

MOM: That way you will have money to use in an emergency

DAD: Or to use to work for you to make more money.

DOUG: Cool.

QUIZY: That's even better than tissue boxes.

NICOLE: It sure is.

GLOSSARY

Bill: A statement of an amount of money due to a business.

Budget: A written plan to allocate money to pay all bills and provide for savings and investment for a specific time period.

Category: A grouping of similar items.

Checkbook: A package of checks grouped together in numerical order that can be used to make payments to other people or businesses.

Checking account: A type of account at a bank in which the bank holds money for a person or business and provides the person with checks and/or debit cards that can be used to easily make payments to others.

Ledger: A book or pages to keep track of money received and paid out.

Overdrawn: When you spend more money in your bank account than you have. The bank will usually charge you a big fee when this happens.

Utility: A service (such as electricity, water, or sewer).

DOING TO UNDERSTAND

The following activities are included as handouts:

1. Create a Budget
2. Career Goal
3. Balance Your Checkbook
4. Board Game

ACTIVITY 1. CREATE A BUDGET

Before you start a budget you need to know two things: your income and your spending. How much money do you receive on an ongoing basis (allowance; jobs; regular payments from investments), and what do you spend your money on? You separate the spending into categories and pre-spend your money.

For an adult these categories include income, giving, taxes, housing, food, transportation, insurance, debts (car loans/credit cards/personal loans), entertainment, clothing, savings, medical, investments, and miscellaneous.

Sometimes "seeing" the money come in and go out will make the budget process easier to understand. Create a budget using made-up amounts for each category. Then print up paper money (see appendix 1) and "pay" each budget item according to your "income."

ACTIVITY 2. CAREER GOAL

Determine a career goal (include what level of education is needed for that career). Do enough research to set a beginning salary for a job in that career. Use that salary as your income basis. Then, using information from the newspaper and your family, fill out a budget. How did you do? Were you able to pay for all the items in the budget and still have money left over?

ACTIVITY 3. BALANCE YOUR CHECKBOOK

Many people like to use credit cards and bank debit cards to pay for things they buy, because they are easy to use. Credit cards charge purchases and then the person pays for all of the purchases at once when he receives the credit card bill. A debit card looks like a credit card, but the amount of each purchase is taken right out of the person's bank account. There is no bill to pay each month. And, even better, the bank does not charge interest on the purchases.

Like using a debit card, payment by check comes out of a buyer's bank account when the seller that receives the check deposits it into its own bank account or cashes it at the bank.

Although many people prefer to use debit cards, checks are still used for many purchases and for paying bills. Part of having a checking account at a bank includes the responsibility to make sure there is enough money in the account to cover the checks and debit charges made.

Each person should check his account each month. Usually this is done by balancing the checkbook. This is how it is done:

1. First make sure that every time you make a payment with your debit card or pay with a check, you note the date and amount in your checkbook ledger. For example, if you write a check on January 3 to Harry's Hardware for $10.26 to buy nails, you would write the date, the amount, the check number, and the recipient in your checkbook. Each check has a number printed on it so you can keep track of the checks you have written.

2. Each time you put money into your account, write a check, or make a debit charge, add or subtract the amount from your total (called your account balance). For example, if you start out your account with $100 and then you deposit (put) $50 into the account, ADD the $50 to the $100 so that your total (balance) now shows $150. Then each time you write a check or charge a debit from your account, SUBTRACT that amount from your balance. That way you will always know how much money is in your account.

3. At the same time each month, the bank will send you a statement of your account. It will show how much money you deposited (put) into your account and all of the checks or debits that were taken out of your account (subtracted) when they were paid by the bank.

4. Look at each item listed on the bank statement and make sure you have written every item in your checkbook ledger. Sometimes the bank makes mistakes, but usually it is the account owner who has forgotten to write down a deposit or a check or debit. Find any errors and correct them.

5. Check your math.

6. Sometimes banks charge a fee to allow you to have a checking account. They may charge this fee every month. Make sure to SUBTRACT that fee (shown on the bank statement) from your account balance.

7. Some banks pay interest on the money in your account. This interest will be shown on the bank statement. Make sure to ADD that interest to your account balance.

ACTIVITY 3. BALANCE YOUR CHECKBOOK (CONT.)

8. It is important to know exactly how much money is in your account, because the bank will usually charge you a big fee if you try to cash a check or make a debit for more than the money in your account. If you try to use more money than you have in your account, the bank says your account "is overdrawn" and will usually charge you a fee. This fee, often called an "overdraft fee," will also be shown on your account statement. Depending on your bank, the bank may transfer money from another account you have at the bank to cover the amount of the check. That way whomever you paid will receive the money. But you will still have to pay your bank a fee for transferring money for you. Make sure you SUBTRACT that amount from your account.

    If you write a check when your account does not have enough money to cover it, the check will "bounce." When a check bounces at a business, that business may also charge you another fee (often $20 or more) PLUS the amount of the check. The business may also report your bad check to the credit reporting bureaus. As a result, you may not be able to get a credit card or a good loan in the future. So it is REALLY important to manage the balance in your checking account.

Using the checkbook ledger on page 161, make up check payments, debit charges, deposits, fees, and interests to an account. Add and subtract the amounts and show your totals. Make sure to fill in all of the information in each column and include at least 10 entries.

CHECKBOOK LEDGER

Enter amounts into the checkbook ledger. In the "Transaction" column write down who the check was paid to and for what, or information about a deposit. Subtract check amounts and fees in the "Check Amount" column from the balance; add interest and deposit amounts in the "Deposit Amount" column to the balance.

Date	Check No.	Transaction	Check Amount ($)	Deposit Amount ($)	Balance ($)
		To:			
		For:			
		To:			
		For:			
		To:			
		For:			
		To:			
		For:			
		To:			
		For:			
		To:			
		For:			
		To:			
		For:			
		To:			
		For:			
		To:			
		For:			
		To:			
		For:			
		To:			
		For:			
		To:			
		For:			

From *Fun with Finance: Math + Literacy = Success* by Carol Peterson. Santa Barbara, CA: Libraries Unlimited. Copyright © 2009.

ACTIVITY 4. BOARD GAME

Budget Bonus

The object of the Budget Bonus board game is to have the most money at the end of the game. This game can be played in small groups of two to four. To play you need:

    a calculator

    a pencil and paper

    small game pieces for each player

    1 die

    1 game board (see appendix 1) for each player

    1 center board (see appendix 1)

    1 bank board (see appendix 1)

    the Star, Moon, Sun, and Flash cards from the handouts (pp. 164–167)

    paper money (see appendix 1)

Set Up

Photocopy one set of cards for each game played. For example, a group of four players will need one set of Star cards, one set of Moon cards, one set of Sun cards, and one set of Flash cards. Place the piles of cards facedown in their boxes on the center board. When players have drawn all the cards in one pile, they should be shuffled and replaced, facedown on the center board, to reuse.

    ☆ STAR CARDS move the game forward

    ☾ MOON CARDS move the game back

    ☼ SUN CARDS help all players

    ⚡ FLASH CARDS speed a player ahead

Cut all cards and money along the lines.
Provide one game board for each player.
Photocopy enough money so there four pages' worth for each player. At the beginning of the game, each player receives one of each of the following bills: $10, $20, $50, $100. The rest of the money is placed on the bank board for use during play.
Use pencil, paper, and calculators, if needed.

ACTIVITY 4. BOARD GAME (CONT.)

Play

Each player rolls the die to find out who plays first; whoever gets the largest number on the die plays first. Play then rotates counterclockwise.

Players travel around the board, moving forward the number of spaces on the die. If a player lands on a space with a symbol on it, that player takes a card from the pile with that symbol and does what the card says.

If a player lands on a Flash space and draws a card that sends him or her across the speed zone, the player moves through the center bar of the dollar sign to the next nearest shaded space at the end of the speed zone.

A player who does not have enough to pay the total owed must pay all he or she has to the bank and then skip one turn.

The game ends when the first person finishes a trip around the board and lands on "Finish." The player does not have to have an exact roll of the die to land on "Finish."

All players then count their money. If they have more than $200 they can bet $200 and keep the rest. If they have $200 or less, they must bet all of it.

Each person then rolls the die. If the player rolls a 1, 2, or 3, he or she has decided to spend all that was bet on something unnecessary. If the player rolls a 4, 5, or 6, he or she has decided to save it and receives another $50 from the bank.

All players count their money again. The person with the most money wins the game.

STAR CARDS FOR BUDGET BONUS GAME

(Photocopy, cut, and place facedown on center board.)

Your budget is working. Receive $50 from the bank. ☆	Your budget is working. Receive $50 from the bank. ☆	Your budget is working. Receive $50 from the bank. ☆
Payday. Receive $100 from the bank. ☆	Payday. Receive $100 from the bank. ☆	Payday. Receive $100 from the bank. ☆
Payday. Receive $100 from the bank. ☆	Payday. Receive $100 from the bank. ☆	Payday. Receive $100 from the bank. ☆

MOON CARDS FOR BUDGET BONUS GAME

(Photocopy, cut, and place facedown on center board.)

Your house payment is due. Pay the bank $200.	Your house payment is due. Pay the bank $200.	Your house payment is due. Pay the bank $200.
Your car payment is due. Pay the bank $100.	Your car payment is due. Pay the bank $100.	Your car payment is due. Pay the bank $100.
Your utility payments are due. Pay the bank $50.	Go to the grocery store. Pay the bank $50.	You need new tires. Pay the bank $50.

From *Fun with Finance: Math + Literacy = Success* by Carol Peterson. Santa Barbara, CA: Libraries Unlimited. Copyright © 2009.

SUN CARDS FOR BUDGET BONUS GAME

(Photocopy, cut, and place facedown on center board.)

EMERGENCY! Everyone needs new shoes. All players pay the bank $50.	EMERGENCY! Everyone goes to the dentist. All players pay the bank $50.	EMERGENCY! Everyone's credit card bill is due. All players pay the bank $50.
Your credit card payment was late! Pay the bank a $50 late fee.	Property tax is due. Pay the bank $100.	You go on vacation. Pay the bank $100.
Your house payment is due. Pay the bank $100.	Your car needs brakes. Pay the bank $100.	You broke your budget. Pay the bank $50.

FLASH CARDS FOR BUDGET BONUS GAME

(Photocopy, cut, and place facedown on center board.)

Your boss pays you a bonus! Advance to nearest speed zone. Cross zone and land on next STAR space after zone. Take a Star card AND receive $100 from the bank.	Your boss pays you a bonus! Advance to nearest speed zone. Cross zone and land on next STAR space after zone. Take a Star card AND receive $100 from the bank.	Your boss pays you a bonus! Advance to nearest speed zone. Cross zone and land on next STAR space after zone. Take a Star card AND receive $100 from the bank.
Your boss pays you a bonus! Advance to nearest speed zone. Cross zone and land on next STAR space after zone. Take a Star card AND receive $100 from the bank.	Your boss pays you a bonus! Advance to nearest speed zone. Cross zone and land on next STAR space after zone. Take a Star card AND receive $100 from the bank.	Your boss pays you a bonus! Advance to nearest speed zone. Cross zone and land on next STAR space after zone. Take a Star card AND receive $100 from the bank.
Take an extra turn.	Take an extra turn.	Take an extra turn.

THINK ABOUT

Some people hate budgets; they feel restricted. But you can also think of budgets as "pre-spending" your income. Before you even get your paycheck, estimate what it will be and determine exactly how it needs to be spent. That way you have planned ahead and know exactly where your money will go so that you don't just spend, spend, spend and then not have enough to pay for what you owe others. That's how people get into debt trouble.

FIND OUT MORE

Resources in Your Community

Find out whether a parent or family friend of a student works in the area of financial advice. Ask that person to visit the class to share experiences or answer questions.

Web Sites

- Go to www.personalbudgeting.com.
- To have Microsoft help you prepare a budget. go to http://office.microsoft.com/en-us/templates/CT101172321033.aspx.
- For a budget template, go to http://financialplan.about.com.

Careers

Related jobs include financial advisor or counselor, bookkeeper, and accountant.

CHAPTER 7

❧ $ ☙

Real Estate Rush

Subject Matter: Real estate (homes, businesses, land) as an investment; the real estate purchase process; loans

Math Standards Addressed:

    Number Sense: computing numbers; decimals; multiplication; fractions

    Data Analysis, Graphs

    Simple Geometry

    Percentage

Literacy Standards Addressed:

    Vocabulary and Concept Development

    Reading Comprehension

    Spelling

Written and Oral English Standards Addressed:

    Listening and Speaking Applications

    Verbal Communication

    Research and Technology

WHAT IS REAL ESTATE?

Real estate includes homes, land, buildings, and businesses. People buy real estate as an investment and hope it increases in value over time. Or they can receive money from other people who use that property, such as when a person pays rent to a landlord for the right to live in an apartment. The owner of the apartment could then use the rent money to pay taxes on the property, to make repairs or improvements, and to pay bank loans. The owner could use any leftover rent to pay her personal bills, just as she could do with income from a job.

When you buy or sell real estate, you must make sure that ownership passes properly from the old owner to the new owner. The process involves a lot of details. Every purchase and sale of real estate is different. But there are common parts to all of them. Let's see how a purchase and sale of a house using a real estate agent might work.

SETTING/PROPS/COSTUMES

This play has seven scenes for ten readers. Doug, Nicole, and their parents, Mr. and Mrs. Smith, are looking to sell their home and buy a new one. Mrs. Roberts, a real estate agent, a home inspector, and Miss Jacobs, an escrow officer, are helping them. Quizy (a friendly alien from another planet) is with them. Props could include telephones, a briefcase, calculators, paper, and pencils. Costumes are not needed. Quizy's clothing and appearance is limited only by students' imagination!

Pronunciation guides may be provided in the script in square brackets. The words are divided into syllables. The syllable to be stressed is in capital letters. For example, the pronunciation guide for Quizy's name would be [QUIZ-ee]. The reader should use the pronunciation guide but not read it aloud.

CHARACTERS

NARRATOR 1

NARRATOR 2

MOM (MRS. SMITH)

DAD (MR. SMITH)

DOUG

NICOLE

MRS. ROBERTS

INSPECTOR

MISS MARTIN

QUIZY (a friendly alien visitor who collects empty tissue boxes)

Old House/ New House

Scene 1: Finding a House to Buy

NARRATOR: Some people think all you need are boxes and a big truck to move to a new house.

NARRATOR: But when you buy a house, you also need paper. Lots of paper.

DOUG: Mom and Dad decided we needed a bigger house.

NICOLE: They're meeting with a lady.

MRS. ROBERTS: Hello, I'm Rona Roberts. I'm a real estate agent.

QUIZY: An "agent"? You don't look like a spy. Where's your secret camera?

MRS. ROBERTS: An agent just means someone who does something on behalf of someone else.

DOUG: So you're here to help us buy a new house?

MRS. ROBERTS: That's right. Let's go find one that's perfect for your family.

NARRATOR 1: Mrs. Roberts drove the Smith family around town.

NARRATOR 2: The Smiths and Mrs. Roberts went inside houses that people wanted to sell.

NICOLE: Wow. These people have really cool stuff!

DOUG: Look, they even have a piano.

QUIZY:	Doug, I'll bet you could make great music. Give us a concert!
NARRATOR 1:	Doug reached out to touch the piano keys.
NICOLE:	Would you like people touching the things in your room?
QUIZY:	Like the models in his room?
DOUG:	Mom, I'll just hang on to your arm.
QUIZY:	Doug, go ahead and play the piano. I know you want to!
DOUG:	I'll put my other hand in my pocket.
NARRATOR 2:	Nicole also wanted to touch the piano.
NICOLE:	I'll put my hands in my pockets, too.
NARRATOR 1:	Another house they visited had striped wallpaper in the kitchen.
QUIZY:	This place makes me dizzy! I'm Dizzy Quizy!
NARRATOR 2:	Another house was almost perfect.
MOM:	This house has no backyard.
DOUG:	No backyard?
NICOLE:	Where would Rascal play?
QUIZY:	No backyard for the dog means nothing to scoop up!
NICOLE:	We have to have a backyard for Rascal.
DAD:	Yes, a backyard is a must.
MRS. ROBERTS:	Then let's look at another house.
NARRATOR 1:	Mrs. Roberts took the Smiths to see the Lees' house.
NARRATOR 2:	Mr. and Mrs. Lee's house was just right.
MOM:	The kitchen is lovely.
DAD:	There's a nice backyard.
NICOLE:	That tree is perfect for climbing.

DOUG: And sitting under.

QUIZY: With Rascal.

Scene 2: Making an Offer

NARRATOR 1: The Smiths and Mrs. Roberts went back to the Smiths' home.

DAD: We'd like to buy the Lees' house.

MRS. ROBERTS: We need to fill out the paperwork.

NARRATOR 2: She pulled out a big packet of papers.

MRS. ROBERTS: These papers are your offer. Let's fill in the blank lines.

NARRATOR 1: The offer told Mr. and Mrs. Lee how much money Mom and Dad were willing to pay for the house . . .

NARRATOR 2: And when the Smiths wanted to move in.

MRS. ROBERTS: Now, if everything looks right, just sign the last page.

DOUG: Mom and Dad are reading all those papers!

QUIZY: That's a lot of paper.

DAD: Sign here?

MOM: Yes, next to the word *buyers*.

MRS. ROBERTS: I'll present the offer to Mr. and Mrs. Lee and let you know what they say.

NARRATOR 1: The next day Mrs. Roberts came back with the papers.

MRS. ROBERTS: Mr. and Mrs. Lee have signed them.

DOUG: Can I see?

MRS. ROBERTS: They signed here next to the word *sellers*.

QUIZY: Like a basement?

DOUG:	Not cellar. "Sellers." Because they're selling the house.
DAD:	Mr. and Mrs. Lee liked our offer.
MOM:	We're going to buy their house!
NICOLE:	Do we get to move in today?
DAD:	No, not today. There's so much to do.
MOM:	Packing and sorting and . . .
MRS. ROBERTS:	Lots and lots of paperwork.
DAD:	And we have to sell this house first.
NARRATOR 2:	Mr. and Mrs. Smith showed Mrs. Roberts around their house.
DOUG:	Why is she asking so many questions about our house?
QUIZY:	Because she's snoopy, that's why.
NICOLE:	No. She needs to know about our house so she can find someone to buy it.
QUIZY:	Someone who doesn't want striped wallpaper in the kitchen!
MRS. ROBERTS:	Mr. and Mrs. Smith, do you have an idea how much you want to sell your house for?
DOUG:	Two hundred bazillion bucks!
NICOLE:	Don't be silly, Doug.
QUIZY:	Yes, don't be silly Doug. You meant three hundred bazillion bucks!
NARRATOR 1:	Mrs. Roberts told the Smiths how much other houses in their town were selling for.
NARRATOR 2:	Then she and Mr. and Mrs. Smith decided on a price for their house.
MRS. ROBERTS:	We will need to fill out the papers to sell your house.

DOUG:	More papers?
QUIZY:	Four hundred bazillion papers!
MRS. ROBERTS:	By signing these papers, you give me the right to help sell your house for you.
NARRATOR 1:	Later that week, Mrs. Roberts brought the Carter family to look at the Smith's house.
QUIZY:	Doug, you'd better follow them so they don't touch anything!
NICOLE:	Look, Mrs. Carter is holding her son's hand.
DOUG:	And he's got his other hand in his pocket!
QUIZY:	I GUESS your stuff is safe . . .

Scene 3: Another Offer

NARRATOR 1:	The next day Mrs. Roberts came back again.
DOUG:	You brought more papers?
QUIZY:	They look just like the ones Mom and Dad signed first.
MRS. ROBERTS:	These are from the Carters. It's their offer.
DAD:	They want to buy our house!
NARRATOR 2:	Mrs. Roberts and Mr. and Mrs. Smith discussed the papers for a long time.
QUIZY:	What's so interesting about those papers? They don't even have pictures.
DOUG:	Shh. I'm trying to listen.
NICOLE:	Look! Dad is signing them.
DOUG:	Where?
QUIZY:	In the basement?
NICOLE:	Next to the word sellers.
DOUG:	I thought Mom and Dad were the buyers.

NICOLE:	They're the buyers of the Lees' house and the sellers of this house.
QUIZY:	But we don't HAVE a basement.
DOUG:	We are going to sell our house to the Carters.
MRS. ROBERTS:	I'll take these papers and open an escrow [ES-krow].
DOUG:	Is that like opening a window?
QUIZY:	All those papers will blow outside!
NICOLE:	What is opening an escrow?
MRS. ROBERTS:	A way to make sure all the paperwork gets done just right.
NICOLE:	How do you do that?
MRS. ROBERTS:	These papers say how the houses will be bought and sold. There are people who make sure everything gets done just like the papers say.
NICOLE:	Who are these people?
QUIZY:	They have to be big so they can act like paperweights.
MRS. ROBERTS:	The people are called escrow officers.
QUIZY:	Escrow officers must be like police officers. They blow a whistle to direct the papers to march around the room.
MRS. ROBERTS:	It's the papers that tell the escrow officers what to do.
NARRATOR 1:	Mrs. Roberts stuffed the packet of papers into her briefcase.
NARRATOR 2:	She had other packets of paper in her briefcase.
NICOLE:	What are all those papers for?
MRS. ROBERTS:	They're for other people who are buying and selling houses.

DOUG: That's a lot of papers.

QUIZY: Maybe having a special place to open an escrow is a good idea.

Scene 4: Bank Papers

NARRATOR 1: After Mrs. Roberts left Mr. and Mrs. Smith called the bank.

DAD: The bank is sending its papers to escrow for us to sign.

NICOLE: Why is the bank sending papers, too?

MOM: Most people don't have enough money to buy a whole house.

DAD: So they pay for some of the house with a down payment and borrow the rest of the money from a bank.

DOUG: How is a down payment different from an up payment?

QUIZY: It has to do with the cellar.

MOM: No, it just means you put some money down—like setting it down on the table—to show that you really intend to buy the house.

DAD: It shows the bank and the sellers you are serious.

MOM: And the down payment pays for part of the cost of the house.

DOUG: And the bank loans you the rest of the money?

DAD: Yes. We'll sign papers in escrow promising to pay back the money.

MOM: A little bit every month.

NICOLE: Will Mr. and Mrs. Carter be signing papers for their bank, too, so they can buy our house?

DAD:	Yes, and we'll sign different papers so that the bank that loaned us money to buy this house will be paid before we start the new loan for the new house.
QUIZY:	Too many papers! I'm dizzy again.
MOM:	And Mr. and Mrs. Lee will sign papers for the bank so they can buy their new house, too.
DOUG:	I never thought of that. Where were Mr. and Mrs. Lee going to live once we bought their house?
QUIZY:	Probably in a cellar.

Scene 5: Getting Ready

NARRATOR 1:	While everyone was filling up the escrow with papers, Mrs. Roberts brought an inspector to the Smiths' house.
NARRATOR 2:	The inspector walked through the house with a clipboard full of papers. He poked at the floor next to the bathtub.
INSPECTOR:	No water damage. I'll just make a note on my papers.
NARRATOR 1:	Then the inspector went outside.
NARRATOR 2:	He dug in the dirt where the walls touched the ground.
INSPECTOR:	Bug free. I'll make another note. No termites.
NARRATOR 1:	Then the inspector took a silver ladder off his truck.
NARRATOR 2:	He leaned the ladder against the house and climbed up to the roof.
QUIZY:	What's he doing up there?
DOUG:	He's looking inside the gutters.
NICOLE:	And under the edge of the roof.
DOUG:	And on top of the roof.

QUIZY:	He would probably check our cellar if we had one.
NICOLE:	Yes, he would.
NARRATOR 1:	The inspector climbed down from the ladder.
NARRATOR 2:	He made more notes on his papers.
INSPECTOR:	I'm done with the inspection.
NARRATOR 1:	He handed Mrs. Roberts a set of papers.
INSPECTOR:	It all looks fine. No repairs are needed.
MRS. ROBERTS:	Great. Make sure you send a copy of your paperwork to escrow.
QUIZY:	Escrow must be full of papers by now!
NARRATOR 1:	The Smiths began to pack for their move.
NARRATOR 2:	They tried to fit everything from their drawers and closets into big boxes.
QUIZY:	Doug, where are you?
DOUG:	Behind this pile of boxes!
QUIZY:	At least you're not IN a box.
NICOLE:	We're almost done packing.
DOUG:	Good. We've been packing for two months. I wonder when we'll move.
QUIZY:	I CAN'T move. I'm stuck behind these boxes.
NARRATOR 1:	Just then the phone rang.
NARRATOR 2:	It was Mrs. Roberts.
DAD:	Escrow is ready to close.
QUIZY:	Like a window?
DOUG:	I sure hope so.

Scene 6: Closing Escrow

NARRATOR 1: The Smiths and Mrs. Roberts went to a big office.

NARRATOR 2: Thick folders full of papers lay on a long table in the center of the room.

DOUG: I'm glad an open escrow isn't like an open window.

QUIZY: We'd be in big trouble.

NARRATOR 1: A woman introduced herself.

MISS MARTIN: I'm Miss Martin—the escrow officer.

QUIZY: Where's her whistle?

MISS MARTIN: I don't have a whistle, only a lot of papers to be signed.

NARRATOR 2: Miss Martin handed the first packet to Mom and Dad.

MISS MARTIN: These papers are your promise to pay back the money you are borrowing.

QUIZY: A bazillion bucks?

MISS MARTIN: Not quite.

NARRATOR 1: Mom and Dad read the bank papers carefully.

NARRATOR 2: Then they signed next to the word *borrowers*.

QUIZY: Does that mean they have to do a lot of digging?

NICOLE: "Borrow," Quizy, not "burrow"!

MISS MARTIN: It means they accept a loan from the bank and promise to pay it back.

NARRATOR 1: Miss Martin handed Mom and Dad another stack of papers.

MISS MARTIN: These papers will change ownership of your house to the Carter family.

NARRATOR 2: Mom and Dad read the papers carefully.

NARRATOR 1: Then they signed next to the word *sellers*.

QUIZY: Like down in the . . .

DOUG: Don't say it!

NARRATOR 2: Miss Martin handed Mom and Dad another stack of papers.

MISS MARTIN: These papers will change the ownership of the new house from Mr. and Mrs. Lee to you.

NARRATOR 1: Mom and Dad read the papers.

NARRATOR 2: Then they signed next to the word *buyers*.

NICOLE: Is the house ours, now?

MRS. ROBERTS: Not yet.

MISS MARTIN: Mr. and Mrs. Lee will sign the papers later this morning.

MRS. ROBERTS: And Mr. and Mrs. Carter will sign their papers this afternoon.

DOUG: Then the house will be ours?

MISS MARTIN: Almost. After everyone has signed the papers, the bank will send the money to escrow.

NICOLE: The bank will bring all that money right here?

QUIZY: All two bazillion bucks?

DOUG: Can we stay and watch? I've never seen that much money before.

MRS. ROBERTS: No, the bank doesn't bring actual money. Sometimes banks pay with a paper check.

MISS MARTIN: And sometimes money is transferred by a computer between the bank and this office.

QUIZY: I wish we had a computer that would send us money, too!

MRS. ROBERTS: Once everyone has all the money they are supposed to get . . .

NICOLE:	THEN the new house will be ours?
MRS. ROBERTS:	Nearly. Some of these papers have to be sent to the government. The papers will prove that your family owns the new house.
MISS MARTIN:	It's called recording the papers.
DOUG:	Recording? Like music?
QUIZY:	Let's dance!
MISS MARTIN:	Recording means to make the change of ownership public. So that everyone knows who owns the houses now.
MRS. ROBERTS:	When the papers are recorded, *then* escrow is closed and the new house is yours.
NICOLE:	There are so many papers.
MRS. ROBERTS:	Yes, but they're important.
MISS MARTIN:	They make sure the money and the ownership are transferred just right.

Scene 7: New House/Our House

NARRATOR 1:	That afternoon the Smith family drove their moving truck to the new house.
NARRATOR 2:	Mrs. Roberts was there.
NARRATOR 1:	She handed a set of shiny keys to Mom.
NARRATOR 2:	And she shook Dad's hand.
MRS. ROBERTS:	Congratulations on your new home.
MOM:	Thank you! It's perfect.
DAD:	Thank you for your help, Mrs. Roberts.
MRS. ROBERTS:	That's my job.
NICOLE:	Did they close the escrow?
MRS. ROBERTS:	Yes, they did.

DOUG: And the house is ours?

MRS. ROBERTS: The house is yours!

DOUG: Come on Rascal. Wait till you see the backyard.

NICOLE: There's a big tree.

DOUG: Paper is made from trees, Rascal.

NICOLE: And you need a lot of paper to buy a house.

DOUG: Don't worry, Rascal. We're not going to make paper from THIS tree.

NICOLE: This tree is all ours.

QUIZY: Piles of paper made sure it was ours!

GLOSSARY

Borrower: A person who borrows money; who takes a loan.

Buyer: A person who buys something.

Closing escrow: Once a sale is done, all papers have been signed and all money and property have been transferred, the escrow is called "closed."

Escrow: A process for handling the paperwork to buy or sell houses.

Escrow officer: The person in charge is called the "escrow officer" and has no personal interest in the house. For example, the seller cannot be the escrow officer because the buyer might not think she would be fair. In some places the escrow officer is a lawyer, in other places it is a person who does nothing else besides handling paperwork to buy and sell houses.

Lender: The person or business that loans money to someone else.

Inspector: A person who checks a building before a sale to make sure it is safe and doesn't need to be fixed. The seller may have to fix something that is broken before the house is sold.

Mortgage: The term used to describe the legal process of obtaining a loan on real estate. If the borrower fails to pay back the loan, the lender takes ownership of the property.

Offer: Papers in which buyers tell sellers how much they are willing to pay for the house and when they want to move in. Sellers can agree to the price, reject the offer, or tell the buyers a different price they are willing to take.

Opening escrow: Starting the process of collecting all the information and papers to buy or sell real estate.

Passive income: Income that you receive without having to do any physical work.

Real estate: Land, houses, offices, or any other kind of building.

Real estate agent: A person with a special license to help people buy and sell houses.

Recording: Filing papers with the government to prove transfer of ownership of property from a seller to a buyer.

Seller: A person who sells something.

Termite: A type of bug that eats wood and can destroy a building. A termite inspection is almost always done on a property to make sure the structure of the building is strong and safe.

DOING TO UNDERSTAND

The following activities are included as handouts:

1. Comparing Home Prices
2. Price per Square Foot
3. Charting Information
4. Board Game

ACTIVITY 1. COMPARING HOME PRICES

Get copies of the local newspaper. Search the want ad section for homes for sale. Find 10 homes to compare. Jot down the price of the home, the number of bedrooms (often shown as bd), and the number of bathrooms (often shown as ba; a ½ bath is a bathroom with a toilet and sink but no shower or tub). List the square footage of each house. This will usually be listed as a number with sf after it. Also list anything that makes this home special, such as a pool, a large backyard, or anything that sounds good to you.

Can you see anything that tells you why the price of one home might be more than another?

ACTIVITY 2. PRICE PER SQUARE FOOT

Part of how a house is priced is based on its square footage. That means how big the house is in terms of floor space. You use geometry to figure out square footage. If a house is 20 feet long and 50 feet wide and has only one floor, this is how you would compute its square footage:

$$\begin{array}{r} 20 \text{ feet long} \\ \times\ 50 \text{ feet wide} \\ \hline 1{,}000 \text{ square feet} \end{array}$$

If the house has two floors that are each 20 feet long and 50 feet wide, the square footage of the house would be calculated like this:

$$\begin{array}{r} 1{,}000 \text{ square feet} \\ \times\ 2 \text{ stories} \\ \hline 2{,}000 \text{ square feet} \end{array}$$

Let's say the price of this house is $100,000. You could compute the price of the home by its square footage, like this:

$$\begin{array}{r} \$100{,}000 \text{ price} \\ \div\ 2{,}000 \text{ square feet} \\ \hline \$50.00 \text{ per square foot} \end{array}$$

The above example tells you the house costs $50.00 for each square foot. Price per square foot is one way to compare prices of different homes.

Using the following table and the homes you picked in Activity 1, fill in the price, the square footage, and the price per square foot for each one. What kind of chart or graph could you create to show the information from this table?

Chart of Homes

Address	Price	Square Feet	Price/Square Foot

ACTIVITY 3. CHARTING INFORMATION

What type of visual representation could you use to show the differences among these 10 homes? Would it be a simple chart? A pie chart? A graph? Review the information on charts and graphs (see appendixes 2–5) to help you decide. As a class, discuss what the information in your "Chart of Homes" tells you about the homes in the town where you live. Vote on which home appears to be the best value for the asking price.

ACTIVITY 4. BOARD GAME

Real Estate Rush

The object of the Real Estate Rush board game is to have the most money at the end of the game. This game can be played in small groups of two to four. To play you need:

a calculator

a pencil and paper

small game pieces for each player

1 die

1 game board (see appendix 1) for each player

1 center board (see appendix 1)

1 bank board (see appendix 1)

the Star, Moon, Sun, and Flash cards from the handouts (pp. 190–193)

paper money (see appendix 1)

Set Up

Photocopy one set of cards for each game played. For example, a group of four players will need one set of Star cards, one set of Moon cards, one set of Sun cards, and one set of Flash cards. Place the piles of cards facedown in their boxes on the center board. When players have drawn all the cards in one pile, they should be shuffled and replaced, facedown on the center board, to reuse.

☆ STAR CARDS move the game forward

☾ MOON CARDS move the game back

☼ SUN CARDS help all players

⚡ FLASH CARDS speed a player ahead

Cut all cards and money along the lines.
Provide one game board for each player.
Photocopy enough money so there are four pages' worth for each player. At the beginning of the game, each player receives one of each of the following bills: $10, $20, $50, $100. The rest of the money is placed on the bank board for use during play.

Play

Each player rolls the die to find out who plays first; whoever gets the largest number on the die plays first. Play then rotates counterclockwise.

Players travel around the board, moving forward the number of spaces on the die. If a player lands on a space with a symbol on it, that player takes a card from the pile with that symbol and does what the card says.

From *Fun with Finance: Math + Literacy = Success* by Carol Peterson. Santa Barbara, CA: Libraries Unlimited. Copyright © 2009.

ACTIVITY 4. BOARD GAME (CONT.)

If a player lands on a Flash space and draws a card that sends him or her across the speed zone, the player moves through the center bar of the dollar sign to the next nearest shaded space at the end of the speed zone.

A player who does not have enough to pay the total owed must pay all he or she has to the bank and then skip one turn.

The game ends when the first person finishes a trip around the board and lands on "Finish." The player does not have to have an exact roll of the die to land on "Finish."

Players then buy as much real estate as they can. Any player can buy as much of the following real estate as she can afford. And more than one player can buy the same type of real estate.

Players add up the value of their real estate using this chart. The player with the most value in real estate plus cash wins the game.

Price Paid by Player	Type of Real Estate	Value of Real Estate
$200	mobile home	$ 20,000
$300	1 acre bare land	$ 30,000
$500	condominium	$ 50,000
$600	lakeside cabin	$ 75,000
$700	1,500-square-foot house	$100,000
$800	2,000-square-foot house	$200,000
$900	fast food business	$250,000
$1,000	3,000-square-foot house	$400,000
$1,500	office building	$400,000
$2,000	apartment building	$500,000

STAR CARDS FOR REAL ESTATE RUSH GAME

(Photocopy, cut, and place facedown on center board.)

Your credit rating is GOOD. Receive $100 from the bank to save for real estate. ☆	Your credit rating is GOOD. Receive $100 from the bank to save for real estate. ☆	Your credit rating is EXCELLENT. Receive $200 from the bank to save for real estate. ☆
Your credit rating is EXCELLENT. Receive $200 from the bank to save for real estate. ☆	You get a raise and decide to save the extra for a house. Receive $100 from the bank. ☆	You get a raise and decide to save the extra for a house. Receive $100 from the bank. ☆
You inherit money from your great-great Aunt Lulu. Receive $100 from the bank. ☆	You win first prize in the Paltry Poetry contest. Receive $100 from the bank. ☆	You sell your solar-powered dishwasher invention. Receive $100 from the bank. ☆

MOON CARDS FOR REAL ESTATE RUSH GAME

(Photocopy, cut, and place facedown on center board.)

A late payment lowers your credit score. Pay the bank $100.	A late payment lowers your credit score. Pay the bank $100.	Your lender loses your loan application. Lose one turn while you send in a new one.
You need to send copies of your bank account statement to your lender. It's a bank holiday. Lose one turn while you wait for your bank to open.	Someone has the same name as you do, and your lender won't approve your loan until they're sure of your identity. Lose one turn.	Real estate taxes are due. Pay the bank $100.
You need to make repairs on your property. Pay bank $100.	Move back 2 spaces.	Move back 2 spaces.

SUN CARDS FOR REAL ESTATE RUSH GAME

(Photocopy, cut, and place facedown on center board.)

It's a buyer's market in real estate. Prices are low! Everyone receives $50 from the bank.	It's a buyer's market in real estate. Prices are low! Everyone receives $50 from the bank.	It's a buyer's market in real estate. Prices are low! Everyone receives $50 from the bank.
It's a buyer's market in real estate. Prices are low! Everyone receives $100 from the bank.	It's a buyer's market in real estate. Prices are low! Everyone receives $100 from the bank.	Loan interest rates are down. Everyone receives $50 from the bank.
Loan interest rates are down. Everyone receives $50 from the bank.	Loan interest rates are down. Everyone receives $50 from the bank.	Loan interest rates are down. Everyone receives $50 from the bank.

FLASH CARDS FOR REAL ESTATE RUSH GAME

(Photocopy, cut, and place facedown on center board.)

Advance to nearest speed zone. Cross zone and land on next STAR space after zone. Take a Star card AND receive $100 from the bank.	Advance to nearest speed zone. Cross zone and land on next STAR space after zone. Take a star card AND receive $100 from the bank.	Advance to nearest speed zone. Cross zone and land on next STAR space after zone. Take a Star card AND receive $100 from the bank.
Your other investments are doing well. Receive $100 from the bank.	Your other investments are doing well. Receive $100 from the bank.	Your other investments are doing well. Receive $100 from the bank.
Your other investments are doing well. Receive $100 from the bank.	Take an extra turn.	Take an extra turn.

THINK ABOUT

Houses aren't the only type of real estate that people can buy for an investment. People also buy apartment buildings as an investment. Although buying an apartment building usually costs much more money than buying a single home, the owner can then rent the apartments to other people. The owner hopes the income she receives from rent will be more than the payments she makes to the bank for the loan. This income is an example of "passive income," which means it is income that you receive without having to do any physical work.

Condominiums and townhouses are another form of real estate. In those types of real estate, a person only buys space between the walls and the use of common area owned together with other people. So if the Martinez family sells the Haddad family their condominium, they are really selling the space inside condo unit 4 and selling the USE of the walls, ceiling, floor, land underneath, and sidewalks and parking lot that other people living in the condo community also share and own together.

Bare land is also a form of real estate investment. Often people will buy land in an area where there may be new homes or businesses in the future. People like to invest in land because it is often less expensive to buy, does not require much upkeep or repair like a building does, yet also often increases in value. Bare land can also be built on. Then the value of the building plus the land is greater than just the value of the land by itself. Sometimes a large piece of land can be divided into smaller pieces. Each piece can then be sold alone. The result may be more profit than if the single large piece of land were sold alone. For example, if Mrs. Singh bought four acres of land for $100,000, she might then subdivide the land into four lots of one acre each. She might then sell each of the four lots for $50,000 each. By doing that, she would make a profit of 100 percent.

$$\begin{array}{r} \$50{,}000 \text{ per lot} \\ \times\ 4 \text{ lots} \\ \hline \$200{,}000 \end{array}$$

$$\begin{array}{r} \$200{,}000 \text{ from the sale of 4 lots} \\ -\$100{,}000 \text{ paid for the initial lot} \\ \hline \$100{,}000 \text{ profit} \end{array}$$

Mrs. Singh would then calculate her return on investment (sometimes called ROI). That is a figure that people want to know when considering whether or not to make a particular investment. In this case, her return on investment was 100 percent. In other words, she made a profit equal to the amount she invested. She would calculate her return on investment by dividing the profit by the investment, like this:

$$\begin{array}{r} \$100{,}000 \text{ profit} \\ \div\ \$100{,}000 \text{ Mrs. Singh's initial \$100{,}000 investment} \\ \hline 1 \text{ (turned into a percentage as 100\%)} \end{array}$$

In other words, Mrs. Singh paid $100,000 and made $100,000.

Businesses are also sold as a form of "real estate." Sometimes the sale of a business will include a building, but not always. For example, if a person sells her restaurant, she may include the building, the furniture inside, the supply of food and paper goods, as well as the business name.

FIND OUT MORE

Resources in Your Community

Find out whether a parent or family friend of a student works in real estate as an agent or with an escrow or title company. Ask that person to visit the class to share experiences or answer questions. Call a bank or local board of realtors and ask if someone can share some blank forms related to a real estate transaction or a home mortgage.

Web Sites

- Visit the National Association of Realtors to see what real estate sales are all about, at http://www.realtor.com/.
- Find out how to qualify for mortgages at http://www.mortgage-calculator-tips.com/.
- Search the Web with keywords "real estate agent," "realtor," "mortgage," and "home loan."

Careers

Related jobs include real estate agent or broker, property manager, title company employee (clerk, escrow officer), county recorder employee, mortgage broker, bank loan officer, home inspector, construction contractor or employee, architect, interior decorator, real estate lawyer, engineer, land surveyor, planning department employee, and blueprint worker.

CHAPTER 8

Stock Stuff

Subject Matter: Stock market; options; indexes; mutual funds

Math Standards Addressed:

    Number Sense: computing numbers; multiplication; decimals

    Data Analysis: tables; charts; graphs

    Percentages

Literacy Standards Addressed:

    Vocabulary and Concept Development

    Reading Comprehension

    Spelling

Written and Oral English Standards Addressed:

    Listening and Speaking Applications

    Verbal Communication

    Research and Technology

WHAT IS STOCK?

A share of *stock* stands for a small percentage of ownership in a company. A company is owned by people who own shares of stock. People often invest in stocks to grow their money. Many companies take part of their profits and give them to shareholders in payments called *dividends*. If a company doesn't pay dividends, people may still invest in a company's stock in the hope that the company will be profitable and the value of the stock they hold will increase.

Most people buy and sell stocks through a stock broker. When prices in the stock market are generally going down, it is called a "bear market." When prices are generally rising, it is called a "bull market." Investors who understand how the stock market works can make money in either a bear market or a bull market.

SETTING/PROPS/COSTUMES

This play has three scenes for seven readers. Several friends—Doug, Nicole, Jacob, and Chandra—are together. Quizy (a friendly alien from another planet) is with them. They're discussing the stock market. Props could include calculators, paper, and pencils. Costumes are not needed. Quizy's clothing and appearance is limited only by students' imagination!

Pronunciation guides may be provided in the script in square brackets. The words are divided into syllables. The syllable to be stressed is in capital letters. For example, the pronunciation guide for Quizy's name would be [QUIZ-ee]. The reader should use the pronunciation guide but not read it aloud.

CHARACTERS

NARRATOR 1

NARRATOR 2

DOUG

NICOLE

JACOB

CHANDRA

QUIZY (a friendly alien visitor who collects empty tissue boxes)

Stocking Up (and Down)

Scene 1: Alien Warnings

NARRATOR 1: Doug, Nicole, Jacob, and Chandra are at the computer.

NARRATOR 2: Here comes Quizy.

NARRATOR 1: He looks scared.

NARRATOR 2: He looks afraid of the computer? Let's find out why.

QUIZY: Watch out!

DOUG: What do you mean, Quizy?

QUIZY: Watch out for the aliens.

NICOLE: What are you talking about?

JACOB: You're an alien.

QUIZY: But I'm a good alien.

CHANDRA: There are bad aliens?

QUIZY: Yes, there are really bad aliens, and they're here.

DOUG: Where?

QUIZY: They have taken over your computer.

NICOLE: Why do you say that, Quizy?

QUIZY: Because of what is on your screen.

JACOB: It's a stock chart.

From *Fun with Finance: Math + Literacy = Success* by Carol Peterson. Santa Barbara, CA: Libraries Unlimited. Copyright © 2009.

QUIZY: No, it's alien writing.

CHANDRA: Why do you think that?

QUIZY: It says things are going to explode.

DOUG: Quizy. We're looking at a stock chart.

QUIZY: Are you sure?

NICOLE: Yes. It's a chart of Roaring Beast Associates.

JACOB: See here, it says the company is RBA.

CHANDRA: RBA is the ticker symbol for the company.

QUIZY: Are you sure it doesn't stand for "really bad aliens"?

DOUG: I'm sure. It's a ticker symbol.

QUIZY: I knew it.

NICOLE: You knew what?

QUIZY: The bad aliens are after your heart.

JACOB: My heart?

CHANDRA: Quizy heard Grandma call her heart a "ticker."

DOUG: Oh. No, Quizy; not "ticker" but "ticker symbol."

NICOLE: A ticker symbol is just a way the stock market keeps track of companies.

JACOB: In a shorter way than writing the whole name of the company.

CHANDRA: It's a little like initials.

QUIZY: My initial is Q.

DOUG: So if you were a stock, your ticker symbol might be Q.

NICOLE: Or QZ

JACOB: Or QZY.

QUIZY: Or QZYTAVWCETB.

DOUG: What?

QUIZY: It stands for "Quizy, the alien visitor who collects empty tissue boxes."

NICOLE: Right.

QUIZY: But why the soup?

CHANDRA: What soup?

QUIZY: Roaring Beasts. They sell soup, right?

DOUG: Why do you ask?

QUIZY: Because it's the STOCK market.

DOUG: What are you talking about, Quizy?

QUIZY: Your mom made chicken stock and then made soup out of it.

NICOLE: Oh. No, this stock is not stock like the base for making soup.

QUIZY: Oh, then the Roaring Beasts are cows.

JACOB: Cows?

CHANDRA: Because cows are beasts?

DOUG: I think Quizy means that cows are cattle.

NICOLE: And cattle are sometimes called stock?

JACOB: Quizy, this is not that kind of stock market, either.

QUIZY: Oh, stock like in Earth history, when they put the bad people in the stockade?

CHANDRA: No, not that kind of stock, either.

QUIZY: Not even if they're bad aliens?

DOUG: No.

QUIZY: Then what is this kind of stock?

NICOLE: A share of stock stands for a little bit of ownership in a company.

QUIZY: Like Roaring Beasts Associates?

JACOB: Yes. If a company has stock, then that company is owned by the people who own the shares of its stock.

Scene 2: The Cost of Stock

NARRATOR 1: I'm sure glad the bad aliens aren't coming to Earth.

NARRATOR 2: Yes, but let's learn more about the stock market.

QUIZY: You mean I could own Roaring Beasts?

CHANDRA: Yes, you could own a little bit of the company by buying some of its stock.

QUIZY: How much does it cost?

DOUG: We were just finding out.

QUIZY: By looking at the computer?

NICOLE: Yes, or you can look in the business part of the newspaper.

JACOB: So how much is the stock?

CHANDRA: Today it is $27.53.

QUIZY: I could buy the whole company for $27.53?

CHANDRA: No, you could just buy a little piece of the company for $27.53.

JACOB: But you could buy several shares of the company.

CHANDRA: That means you could buy several little pieces of the company.

QUIZY: For $27.53 a piece?

CHANDRA: That's the price today.

QUIZY: What do you mean today?

DOUG: Well, yesterday the stock cost only $27.43.

QUIZY: Then you should have bought it yesterday.

NICOLE: Maybe. Or maybe if we buy it today, it'll cost more tomorrow.

JACOB: You'd be happy tomorrow if you already owned it today.

CHANDRA: You could sell it for more than you bought it.

QUIZY: Why would you do that?

DOUG: To make a profit.

QUIZY: But didn't you want to own the company?

NICOLE: Yes, but some people buy and sell stock to make money.

QUIZY: Is this about money working for you again?

JACOB: Yes. The stock market can be a type of investment.

CHANDRA: So you can buy stock and sell it.

DOUG: Or buy stock and keep it.

QUIZY: But if the stock price goes down, wouldn't I lose money?

NICOLE: Maybe. But it may go up again over time.

JACOB: Or you may want to hold on to your stock for the dividends.

QUIZY: Is that some kind of alien math?

CHANDRA: No. A dividend is when a company takes part of its profit . . .

DOUG: And gives it to the people who own the stock.

JACOB: It's like a bonus.

NICOLE: The people who own the stock are called shareholders.

QUIZY: Is that like a potholder?

JACOB: No.

QUIZY: Is it like a candle holder?

CHANDRA: No.

QUIZY: Is it like a pencil holder?

DOUG: No.

QUIZY: Is it like a cup holder?

NICOLE: No.

QUIZY: Is it like a folder holder?

JACOB: A folder holder? No.

QUIZY: Is it like a boulder holder? A colder holder? An older holder? A . . .

CHANDRA: It's just a person who owns the stock.

DOUG: He "holds" the stock.

QUIZY: Does everyone get a dividend?

NICOLE: No, not all companies pay dividends.

CHANDRA: Why would you buy a stock that didn't pay a dividend?

DOUG: Because buying and selling stock is a way to grow money.

QUIZY: I love your Earth trees.

NICOLE: What trees?

QUIZY: Your dad said money grows on trees.

JACOB: Actually, he said money DOESN'T grow on trees.

QUIZY: So it grows on stockholders?

CHANDRA: No, but it grows on Wall Street.

QUIZY: Where's that?

DOUG: Wall Street is in New York City.

JACOB: Where the stock exchange is located.

NICOLE: The stock exchange is the place stock is bought and sold.

CHANDRA: But "Wall Street" is also just a way of talking about the stock market.

JACOB: There are actually many stock markets all over the world.

QUIZY: That's a lot of stock.

CHANDRA: So you can invest in American companies.

DOUG: Or Canadian companies.

NICOLE: Or Chinese companies.

JACOB: Or Brazilian companies.

CHANDRA: Or Japanese companies.

QUIZY: Or alien companies?

DOUG: Not yet.

Scene 3: Buying Stock

NARRATOR 1: I'd like to invest in companies, too.

NARRATOR 2: I wonder how we do it.

QUIZY: How can I buy some stock?

NICOLE: You call your broker.

QUIZY: No way!

JACOB: Why not, Quizy?

QUIZY: Why would I call a broker? I want to make money.

CHANDRA: Your broker can help you buy stock.

QUIZY: I'm not going to give money to someone who is broke!

DOUG: A broker is not broke.

NICOLE: That's just what he's called.

JACOB: It means he has a special license to be able to help people buy and sell stocks.

QUIZY: Well, it's a silly name.

CHANDRA: Maybe, but that's still what he's called.

DOUG: Quizy, why are you so quiet?

QUIZY: I'm looking at that stock chart.

NICOLE: What are you thinking?

QUIZY: I don't like it.

JACOB: Why not?

QUIZY: It looks like a row of higher mountains.

CHANDRA: You mean because the lines are going uphill?

QUIZY: Yes. Uphill is bad.

DOUG: Why?

QUIZY: When I climb up the hill I get tired.

NICOLE: But Quizy . . .

QUIZY: Downhill is much easier.

JACOB: But Quizy . . .

QUIZY: Besides, you earthlings say that bad things are an uphill battle.

CHANDRA: But Quizy . . .

QUIZY: And when it's "all downhill from here," that's a good thing.

DOUG: But Quizy . . .

QUIZY: And if you're over the hill, you're old and tired out.

NICOLE: But Quizy . . .

QUIZY: What?

JACOB: The chart is showing that the price for Roaring Beasts has been going up.

QUIZY: Up?

CHANDRA: Yes, it has been going up.

DOUG: And going up is a good thing in the stock market.

NICOLE: Yes it is.

QUIZY: So I don't have to go hiking?

JACOB: Not today.

CHANDRA: An uphill chart is good.

DOUG: If the chart looked like it was downhill, it would mean the price was going down.

NICOLE: If the whole stock market was going down, it would mean it was a bear market.

JACOB: And if the stock market was going up, it would mean it was a bull market.

QUIZY: I knew it!

CHANDRA: You knew what?

QUIZY: They're selling cows after all!

DOUG: What?

QUIZY: I don't know about the bears, but the bulls! The bulls! The STOCK market sells cattle.

NICOLE: No, Quizy. That's just what they say.

JACOB: A bear market means that prices are going down.

CHANDRA: And a bull market means that prices are going up.

QUIZY: Earthlings say funny things.

DOUG: Yes, we do.

NICOLE: Then again, aliens say funny things, too.

QUIZY: Then I'll call the guy who is broke . . .

JACOB: The broker.

QUIZY: And buy the stock that is on the way to being over the hill.

CHANDRA: You mean the price is going up.

DOUG: Which is bullish.

NICOLE: Right.

QUIZY: Then this is the perfect stock.

JACOB: Why?

QUIZY: The Roaring Beasts are bulls.

CHANDRA: At least they're not bad aliens.

GLOSSARY

Call: An option. Buying a call gives you the right but not the obligation to buy a stock at a certain price on or before a specified date. Selling a call gives you the obligation to sell a stock at a specified price on a specified date.

Charts: Graphics that show the movement of a stock. Bars (sometimes called "candles") show the daily open, close, high, and low price of a company's stock. White or green bars show upward movement (increase in price). Black or red bars show downward movement (decrease in price).

Diversify: To make different types of investments to limit the risk if one investment does badly, in the hope that the other investments will make up for any loss in some areas.

Dow Jones Industrial Average: Often called "the Dow." The most quoted indicator of the stock market, which helps people sense generally if the stock market is going up or down. It is an average of the stock prices of 30 specific companies.

Expiration: The date options expire. It is usually the third Friday of the month. On that day a buyer and seller of an option must exercise it (actually buy or sell the stock) or allow it to expire without exercising the option

Fundamentals: Information that shows how well run the company has been in the past. May indicate how well a company's stock may do in the future.

Index: A group of stocks traded together as one stock.

Industry: A group of stocks that have similar products or services.

Institutional investors: Investors such as pension funds, mutual funds, and insurance companies that invest huge sums of money at once and can influence the stock market. They are sometimes called "big money."

Margin: When you borrow money from the broker, you go into debt for part of what you pay for a stock or option.

Mutual fund: A collection of stocks or bonds bought by a group of investors. A mutual fund is managed by a professional money manager, who is usually paid a yearly management fee. Mutual funds allow you to diversify by investing in a number of stocks or industries or companies at one time.

Options: The right but not the obligation to buy or sell stocks until a certain time. An option is like a discount coupon that has an expiration date. You have the right to take the coupon to the store and buy that item at the discounted price until the expiration date. You don't HAVE TO buy it, but you can. Or you can sell the coupon to someone else. That person then has the right to buy the item at that discounted price.

Put: A type of option. Buying a put gives you the right, but not the obligation, to force the seller of a put to buy your stock at a specified price on or before a specified date. Selling a put gives someone else the right, but not the obligation, to make you buy a stock at a specified price on a specified date.

Resistance: The point to which a stock tends to rise and then resists going above. It is affected by the psychology of buyers in the marketplace.

Support: The level to which a stock tends to fall and then won't go below. It is affected by the psychology of buyers in the marketplace.

Technicals: What can be seen on a stock chart that may show what things may affect the stock price's ability to rise or fall, including support, resistance, and volume of shares traded.

Ticker symbol: Several letters that stand for a company's full name. It is how the company's stock is listed on the stock exchanges.

Trend: The general direction the stock is going—either up, down, or sideways. A stock tends to continue its trend in the direction it has been going until it meets support or resistance.

DOING TO UNDERSTAND

The following activities are included as handouts:

1. Paper Money Trade
2. Watch List
3. Conduct a Fundamental Analysis
4. Conduct a Technical Analysis
5. Portfolio Management
6. Chart Information
7. Board Game

ACTIVITY 1. PAPER MONEY TRADE

Select a stock and analyze the company's strength. How much money did it make in the last three months, the last year, and the last five years? "Buy" shares of the company using pretend money. Then track the price of the stock over time and sell it at a specific date. Chart your profit or loss. Allow at least one month for the trade.

ACTIVITY 2. WATCH LIST

You can't get to know all the thousands of stocks in the market. What many investors do is become familiar with 20 to 50 stocks that they like. Then they create a "watch list." The stocks on their watch list are those that they "watch" every day or two to see if and when they should invest in them.

Create your own watch list. First decide what industry or industries you want to watch. The *industry* is a group of stocks that have similar products or services. Stocks tend to trend (go up or down) in a way that is similar to the whole industry. You might look at the financial industry (banks, savings and loans, mortgage companies). Or you might look at the energy sector of the market (oil, coal, solar energy), agricultural commodities, gold, transportation, consumer staples (food, clothing), or technology (computer hardware and software).

Look at the industries and market sectors and find companies you think will do well in the future. Place their ticker symbols on your watch list and track their progress over time. Watch for any news about the sector, the industry, or the company. Note what the price of the stock does over time. Did the stock trend up or down or generally sideways over the past week? Over the past three months? Over the past year? Over the past five years? Would you buy any of those stocks? When would you have bought them?

ACTIVITY 3. CONDUCT A FUNDAMENTAL ANALYSIS

A fundamental analysis shows you how well the company is managed. Select five companies whose stocks are sold on the stock market. Go to each company's Web site or find information on a brokerage site. Financial information shows how well the company has done in the past. How well it has done in the past indicates how well it COULD do in the future. Look for any news that tells what is happening in the company. The news could be good, such as a contract or new product. Or the news could be bad, such as a new product that doesn't work as expected or a lawsuit against the company. Look also at earnings announcement dates. Prices may go up or down dramatically based on the earnings announcements.

Create a scoring method, such as A, B, C, D, F, or a number from 1 to 5. Rate each company based on several things: return on investment, price/earnings, and profits last quarter over the previous quarter. These pieces of information are often available on the company Web site or a brokerage site. Also rate any news on the company or on the industry the company is in. Which companies look best?

ACTIVITY 4. CONDUCT A TECHNICAL ANALYSIS

A technical analysis looks at the price and volume of a stock based on its chart. By looking at the chart, often you can "see" the stock's support and resistance. Support is the lower level at which the stock price tends to settle again and again before heading back up. Resistance is the upper level to which the price tends to rise to, hit, and then fall back below. Stocks tend to have "personalities" and tendencies in how their prices act.

Look also at how many shares of stock are traded every day. This information should also be available at a brokerage site for each stock. If a stock trades over one million shares a day, that will show you that the investors generally like buying and selling that stock. If the number of shares is traded much more than usual on one day, look to see if the price rose or fell that day. If the stock rose one day when more than 1.5 times as many investors as usual traded it, it suggests that investors think the stock is a good investment. Chances are the stock will continue to increase in price and value. If more than 1.5 times as many people SOLD the stock on a day when the price fell, chances are investors no longer think that stock is a good investment.

ACTIVITY 5. PORTFOLIO MANAGEMENT

Portfolio management is how to monitor the stocks you own. The basic rules of portfolio management are not to buy too many shares and to diversify your account by buying stocks in different industry groups so that if one industry is doing badly, your entire portfolio won't suffer too much. For example, if all the stocks you own are airline stocks and the price of oil rises, the cost of fuel for airplanes will be very high. Higher costs reduce profits the airlines can make. Therefore the price of airline stocks may fall. But if you own one airline stock and the other stocks you own are in technology, health care, retail stores, and banking, your portfolio will not be hurt as badly by the increased cost of oil.

Portfolio management also means knowing ahead of time what to do if the stock does not do what you think it should. For example, if you believe the stock will go up, know ahead of time when you will sell the stock if it goes down instead of up. Use support levels on your chart to help you decide. For example, assume you buy a stock for $107 a share. Before you bought the stock, you saw from the chart that the stock tended to return to $100 before rising again. You may want to decide before you buy the stock that if the price falls 3 percent below $100 a share (or $100 minus $3 = $97), you will sell the stock and take a smaller loss than if you held the stock and it continued to go down.

ACTIVITY 6. CHART INFORMATION

After doing the three previous activities over a period of at least one month, create a chart like the following one. What did you learn in this trade that you would do or not do in the future? What kind of chart or graph could you create to show the information from this table?

Stock Tracking Sheet

Stock Name and Ticker Symbol	
Industry	
Fundamentals and Score	
Support Levels	
Resistance Levels	
News	
Date You Bought Stock	
Price of Stock Bought	
Number of Shares Bought	
Date You Sold Stock	
Price at Which You Sold Stock	
Your Profit or Loss	
What You Learned About This Stock or This Trade	

ACTIVITY 7. BOARD GAME

Stock Stuff

The object of the Stock Stuff board game is to have the most money at the end of the game. This game can be played in small groups of two to four. To play you need:

a calculator

a pencil and paper

small game pieces for each player

1 die

1 game board (see appendix 1) for each player

1 center board (see appendix 1)

1 bank board (see appendix 1)

the Star, Moon, Sun, and Flash cards from the handouts (pp. 219–222)

paper money (see appendix 1)

Set Up

Photocopy one set of cards for each game played. For example, a group of four players will need one set of Star cards, one set of Moon cards, one set of Sun cards, and one set of Flash cards. Place the piles of cards facedown in their boxes on the center board. When players have drawn all the cards in one pile, they should be shuffled and replaced, facedown on the center board, to reuse.

☆ STAR CARDS move the game forward

☾ MOON CARDS move the game back

Cut all cards and money along the lines.
Provide one game board for each player.
Photocopy enough money so there are four pages' worth for each player. At the beginning of the game, each player receives one of each of the following bills: $10, $20, $50, $100. The rest of the money is placed on the bank board for use during play.

Play

Each player rolls the die to find out who plays first; whoever gets the largest number on the die plays first. Play then rotates counterclockwise.

Players travel around the board, moving forward the number of spaces on the die. If a player lands on a space with a symbol on it, that player takes a card from the pile with that symbol and follows the instructions on that card.

ACTIVITY 7. BOARD GAME (CONT.)

If a player lands on a "Flash" space and draws a card that sends him or her across the speed zone, the player moves through the center bar of the dollar sign to the next nearest shaded space at the end of the speed zone.

A player who does not have enough to pay the total owed must pay all he or she has to the bank and then skip one turn.

The game ends when the first person finishes a trip around the board and lands on "Finish." The player does not have to have an exact roll of the die to land on "Finish."

All players then count their money. The person with the most money (NOT the first player to finish) wins the game.

STAR CARDS FOR STOCK STUFF GAME

(Photocopy, cut, and place facedown on center board.)

Dip and Drip has a new BBQ sauce. Stock jumps. Receive $200 from the bank. ☆	Puppy Pants' disposable doggie diapers earn the company record earnings! Receive $50 from the bank. ☆	Hot and Cold Heating and Air introduces fans cooled by ice cubes. Stock jumps. Receive $50 from the bank. ☆
Cure-It-All Company's new medicine is approved by the FDA. Stock shoots higher. Receive $200 from the bank. ☆	Choo-Choo Locomotive merges with Little Red Caboose. Stock climbs after the merger. Receive $100 from the bank. ☆	Computer Concepts invents a waterproof laptop for swimmers. Stock climbs. Receive $100 from the bank. ☆
Pork & Bean Gas Company has record output. Stock rises. Receive $50 from the bank. ☆	Mostly Healthy Snack Foods launches zero calorie banana splits. Stock zooms. Receive $200 from the bank. ☆	You sell a put on Q-T-Pie Company and stock jumps up. Receive $50 from the bank from selling the put and another $100 when the stock rises. ☆

From *Fun with Finance: Math + Literacy = Success* by Carol Peterson. Santa Barbara, CA: Libraries Unlimited. Copyright © 2009.

MOON CARDS FOR STOCK STUFF GAME

(Photocopy, cut, and place facedown on center board.)

You hear a hot tip from your mailman that Go Go Juice, Inc.'s stock will go down, so you sell the stock short. Everyone loves their new dill pickle flavor juice, and the stock jumps UP! You lose. Pay the bank $100.	Crazy Car Company has a new car that runs on banana peels. But an increase in the monkey population means not enough bananas for fuel. Crazy Car goes bankrupt. Pay the bank $200.	Classy Clothes' new clothing line isn't classy. Stock drops. Pay the bank $100.
The market drops 500 points. Pay the bank $100.	The market drops 600 points. Pay the bank $150.	The market drops 700 points. Pay the bank $200.
Your call options expire, but the stock went down. Pay the bank $50.	Your put options expire, but the stock went up. Pay the bank $50.	The market fell so far that the stock market closed "lock limit down." Pay the bank $200.

From *Fun with Finance: Math + Literacy = Success* by Carol Peterson. Santa Barbara, CA: Libraries Unlimited. Copyright © 2009.

SUN CARDS FOR STOCK STUFF GAME

(Photocopy, cut, and place facedown on center board.)

The stock market closes 100 points higher. Everyone receives $50 from the bank.	The stock market closes 100 points higher. Everyone receives $50 from the bank.	The stock market closes 100 points higher. Everyone receives $50 from the bank.
The stock market closes 400 points higher. Everyone receives $100 from the bank.	The stock market closes 400 points higher. Everyone receives $100 from the bank.	The stock market closes 400 points higher. Everyone receives $100 from the bank.
Jupiter Explorations pays dividends. Everyone receives $50 from the bank.	George Washington's River Boat Tours pays dividends. Everyone receives $50 from the bank.	3 Little Pig Building Materials pays dividends. Everyone receives $20 from the bank.

FLASH CARDS FOR STOCK STUFF GAME

(Photocopy, cut, and place facedown on center board.)

Advance to nearest speed zone. Cross zone and land on next STAR space after zone. Take a Star card AND receive $100 from the bank.	Advance to nearest speed zone. Cross zone and land on next STAR space after zone. Take a Star card AND receive $100 from the bank.	Summer Sailboats pays dividends of 10 cents a share. Roll die to see how many hundred shares you own. Multiply that number of shares by 10 cents (.10 or 1/10) and receive that amount from the bank.
Water Wheel Hydroelectric pays dividends of 50 cents a share. Roll die to see how many hundred shares you own. Multiply that number of shares by 50 cents (.50 or ½) and receive that amount from the bank.	Windy Turbine pays dividends of 50 cents a share. Roll die to see how many hundred shares you own. Multiply that number of shares by 50 cents (.50 or ½) and receive that amount from the bank.	East West Travel pays dividends of 20 cents a share. Roll die to see how many hundred shares you own. Multiply that number of shares by 20 cents (.20 or 1/5) and receive that amount from the bank.
Take an extra turn.	Take an extra turn.	Take an extra turn.

THINK ABOUT

Investing in the stock market offers the reward of making money. However, there is also the risk of losing money. You should never invest money in the stock market that you CAN'T afford to lose. The stock market is not a quick gamble. It may take a long time to make money. Don't try to use strategies you don't understand; focus on what you do understand. The best investors have a plan and rules and stick with them.

One long-term strategy is to buy a stock in a good company and hold it over several years. Over the past 50 to 70 years, the stock market has averaged 10 to 12 percent growth annually. Although that information doesn't guarantee that you would get 10 to 12 percent too, it is an average rate to look for. For example, if you bought 100 shares of WWW stock 50 years ago and had paid $10 a share, today your 100 shares might be worth $6,000 to $7,000. Certain stocks that have done well over time and are from good companies that have been well run for many years are called "blue chip stocks."

In addition to buying and selling shares of stock, investors can also buy and sell "options." Options are the right, but not the obligation, to buy or sell a specific stock at a specific price on or before a specific date. Basically when you buy and sell options, you are really buying and selling rights or obligations and time.

Options were originally used by investment companies as a way to protect themselves against a price drop in the market. Stocks can go up, down, or sideways, but only up is good if you own a stock. With options, you can make money even if the price of the stock goes down or sideways. You can also lower the amount of money you risk to only what you paid for the option. When you own the stock, the price of the stock is generally much larger than the price of the option, which means you can lose more money if you buy the stock. When you own an option, you still "control" the stock.

Buying and selling options is generally shorter term than buying a stock and holding on to it. An options trade may be for a few days or several months. Some stocks have options, known as LEAPS (long term equity anticipation securities) that can be bought or sold several years out.

FIND OUT MORE

Resources in Your Community

Find out whether a parent or family friend of a student works in the stock market or a brokerage firm or invests in stock directly. Ask that person to visit the class to share experiences or answer questions.

Web Sites

- To learn more about stock, visit MSM at moneycentral.msn.com/investor/market/home or finance.yahoo.com/.

- Go to the online *Wall Street Journal* at www.online.wsj.com.

- Go to the Chicago Board of Options Exchange Web site at www.CBOE.com for information on trading stock options.

- If you want to learn about a specific company, you can search the Web for that company's site and find information about how well the company is run and its profits and losses.

Careers

Related jobs include stock trader, broker, investment counselor, investment advisor, and market analyst.

CHAPTER 9

Building with Bonds

Subject Matter: Corporate, municipal, U.S., special voter bonds

Math Standards Addressed:

    Number Sense: computing numbers; multiplication; decimals; fractions

    Data Analysis: tables; charts; graphs

    Percentages

Literacy Standards Addressed:

    Vocabulary and Concept Development

    Reading Comprehension

    Spelling

Written and Oral English Standards Addressed:

    Listening and Speaking Applications

    Verbal Communication

    Research and Technology

WHAT ARE BONDS?

When you buy a *bond*, you own someone else's debt; you have loaned money to the government or a company that issued the bond. The government or company then pays you interest. You expect to receive regular interest payments as long as you own the bond.

Each bond is for a specific period of time. A BILL may be for one year or less; a NOTE is usually for one to ten years; a BOND is for more than ten years. A U.S. Savings Bond is an example of a government bond. It has a date of maturity when it expires and the borrower must repay the loan.

Municipal bonds are issued by governments that are smaller than the federal government. They may be state or county or city bonds and may be used to pay for specific projects such as a new school or park.

SETTING/PROPS/COSTUMES

This play has three scenes for seven readers. Several friends—Doug, Nicole, Jacob, and Chandra—are together. Quizy (a friendly alien from another planet) is with them. They're discussing bonds. Props could include calculators, paper, and pencils. Costumes are not needed. Quizy's clothing and appearance is limited only by students' imagination!

Pronunciation guides may be provided in the script in square brackets. The words are divided into syllables. The syllable to be stressed is in capital letters. For example, the pronunciation guide for Quizy's name would be [QUIZ-ee]. The reader should use the pronunciation guide but not read it aloud.

CHARACTERS

NARRATOR 1

NARRATOR 2

DOUG

NICOLE

JACOB

CHANDRA

QUIZY (a friendly alien visitor who collects empty tissue boxes)

Bonding with Friends

Scene 1: The Election

NARRATOR 1: What's everybody talking about?

NARRATOR 2: I don't know. Let's listen.

DOUG: Tomorrow is Election Day.

QUIZY: Are you running for King of Earth?

NICOLE: No, of course he's not.

QUIZY: Then why do you care?

JACOB: Because of the bond measure.

CHANDRA: What is the bond measure?

DOUG: Our city is voting on whether or not to have a new bond.

CHANDRA: What is a bond?

NICOLE: It's like a loan.

QUIZY: The city is going to loan us money?

DOUG: No, the city is going to borrow money.

CHANDRA: From whom?

NICOLE: There are people who loan the government money.

QUIZY: They must be really rich people.

JACOB: Not always. Some are rich, but not everyone.

CHANDRA: Who are they then?

DOUG: Investors.

QUIZY: It's too hot.

NICOLE: Quizy, what are you talking about?

QUIZY: Investors. It's too hot to be an investor.

CHANDRA: Do you know who an investor is?

QUIZY: It's a person who wears a vest. He's "in" a vest.

DOUG: No, Quizy.

NICOLE: That's not who an investor is.

QUIZY: Who is it then?

JACOB: An investor is a person who puts his money to work for him.

QUIZY: I thought YOU work to GET money.

CHANDRA: Yes, but after you get the money, then your money can work for you.

QUIZY: What do you mean?

DOUG: A person may put money into a bank . . .

NICOLE: And receive interest.

JACOB: Or a person may buy a house . . .

CHANDRA: And the value of the house may increase over time.

DOUG: Or a person may buy stocks in a company . . .

NICOLE: And receive profits when the company grows.

QUIZY: Oh, a money worker. Do you know what we call an investor on my planet?

CHANDRA: What?

QUIZY: Smart.

Scene 2: How a Bond Works

NARRATOR 1: Quizy is right.

NARRATOR 2: An investor IS smart.

NARRATOR 1: But I'm still not sure how a bond works.

NARRATOR 2: Neither am I. Let's listen.

QUIZY: Why would anyone want to loan money to the government?

DOUG: What do you mean?

QUIZY: Isn't a loan debt?

NICOLE: Yes, it is.

QUIZY: Isn't debt bad?

JACOB: Too much debt can be bad, yes.

CHANDRA: But sometimes a little debt can be good.

QUIZY: When?

DOUG: When you want to buy a house but don't have all the money to buy it.

NICOLE: As long as you can afford to make the payments.

QUIZY: There's always a catch, isn't there?

JACOB: A little debt is also good now.

QUIZY: How?

CHANDRA: You've visited our school, Quizy.

QUIZY: Yes, there are lots of kids in every class.

DOUG: Too many.

NICOLE: Mrs. Ramirez looked a little crazy yesterday.

QUIZY: Mrs. Ramirez looks a little crazy most days.

JACOB: She won't look so crazy if there are fewer students in her class.

CHANDRA: She can give each student more time.

DOUG: Without going crazy.

QUIZY: So the city wants to borrow money to send Mrs. Ramirez on a vacation?

NICOLE: No, the city wants to borrow money to build a new school.

JACOB: So some of the kids from our school can go to the new school.

CHANDRA: That sounds like a good thing.

QUIZY: I get it now.

DOUG: Are you sure you get it, Quizy?

QUIZY: Yes. Investors want to build a school so they can sell the school when it is worth more.

NICOLE: No. Investors don't actually buy the school; they just loan money to the city.

JACOB: The city owns the school.

QUIZY: What do the investors get out of it other than not having a crazy person living in the city?

DOUG: They receive interest.

CHANDRA: Like the bank?

NICOLE: Yes. The bank PAYS interest to people who save their money at the bank.

JACOB: And the bank loans that money to other people.

CHANDRA: And those people pay the bank interest.

DOUG: More interest than the bank pays the savers.

CHANDRA: Why doesn't the city just get a loan from the bank?

NICOLE: Cities, companies, and other parts of the government do sometimes borrow money through banks.

DOUG:	But they also borrow through bonds.
QUIZY:	Ah. I know.
JACOB:	You know what, Quizy?
QUIZY:	I know the government's spies do that.
CHANDRA:	Do what?
QUIZY:	Borrow with bonds.
DOUG:	What are you talking about, Quizy?
QUIZY:	Bonds. James Bonds.
NICOLE:	No, that's not what we mean, Quizy.
JACOB:	A bond is just a way to loan money.
DOUG:	People buy the bonds.
NICOLE:	Then after a certain amount of time, the city pays back that amount.
JACOB:	Plus some extra interest.
CHANDRA:	The city pays the interest as regular payments to the investor.
QUIZY:	But the city doesn't pay back the loan?
DOUG:	The city pays the loan at the end of the time.
CHANDRA:	That's different from a bank loan.
NICOLE:	Yes, for most bank loans, you pay the interest plus part of the debt each month.

Scene 3: Types of Bonds

NARRATOR 1:	So a bond is a type of loan.
NARRATOR 2:	And an investor can buy that loan and receive interest.
NARRATOR 1:	But you have to hold the bond for some amount of time.

NARRATOR 2: I wonder how long. Let's find out.

CHANDRA: How long does a bond last?

JACOB: Different times.

DOUG: If the bond is for less than a year, it's called a Bill.

QUIZY: I don't know Bill.

NICOLE: Not Bill the person. A Bill is a bond that is less than a year.

CHANDRA: Isn't a bill something you have to pay?

JACOB: Yes, but in this case, the Bill is what someone ELSE has to pay.

DOUG: If you own the Bill, you are the one getting paid.

CHANDRA: I understand.

NICOLE: If the bond is for one to ten years, it is called a note.

QUIZY: La-la-la.

JACOB: What are you doing, Quizy?

QUIZY: Singing.

CHANDRA: Why are you singing?

QUIZY: Because bonds for one to ten years are called notes.

DOUG: Not musical notes.

NICOLE: These notes are a kind of bond.

CHANDRA: What if the bond is for more than 10 years?

JACOB: It's called a bond.

CHANDRA: Yes. But what is it called?

DOUG: It's just called a bond.

QUIZY: I'm going to call it a James Bond.

NICOLE: There are other bonds, too.

QUIZY: Like what?

JACOB:	Corporate bonds.
CHANDRA:	Corporate like in "corporation"?
JACOB:	Yes. A corporation might sell a bond to raise money.
QUIZY:	Instead of selling a product?
DOUG:	No, to raise money for other things, like researching a new product.
NICOLE:	Such as a new product that will make the company more money.
JACOB:	Or they might sell a bond to raise money to open more stores to sell the products they already have.
CHANDRA:	And make more money that way.
QUIZY:	They could sell glue.
DOUG:	Why glue?
QUIZY:	Because glue is good for bonding things together.
NICOLE:	OK, but where are you going, Quizy?
QUIZY:	I have to change clothes.
JACOB:	Why?
QUIZY:	I have to put on my vest.
CHANDRA:	To be an investor?
QUIZY:	Yes. And then get my coat.
DOUG:	Your coat?
NICOLE:	Quizy, you'll be too hot.
JACOB:	What kind of coat are you going to wear?
QUIZY:	My trench coat.
CHANDRA:	I don't think I want to ask, but why?
QUIZY:	So I can invest in the city's bond.
DOUG:	But why the coat?

QUIZY: So I can be like him.

NICOLE: Like who?

QUIZY: Bond.

ALL TOGETHER: James Bond.

GLOSSARY

Bill: A bond with a term under one year.

Bond: A type of loan made to a government or company.

Bond measure: A question placed on the ballot for voters to decide whether or not the government should go into debt with a bond.

Corporate bonds: Bonds issued by companies.

Investor: A person who tries to make money, for example by buying bonds and earning interest on the money lent.

Issuer: An entity that issues, and is obligated to pay principal and interest on, a debt security.

Maturity date: The date when the borrower must repay the bond loan.

Municipal bonds: Bonds issued by state and local governments.

Note: A bond with a term between one and ten years.

Payments: Sometimes called coupon payments. The amount of interest paid on each interest period.

Rate: Sometimes called coupon rate. The interest rate paid to the investor on the bond value.

Term: The amount of time the bond covers.

Treasuries: Bonds issued by the U.S. government.

Value: Sometimes called face value or par value. The amount of money you will be paid on the bond maturity date.

Zero coupon: A bond on which no periodic interest payments are made. The investor receives one payment—which includes principal and interest—at the end of the term.

DOING TO UNDERSTAND

The following activities are included as handouts:

1. Understanding Savings Bonds
2. Bank Bonds
3. Municipal Bonds
4. Laddering
5. What Are Your Savings Bonds Worth?
6. Board Game

ACTIVITY 1. UNDERSTANDING SAVINGS BONDS

U.S. Savings Bonds are a type of bond issued by the U.S. government. That means they are treasuries. Usually you can buy a savings bond for half the face value of the bond. For example, you can buy a $100 savings bond for $50. You receive the full $100 when the bond has completely matured. But you can sell the bond at any time and get the amount of money the bond is worth at that time.

U.S. savings bonds (sometimes called series EE bonds) mature at various times because the interest rates change over time. If you purchased a $100 savings bond and paid $50 for it, and held it until maturity, how much interest would you make? Divide the amount of interest by the number of years you held the bond. That figure will tell you how much interest you made each year.

Phone your local bank and find out the interest rate for their savings account and T-bills. How do the interest rates compare with what you might get for a U.S. Savings Bond? You often have to invest a larger amount of money for a T-bill than for a savings bond or savings account. So your bank's choice for you right now might only be the savings bond or the savings account.

ACTIVITY 2. BANK BONDS

Phone several banks. Find out what T-bills are available. Create a chart showing the amount required to purchase each T-bill; its face value, its interest rate, and its maturity date. Which T-bill appears to be the best investment?

Fill out the following table with what you found out. What kind of chart or graph could you create to show the information from this table?

T-Bill Comparison (Assume $50,000 to Invest)

Name of Bank: _____

T-Bill Name	Term	Interest Rate	Amount Required to Invest

ACTIVITY 3. MUNICIPAL BONDS

Call your city clerk. Find out what bonds the city has and whether it is considering issuing any bonds in the future. Find out how much (usually a percentage) of taxes paid by homeowners goes to repay those bonds.

Find out if there are any bond measures coming up in local elections. What will the money be used for?

Interview adults you know to find out whether they think the new bonds are needed and whether they support or oppose the bond measure.

Choose a side yourself and have a mock election in class. Did the bond measure pass or fail in your classroom?

ACTIVITY 4. LADDERING

One aspect of bonds is that they are for a specified period of time (the bond's term). Because this term may be a number of years, the money you invest in the bond cannot be used until the end of the term. Part of a total investment plan is to prepare for unexpected events. Laddering bonds is one way investors try to prepare for the future while still making their money work for them.

Laddering bonds means buying different bonds that expire at different points in time. Generally, the longer the term, the higher the percentage rate the bond will pay. Investors like to receive as high a percentage as they can without tying up their money for too long.

So instead of putting all of her money into one ten-year bond, an investor might ladder bonds. She might buy a smaller bond with a term of ten years that pays 10 percent, a bond with a term of seven years that pays 8 percent, a bond with a term of five years that pays 6 percent, a bond with a term of three years that pays 5 percent, and a bond with a term of one year that pays 4 percent. Then if she needs money for something unexpected after one year, she can redeem the one-year bond. If she does not need the money at that time, she can then buy another ten-year bond that pays a higher interest rate.

As the term of each bond expires, the investor can determine whether or not that money is needed for something. If not, it can be reinvested into a new longer-term bond that pays a higher interest rate. After 10 years, if the investor has continued to ladder her bonds, ALL of her bonds will now be at a higher interest rate.

Using the chart you completed in Activity 2, complete the table below, showing how you might ladder your bonds if you had $50,000 to invest. What kind of chart or graph could you create to show the information from this table?

Laddering Bonds (Assume $50,000 to Invest in Bonds)

Bond Name	Term	Interest	Amount Required to Invest	Amount Invested

ACTIVITY 5. WHAT ARE YOUR SAVINGS BONDS WORTH?

Do you or someone in your family already own U.S. Savings Bonds? They are often given as gifts when a child is born because they must sit many years before they are worth the value stated on their face. If you have a savings bond, you can find out how much it is worth today. If you needed to turn it in for cash, you would not receive the face value of the bond until it had completely matured. But you can go to the U.S. Treasury Department's Web site and use their online calculator to find out how much it is worth now. Go to http://www.treasurydirect.gov/indiv/tools/tools_savingsbondcalc.htm. On the bond is the date it was issued. What is that date? How much is your bond presently worth? How much will it be worth at maturity? How many years is that? Do you think it is worth waiting?

ACTIVITY 6. BOARD GAME

Building with Bonds

The object of the Building with Bonds board game is to have the most money at the end of the game. Money is received based on interest from different types of bonds. This game can be played in small groups of two to four. To play you need:

    a calculator

    a pencil and paper

    small game pieces for each player

    1 die

    1 game board (see appendix 1) for each player

    1 center board (see appendix 1)

    1 bank board (see appendix 1)

    the Star, Moon, Sun, and Flash cards from the handouts (pp. 243–246)

    paper money (see appendix 1)

Set Up

Photocopy one set of cards for each game played. For example, a group of four players will need one set of Star cards, one set of Moon cards, one set of Sun cards, and one set of Flash cards. Place the piles of cards facedown in their boxes on the center board. When players have drawn all the cards in one pile, they should be shuffled and replaced, facedown on the center board, to reuse.

    ☆ STAR CARDS move the game forward

    ☾ MOON CARDS move the game back

    ☼ SUN CARDS help all players

    ⚡ FLASH CARDS speed a player ahead

Cut all cards and money along the lines.
Provide one game board for each player.
Photocopy enough money so there four pages' worth for each player. At the beginning of the game, each player receives one of each of the following bills: $10, $20, $50, $100. The rest of the money is placed on the bank board for use during play.

Play

Each player rolls the die to find out who plays first; whoever gets the largest number on the die plays first. Play then rotates counterclockwise.

Players travel around the board, moving forward the number of spaces on the die. If a player lands on a space with a symbol on it, that player takes a card from the pile with that symbol and does what the card says.

ACTIVITY 6. BOARD GAME (CONT.)

If a player lands on a Flash space and draws a card that sends him or her across the speed zone, the player moves through the center bar of the dollar sign to the next nearest shaded space at the end of the speed zone.

A player who does not have enough to pay the total owed must pay all he or she has to the bank and then skip one turn.

The game ends when the first person finishes a trip around the board and lands on "Finish." The player does not have to have an exact roll of the die to land on "Finish."

All players then count their money. The person with the most money (NOT the first player to finish) wins the game.

STAR CARDS FOR BUILDING WITH BONDS GAME

(Photocopy, cut, and place facedown on center board.)

Your savings bonds mature. Receive $50 from the bank.	Your savings bonds mature. Receive $50 from the bank.	Your T-bills mature. Receive $100 from the bank.
Your T-bills mature. Receive $100 from the bank.	Your corporate bonds mature. Receive $200 from the bank.	Your corporate bonds mature. Receive $200 from the bank.
Your municipal bonds mature. Receive $200 from the bank.	Your municipal bonds mature. Receive $200 from the bank.	Your note matures. Receive $50 from the bank.

From *Fun with Finance: Math + Literacy = Success* by Carol Peterson. Santa Barbara, CA: Libraries Unlimited. Copyright © 2009.

MOON CARDS FOR BUILDING WITH BONDS GAME

(Photocopy, cut, and place facedown on center board.)

You cash in your savings bonds early and lose interest. Pay the bank $50.	You cash in your savings bonds early and lose interest. Pay the bank $50.	You cash in your savings bonds early and lose interest. Pay the bank $50.
You cash in your corporate bonds early and lose interest. Pay the bank $200.	You cash in your corporate bonds early and lose interest. Pay the bank $100.	You cash in your municipal bonds early and lose interest. Pay the bank $200.
You cash in your municipal bonds early and lose interest. Pay the bank $100.	You cash in your T-bills early and lose interest. Pay the bank $100.	You cash in your T-bills early and lose interest. Pay the bank $100.

SUN CARDS FOR BUILDING WITH BONDS GAME

(Photocopy, cut, and place facedown on center board.)

Interest rates on bonds increase! Everyone receives $100 from the bank.	Interest rates on bonds increase! Everyone receives $100 from the bank.	Everyone receives $20 from the bank for savings bonds.
Everyone receives $20 from the bank for savings bonds.	Everyone receives $50 from the bank for municipal bonds.	Everyone receives $50 from the bank for municipal bonds.
Everyone receives $50 from the bank for corporate bonds.	Everyone receives $20 from the bank for corporate bonds.	Everyone receives $20 from the bank for corporate bonds.

From *Fun with Finance: Math + Literacy = Success* by Carol Peterson. Santa Barbara, CA: Libraries Unlimited. Copyright © 2009.

FLASH CARDS FOR BUILDING WITH BONDS GAME

(Photocopy, cut, and place facedown on center board.)

Advance to nearest speed zone. Cross zone and land on next STAR space after zone. Take a Star card AND receive $100 from the bank.	Advance to nearest speed zone. Cross zone and land on next STAR space after zone. Take a Star card AND receive $100 from the bank.	Advance 1 space.
Advance 1 space.	Advance 1 space.	Advance 3 spaces.
Advance 3 spaces.	Take an extra turn.	Take an extra turn.

THINK ABOUT

Bonds are thought of as a very safe investment. U.S. government bonds in particular are nearly "guaranteed." That means those bonds are almost 100 percent sure to be repaid. Most municipal bonds are also fairly safe, because most local and state governments have enough money to repay the bonds or can raise taxes to be able to pay them.

Corporate bonds carry more risk. A good idea when thinking about investing in a company is to learn as much as you can about the company. How well has it been run? Has it been profitable? That means, has it made money from its business, or is it losing money? What will the money from the bond be used for? Will it be used to research new products or expand its business, which will mean possible future profit?

There are different things to consider when thinking about investing in corporate or government bonds. Corporate bonds usually pay a higher interest rate than U.S. or municipal bonds but are a more risky investment. Would you prefer a possible higher rate or a more secure investment? An investor must do her homework and decide for herself whether she wants a higher rate and more risk or less interest and more safety.

FIND OUT MORE

Resources in Your Community

Find out whether a parent or family friend of a student works with bonds. Ask that person to visit the class to share experiences or answer questions.

Web Sites

- Go to the U.S. Department of the Treasury for more information about U.S. Savings Bonds, at http://www.treas.gov/ or the children's website at http://www.ustreas.gov/kids/.

- Go to www.treasurydirect.gov/BC/SBCPrice to find out prices of savings bonds.

- Go to the online *Wall Street Journal* at www.online.wsj.com.

Careers

Related jobs include investment broker and government employee in the finance department.

CHAPTER 10

ഩ $ ര

Commodity Commotion

Subject Matter: Gold, agriculture, and other commodities as a market for investment; futures as a market for investment

Math Standards Addressed:

    Number Sense: computing numbers; multiplication; decimals; fractions

    Data Analysis: tables; charts; graphs

    Percentages

Literacy Standards Addressed:

    Vocabulary and Concept Development

    Reading Comprehension

    Spelling

Written and Oral English Standards Addressed:

    Listening and Speaking Applications

    Verbal Communication

    Research and Technology

WHAT ARE COMMODITIES?

    A *commodity* in the investment world is a product, usually in agriculture or mining, that has value. There is an international market, both separate from and part of the stock market, in which people can buy and sell commodities. People do not actually buy the physical commodity. Instead, they buy and sell the right to own the commodity. When an investor buys and sells commodities within the stock market, he or she usually buys or sells stock in a company or group of companies that produce those commodities. Some commodities that are widely traded are gold, oil, chemicals, steel, and coal.

WHAT ARE FUTURES?

A *futures* contract is an agreement to buy or sell a specific amount of a commodity or group of stocks by a specific date in the future at a specific price. These futures contracts are traded in a special market, similar to the stock market. Futures contracts for agricultural commodities have been traded in the United States for more than 100 years. Today futures include oil, natural gas, foreign currencies, government securities, and groups of stock (called indices).

SETTING/PROPS/COSTUMES

This play has three scenes for seven readers. Several friends—Doug, Nicole, Jacob, and Chandra—are together. Quizy (a friendly alien from another planet) is with them. They're discussing savings. Props could include calculators, paper, and pencils. Costumes are not needed. Quizy's clothing and appearance is limited only by students' imagination!

Pronunciation guides may be provided in the script in square brackets. The words are divided into syllables. The syllable to be stressed is in capital letters. For example, the pronunciation guide for Quizy's name would be [QUIZ-ee]. The reader should use the pronunciation guide but not read it aloud.

CHARACTERS

NARRATOR 1

NARRATOR 2

DOUG

NICOLE

JACOB

CHANDRA

QUIZY (a friendly alien visitor who collects empty tissue boxes)

Just Drop It

Scene 1: Quizy Learns about Commodities

NARRATOR 1: Oh, look. There are Doug, Nicole, Jacob, Chandra, and Quizy.

NARRATOR 2: What is Quizy doing?

NARRATOR 1: It's hard to tell.

NARRATOR 2: Let's find out.

QUIZY: Ouch!

DOUG: Quizy, what are you doing?

QUIZY: Dropping this barrel of oil.

NICOLE: On your foot?

QUIZY: Yes. Ouch!

JACOB: Now what are you doing?

QUIZY: Dropping this bushel of corn.

CHANDRA: On your foot?

QUIZY: Yes. Ouch!

DOUG: Now what are you doing?

QUIZY: Dropping this bag of fertilizer.

NICOLE: Why are you dropping everything?

QUIZY: To learn.

JACOB: What do you want to learn?

QUIZY: About commodities.

CHANDRA: Commodities?

QUIZY:	Yes. I want to invest in commodities.
DOUG:	So?
QUIZY:	I heard that a commodity is something you can drop on your foot.
NICOLE:	Quizy, there's an easier way to pick how to invest in commodities.
QUIZY:	It's OK. I'm going to try dropping feathers next.
JACOB:	Feathers?
CHANDRA:	At least they won't hurt.
DOUG:	But I'm not sure you want to invest in feathers anyway.
QUIZY:	Why not?
NICOLE:	There may not be much of a market for them.
QUIZY:	People would rather drop barrels of oil on their feet?
JACOB:	Quizy, you don't have to drop anything on your feet.

Scene 2: The Commodities Market

NARRATOR 1:	Quizy wants to learn the hard way.
NARRATOR 2:	The painful way!
NARRATOR 1:	I've heard that saying about dropping things on your feet, too.
NARRATOR 2:	You have?
NARRATOR 1:	Yes, but I think I'd like to hear Jacob's idea.
NARRATOR 2:	Me, too. Let's listen.
QUIZY:	What do I do to learn about commodities?
JACOB:	Check out the commodities market.
QUIZY:	I did.

CHANDRA: You did?

QUIZY: Yes, I went to the market and bought all this stuff.

DOUG: That's not the commodities market.

NICOLE: That's just the store.

QUIZY: How do I find the commodities market?

JACOB: You can look in the same place as the stock market.

QUIZY: Oh, by calling that guy who is broke?

CHANDRA: What guy?

QUIZY: The broker.

DOUG: Yes, the broker. But he's not broke.

NICOLE: That's just what he's called.

JACOB: He has a special license to be able to buy and sell commodities.

CHANDRA: That's what a broker is.

QUIZY: He must be very strong.

DOUG: Why?

QUIZY: To be able to lift all this stuff.

NICOLE: Quizy . . .

QUIZY: And he must have big shoes.

JACOB: Quizy, you don't have to drop these things any more.

QUIZY: What about a hint?

CHANDRA: A hint for what?

QUIZY: Anything. You can drop a hint, can't you?

DOUG: Yes, but a hint isn't a commodity.

QUIZY: OK, just tell me where the commodities market is and I'll go buy some oil.

NICOLE:	You don't have to go anywhere or actually buy any barrels of oil.
QUIZY:	But I want to invest in oil.
JACOB:	Then all you have to do is buy a little bit of some companies that sell oil.
CHANDRA:	Or companies that find oil.
DOUG:	Or companies that refine oil.
QUIZY:	Isn't that like buying stock?
NICOLE:	Yes, you can buy stock in an oil company.
JACOB:	Or you can buy shares of a group of companies that have oil.
CHANDRA:	Or you can invest in the futures of oil.
QUIZY:	Doesn't future mean time?
DOUG:	Yes, it does.

Scene 3: The Future

NARRATOR 1:	I'm glad Quizy stopped dropping things on his feet.
NARRATOR 2:	Me, too. But how can you invest in the future?
NARRATOR 1:	I don't know.
NARRATOR 2:	Let's find out.
QUIZY:	I can buy time?
NICOLE:	Sort of.
QUIZY:	By buying a clock?
JACOB:	No. You can invest in oil based on whether you think the price of oil will go up or down in the future.
QUIZY:	Then what I really want to invest in are "B-balls".
CHANDRA:	"B-Balls"? Basketballs are not commodities.

QUIZY:	I don't want to invest in basketballs.
DOUG:	Baseballs are not commodities, either.
QUIZY:	I don't want to invest in baseballs.
NICOLE:	Bowling balls are not commodities, either.
QUIZY:	I don't want to invest in bowling balls.
JACOB:	What kind of "B-balls" do you mean?
QUIZY:	I don't remember. I just know they start with the letter "B".
CHANDRA:	Quizy, sometimes you don't make any sense.
DOUG:	There are no kinds of sporting goods that are commodities.
QUIZY:	You don't use these balls in sports.
NICOLE:	Where are they used then?
QUIZY:	They're used by fortune-tellers.
JACOB:	Crystal balls?
QUIZY:	Yes!
CHANDRA:	Crystal starts with the letter C, Quizy, not B.
QUIZY:	Yes, but "breakable" starts with B.
DOUG:	A crystal ball isn't used in investing.
QUIZY:	Too bad.
NICOLE:	Yes, it is.
QUIZY:	Then how can I know whether the commodities will go up or down in the future?
NICOLE:	You can't "know."
DOUG:	But you can make a prediction based on what you think might happen.
JACOB:	A lot of it has to do with supply and demand.

QUIZY: Is that when someone demands a supply of commodities?

CHANDRA: No, it has to do with economics.

QUIZY: What is economics? Is it a fancy harmonica?

DOUG: Economics is the study of the production, distribution, and consumption of goods and services.

QUIZY: Are you speaking Earth-ish?

NICOLE: It means how things are made, circulated, and used.

JACOB: The price of something has a lot to do with how much of it there is.

CHANDRA: And how many people want to buy it.

DOUG: For example, lots of people in the world have cars.

NICOLE: And there's only so much gasoline.

JACOB: So there's a lot of demand

CHANDRA: And not as much supply.

QUIZY: So the price goes up!

DOUG: That's right, Quizy.

NICOLE: But for something like feathers, well . . .

JACOB: There are a lot of feathers,

CHANDRA: But not a lot of people are out buying bushels of them.

DOUG: So they're cheap.

QUIZY: I've changed my mind.

CHANDRA: You don't want to invest in commodities?

QUIZY: Yes, I do.

DOUG: But not oil?

QUIZY: No. Something else.

NICOLE: What then?

QUIZY: Feathers.

JACOB: But Quizy, we just told you there's not a big demand for feathers.

CHANDRA: And feathers really aren't a commodity, Quizy.

QUIZY: I know. But I think feathers will be a great investment anyway.

DOUG: Why?

NICOLE: Because commodity traders are tired of dropping heavy things on their feet?

QUIZY: No, because everyone needs a nice soft pillow to rest their feet on after they're finished dropping heavy things all day.

JACOB: You surprise me, Quizy.

CHANDRA: Yes, Quizy. Sometimes you even make sense!

GLOSSARY

Commodities market: A market like the stock market, in which shares in companies or groups of companies that produce commodities can be traded.

Commodity: A product of agriculture or mining.

Cyclical sectors: Cyclical sectors move up and down based on other factors. They include materials, transportation, finance, health care, technology, finance, capital goods, consumer cyclical, and energy.

Defensive sectors: Utilities and consumer staples such as food and clothing. People will continue to need these products and services, so the stock in the companies should stay up even if the overall market goes down.

Demand: The willingness to purchase a good or service.

Economics: Analysis of how goods are produced, distributed, and used.

Futures: Part of the market for commodities (and also for groups of stocks) in which investors can buy and sell prices of commodities and stock based on what they think the price will be in the future.

Sector: Companies grouped together in similar industries so they can be compared. They are usually divided into two "defensive" sectors and nine "cyclical" sectors.

Supply: To make goods or services available.

DOING TO UNDERSTAND

The following activities are included as handouts:

1. Create a List of Commodities
2. Find Commodities
3. Board Game

ACTIVITY 1. CREATE A LIST OF COMMODITIES

Make a list of all the commodities you can think of. Or go to a commodities Web site to see what types of things can be traded. What would you trade, and why? Pick one or two commodities and follow their prices for several days or weeks.

ACTIVITY 2. FIND COMMODITIES

Think about the definition of a commodity. Look in the newspaper or an online brokerage site and find commodities. List several commodity groups (called sectors), such as agriculture, energy, or mining. Then list the individual commodities you find, such as corn, agricultural chemicals, oil, coal, or gold. Compare the prices of the commodities. Compare the prices again one week later. Fill in the following table. What kind of chart or graph could you create to show the information from this table?

Commodities

Sector: _____

Commodity	Price Week 1	Price Week 2	Price Moving Up or Down?

ACTIVITY 3. BOARD GAME

Commodity Commotion

The object of the Commodity Commotion board game is to have the most money at the end of the game. This game can be played in small groups of two to four. To play you need:

    a calculator

    a pencil and paper

    small game pieces for each player

    1 die

    1 game board (see appendix 1) for each player

    1 center board (see appendix 1)

    1 bank board (see appendix 1)

    the Star, Moon, Sun, and Flash cards from the handouts (pp. 263–266)

    paper money (see appendix 1)

Set Up

Photocopy one set of cards for each game played. For example, a group of four players will need one set of Star cards, one set of Moon cards, one set of Sun cards, and one set of Flash cards. Place the piles of cards facedown in their boxes on the center board. When players have drawn all the cards in one pile, they should be shuffled and replaced, facedown on the center board, to reuse.

    ☆ STAR CARDS move the game forward

    ☾ MOON CARDS move the game back

    ☼ SUN CARDS help all players

    ⚡ FLASH CARDS speed a player ahead

Cut all cards and money along the lines.
Provide one game board for each player.
Photocopy enough money so there four pages' worth for each player. At the beginning of the game, each player receives one of each of the following bills: $10, $20, $50, $100. The rest of the money is placed on the bank board for use during play.

Play

Each player rolls the die to find out who plays first; whoever gets the largest number on the die plays first. Play then rotates counterclockwise.

Players travel around the board, moving forward the number of spaces on the die. If a player lands on a space with a symbol on it, that player takes a card from the pile with that symbol and does what the card says.

ACTIVITY 3. BOARD GAME (CONT.)

If a player lands on a Flash space and draws a card that sends him or her across the speed zone, the player moves through the center bar of the dollar sign to the next nearest shaded space at the end of the speed zone.

A player who does not have enough to pay the total owed must pay all he or she has to the bank and then skip one turn.

The game ends when the first person finishes a trip around the board and lands on "Finish." The player does not have to have an exact roll of the die to land on "Finish."

All players then count their money. The person with the most money (NOT the first player to finish) wins the game.

STAR CARDS FOR COMMODITY COMMOTION GAME

(Photocopy, cut, and place facedown on center board.)

You bought gold commodities before they closed higher. Receive $200 from the bank. ☆	You bought corn commodities before they closed higher. Receive $50 from the bank. ☆	You bought oil commodities before they closed higher. Receive $200 from the bank. ☆
You bought coal commodities before they closed higher. Receive $100 from the bank. ☆	You bought silver commodities before they closed higher. Receive $100 from the bank. ☆	You bought wheat commodities before they closed higher. Receive $50 from the bank. ☆
You bought soybean commodities before they closed higher. Receive $100 from the bank. ☆	You bought iron commodities before they closed higher. Receive $100 from the bank. ☆	You bought copper commodities before they closed higher. Receive $500 from the bank. ☆

MOON CARDS FOR COMMODITY COMMOTION GAME

(Photocopy, cut, and place facedown on center board.)

Gold prices drop. Pay the bank $100.	Steel prices drop. Pay the bank $100.	Oil prices drop. Pay the bank $100.
Corn prices go down. Pay the bank $50.	Silver prices go down. Pay the bank $50.	Coal prices go down. Pay the bank $50.
The market drops 500 points. Pay the bank $100.	The market drops 600 points. Pay the bank $150.	The market drops 700 points. Pay the bank $200.

SUN CARDS FOR COMMODITY COMMOTION GAME

(Photocopy, cut, and place facedown on center board.)

The commodities market closes 100 points higher. Everyone receives $50 from the bank.	The commodities market closes 100 points higher. Everyone receives $50 from the bank.	The commodities market closes 100 points higher. Everyone receives $50 from the bank.
Corn goes up in price. Everyone receives $100 from the bank.	Fertilizer goes up in price. Everyone receives $100 from the bank.	Steel goes up in price. Everyone receives $100 from the bank.
Gold goes up in price. Everyone receives $50 from the bank.	Oil goes up in price. Everyone receives $50 from the bank.	Coal goes up in price. Everyone receives $20 from the bank.

From *Fun with Finance: Math + Literacy = Success* by Carol Peterson. Santa Barbara, CA: Libraries Unlimited. Copyright © 2009.

FLASH CARDS FOR COMMODITY COMMOTION GAME

(Photocopy, cut, and place facedown on center board.)

Advance to nearest speed zone. Cross zone and land on next STAR space after zone. Take a Star card AND receive $100 from the bank.	Advance to nearest speed zone. Cross zone and land on next STAR space after zone. Take a Star card AND receive $100 from the bank.	Advance to nearest speed zone. Cross zone and land on next STAR space after zone. Take a Star card AND receive $100 from the bank.
Take an extra turn.	Take an extra turn.	Take an extra turn.
Take an extra turn.	Take an extra turn.	Take an extra turn.

THINK ABOUT

Commodities are often tied in with other similar commodities. They may also affect the prices of other areas of the market. For example, the price of gold and the price of silver often rise and fall together. When the price of gasoline goes up, the cost of travel or transportation also goes up, which means that the value of companies such as airlines and stores may go down. Part of investing in commodities is understanding how the commodities work together and with other parts of the economy.

FIND OUT MORE

Resources in Your Community

Find out if a parent or family friend of a student works in the field of commodities or trades commodities personally. Ask that person to visit the class to share experiences or answer questions.

Web Sites

- Visit the U.S. Commodities Futures Trading Commission at http://www.cftc.gov/.
- Go to finance.yahoo.com/indices?e=trea for information on indices, commodities, futures, and treasury bonds.
- Go to the online *Wall Street Journal* at www.online.wsj.com.
- Search the Web using the keywords "commodities" and "commodity trading."

Careers

Related jobs include commodity broker and commodity trader.

CHAPTER 11

ॐ $ ॐ

Collecting Can Count

Subject Matter: Collections as an investment (stamps, coins, artwork, antiques)

Math Standards Addressed:

   Number Sense: computing numbers; multiplication; decimals

   Data Analysis: tables; charts; graphs

Literacy Standards Addressed:

   Vocabulary and Concept Development

   Reading Comprehension

   Spelling

Written and Oral English Standards Addressed:

   Listening and Speaking Applications

   Verbal Communication

   Research and Technology

WHAT IS AN INVESTMENT COLLECTION?

Collecting can be another way to create wealth. For example, many people collect stamps or rare coins. Because the stamps or coins are no longer being made the same way they once were, they increase in value. Other things increase in value because of the completeness of the collection. For example, a complete collection of baseball cards for one year is worth a great deal more than any one baseball card from that year, not just because there are more of them, but because the collection for that year is complete.

The value of a collection depends on two things: supply and demand. If the supply of the item (the number of those particular things other collectors could own) is low, then the value and cost of the item goes up. If there is a large supply of the item (lots of them are available), like seashells or shiny rocks, then the value and cost of the item goes down. That is why old things such as stamps, coins, and antiques increase in value—because many similar ones have been lost or destroyed over time, which reduces the supply available to people who want them.

If there is a big demand for an item, the value and cost also increase. Many people like to collect old coins, for example, so the demand is high. But not too many people like to collect used matches. So the value and cost of used matches is low. Supply and demand work together to create value and cost of items that people collect.

SETTING/PROPS/COSTUMES

This play has four scenes for seven readers. Several friends—Doug, Nicole, Jacob, and Chandra—are together. Their friend, Quizy (a friendly alien from another planet) is with them. They're discussing collections. Props could include calculators, paper, and pencils. Costumes are not needed. Quizy's clothing and appearance is limited only by students' imagination!

Pronunciation guides may be provided in the script in square brackets. The words are divided into syllables. The syllable to be stressed is in capital letters. For example, the pronunciation guide for Quizy's name would be [QUIZ-ee]. The reader should use the pronunciation guide but not read it aloud.

CHARACTERS

NARRATOR 1

NARRATOR 2

DOUG

NICOLE

JACOB

CHANDRA

QUIZY (a friendly alien visitor who collects empty tissue boxes)

Quizy's Collection

Scene 1: Nicole's Collection

NARRATOR 1: Do you collect anything?

NARRATOR 2: I collect pretty rocks.

NARRATOR 1: I collect seashells.

NARRATOR 2: I'd like to collect something that would be worth money one day.

NARRATOR 1: Nicole is collecting something.

NARRATOR 2: Let's find out what it is.

DOUG: What are you doing?

NICOLE: Organizing my stamps.

JACOB: They're pretty.

CHANDRA: Why are you organizing them?

NICOLE: I collect them.

DOUG: What kind of collection?

NICOLE: I get stamps from around the world.

QUIZY: So that wherever you go, you can send letters to your friends?

NICOLE: No. I try to get stamps from everywhere just to have them.

QUIZY: Why?

JACOB: To keep them.

CHANDRA: Why?

NICOLE: Because one day I hope my collection will be valuable.

QUIZY: For when you want to send letters to your friends?

DOUG: No, because sometimes stamp collections become valuable.

CHANDRA: To who?

JACOB: To other people who collect stamps

CHANDRA: How would they be valuable?

NICOLE: Let's say I wanted to have a stamp from every country in the world.

QUIZY: OK. "I wanted to have a stamp from every country in the world." Hey, you didn't say it with me.

NICOLE: Quizy . . . never mind. Pretend I didn't have a stamp from Argentina.

CHANDRA: So you would travel there and buy one?

DOUG: No, that would cost too much money.

QUIZY: Tough luck. Your collection isn't very good.

JACOB: But there's another way to get one.

QUIZY: How?

NICOLE: I could buy one from someone who already has a stamp from Argentina.

CHANDRA: Why would he sell it to you?

DOUG: To make money for himself.

CHANDRA: You mean he would charge you extra?

JACOB: Probably.

CHANDRA: Why would you pay extra money for a stamp?

NICOLE: Because then my collection would be worth more.

QUIZY: Why?

DOUG: Because it would be complete.

Scene 2: Increasing in Value

NARRATOR 1: Maybe we should collect stamps, too.

NARRATOR 2: That sounds interesting.

NARRATOR 1: I wonder what else Nicole knows about collections.

NARRATOR 2: Let's find out.

JACOB: What would you do with your collection when it's complete?

NICOLE: I could keep it.

DOUG: Or you could sell it to someone else.

NICOLE: Or I could hold on to it and it might become worth even more.

CHANDRA: Why would it be worth more?

DOUG: Because over time, the stamps would be old.

QUIZY: Wouldn't that make them be worth less?

JACOB: Usually they're worth more when they're old.

CHANDRA: Why?

NICOLE: Because as new stamps are made with new designs, the old ones are no longer printed.

DOUG: And most people who bought the old ones have already used them on their letters.

JACOB: And then thrown them away.

NICOLE: So if there are not very many of the old stamps, then they are worth more than when you first bought them.

QUIZY: It's an investment.

DOUG: Yes, Quizy.

QUIZY: Are stamps the only thing you can collect?

CHANDRA: People collect lots of things, but not everything increases in value.

QUIZY: Like what?

JACOB: Well, I know someone who collects empty tissue boxes.

QUIZY: Hey, that's me!

NICOLE: Why do you collect them, Quizy?

QUIZY: They're cool, and now that I know about collections I'm really glad I have them.

DOUG: What do you mean?

QUIZY: Well, I'm the only one on Earth who collects empty tissue boxes.

JACOB: Probably.

QUIZY: Aha! That means I have the only supply of empty tissue boxes.

CHANDRA: Yes . . .

QUIZY: So when everyone else on Earth discovers that I have them all, they'll be worth gazillions!

Scene 3: Supply and Demand

NARRATOR 1: Do you think Quizy understands the concept of supply and demand?

NARRATOR 2: I'm not sure I understand it myself.

NARRATOR 1: Then we'd better listen to what they have to say.

NARRATOR 2: Good idea!

NICOLE: There's a problem in your thinking, Quizy.

DOUG: As usual.

QUIZY: What's the problem?

JACOB: You're forgetting about supply and demand.

CHANDRA: Look first at demand.

NICOLE: There's not a lot of chance that everyone on Earth will WANT to buy your empty tissue boxes.

DOUG: There's no demand.

JACOB: And in the second place, look at supply.

CHANDRA: If people wanted their own empty tissue boxes, they could just start blowing their noses.

DOUG: And create their own empty tissue boxes.

QUIZY: My secret is out!

JACOB: But there are other things you could collect that could become more valuable.

QUIZY: Like what?

CHANDRA: Lots of people collect coins.

QUIZY: You mean they collect money?

NICOLE: Well, yes, coins are money.

DOUG: But people often just collect individual coins that will increase in value.

QUIZY: How?

JACOB: Because governments make new coins just like they make new stamps.

CHANDRA: Then the old coins become more valuable.

NICOLE: Because there is no longer a new supply of them.

QUIZY: What do you mean?

DOUG: My dad has an old nickel that his dad gave him.

QUIZY: Big deal—a WHOLE nickel?

DOUG: This nickel is over a hundred years old.

QUIZY: Then it must not be worth much.

JACOB: Actually it is worth about $10.00.

CHANDRA: Why is it worth more than a nickel?

DOUG: Because it has a buffalo on it.

QUIZY: Why doesn't he put the buffalo in the zoo?

JACOB: Not a real buffalo.

DOUG: There's a picture of a buffalo on the nickel.

CHANDRA: I've never seen a nickel like that.

JACOB: Because the U.S. Treasury doesn't make nickels like that anymore.

NICOLE: Since those nickels are no longer made . . .

DOUG: There is a small supply of them available

JACOB: For other collectors to own.

CHANDRA: That means that if someone wants to own a buffalo nickel, he has to buy it for more than five cents.

NICOLE: And because there are a lot of people who collect coins . . .

DOUG: There is a pretty good demand for the nickels that aren't being made any more.

JACOB: Supply and demand again.

Scene 4: Things to Collect

NARRATOR 1: I think I understand supply and demand.

NARRATOR 2: Me too, but I want to find out what else I could collect.

DOUG: What else could we collect?

CHANDRA: Antiques.

QUIZY: What are antiques?

CHANDRA: Antiques are things that are really old.

QUIZY: Like Grandpa?

DOUG: No, not old people.

JACOB: Old furniture or jewelry or dishes.

QUIZY: Isn't new better?

NICOLE: Sometimes new is better, but some people love old things.

QUIZY: Like Grandpa.

DOUG: Because they're not made any more.

JACOB: Or because they like the style.

CHANDRA: Or because they want to invest in something that becomes more valuable over time.

NICOLE: Because they're not made any more.

DOUG: That's supply.

JACOB: And lots of people want them.

CHANDRA: That's demand.

QUIZY: OK, then I'll collect soda cans.

NICOLE: What?

QUIZY: Don't a lot of people want soda?

DOUG: Yes, but soda is easy to buy.

JACOB: So there is lots of supply.

QUIZY: Then I'll collect lizard tails.

CHANDRA: Quizy!

QUIZY: Just the ones that fall off the lizards anyway.

NICOLE: Quizy, that's not a good thing to collect, either.

QUIZY: Why not? They are very short in supply!

DOUG: But nobody wants them!

JACOB: There is no demand.

QUIZY: Then my collection is perfect.

CHANDRA: What collection?

QUIZY: Empty tissue boxes.

NICOLE: But Quizy, there is already lots of supply.

DOUG: And no demand.

QUIZY: You're missing the point.

JACOB: Is there actually a point, Quizy?

QUIZY: Yes! When I finally decide what to collect . . .

CHANDRA: Yes . . .

QUIZY: I'll be ready.

NICOLE: For what?

QUIZY: I'll have all those perfect tissue boxes to keep my collection in.

CHANDRA: Quizy, for once you have made some sense.

QUIZY: And there's not even a buffalo sitting on my cents.

GLOSSARY

Antique: An item made more than 100 years ago.

Collection: A group of similar items.

Demand: The willingness to purchase a good or service.

Economics: Analysis of how goods are produced, distributed, and used.

Insurance: Reimbursement for the cost of a collection or item if it is lost, stolen, or destroyed in exchange for the payment (monthly or yearly) of a premium.

Premium: An amount of money paid for insurance.

Secondary market: Where items are resold to others.

Supply: To make goods or services available.

DOING TO UNDERSTAND

The following activities are included as handouts:

1. Collections
2. Value of Collections
3. Collection Display and Catalog
4. Board Game

ACTIVITY 1. COLLECTIONS

What types of things do you collect? How do you store and display your collection? Does anyone you know collect something as an investment? Interview that person and find out why he chose that item to collect. How long has he been collecting? How much has the collection cost him? How much has his collection increased in value over what he paid for it? What does he hope to do with the collection in the future?

Have students bring in their collections to share with the class. Or have students poll each other to find out what things they collect. Have them create a table of the types of collections they have and then create a chart or graph based on that table.

ACTIVITY 2. VALUE OF COLLECTIONS

Have students choose a specific type of collection. Make the selection as specific as possible, such as U.S. buffalo nickels. Have them research the cost of purchasing 10 of those items based on quality and age. Have them create a chart indicating quality, age, and price. Discuss what they find and the relationship between the findings.

The class might decide to select a collection based on it being a limited edition. This refers to an item (usually a work of art such as a painting or plate or sculpture) of which only a limited number is produced, rather than thousands. This makes each item more valuable based on the principle of supply and demand. The maker may number each item or limit the number of items produced per year.

ACTIVITY 3. COLLECTION DISPLAY AND CATALOG

Many collectors keep records of the items in their collections. They include the details of each purchase such as the price they paid for the item, whom they bought it from, and when they bought it. They also record a description of the item and the condition it was in when purchased. They will keep any receipts and information about cleaning the item that may help them resell the item in the future. They may also photograph the item and keep both the photograph and the record in a safe place. Keeping records helps collectors understand how their collections may increase in value and is helpful to insurance companies and police in case of theft. Start keeping a record of your collection now using the following table.

Collection Record

Type of Collection: _____

Item	Date Obtained	Place Obtained	Price	Description/Condition

If you have a collection, do you have a way to display it? Share ideas with your class on your display and how others might display their collections.

ACTIVITY 4. BOARD GAME

Collecting Can Count

The object of the Collecting Can Count board game is to have a collection worth the most money at the end of the game. This game can be played in small groups of two to four. To play you need:

- a calculator
- a pencil and paper
- small game pieces for each player
- 1 die
- 1 game board (see appendix 1) for each player
- 1 center board (see appendix 1)
- 1 bank board (see appendix 1)
- the Star, Moon, Sun, and Flash cards from the handouts (pp. 285–288)
- paper money (see appendix 1)

Set Up

Photocopy one set of cards for each game played. For example, a group of four players will need one set of Star cards, one set of Moon cards, one set of Sun cards, and one set of Flash cards. Place the piles of cards facedown in their boxes on the center board. When players have drawn all the cards in one pile, they should be shuffled and replaced, facedown on the center board, to reuse.

- ☆ STAR CARDS move the game forward
- ☾ MOON CARDS move the game back
- ☀ SUN CARDS help all players
- ⚡ FLASH CARDS speed a player ahead

Cut all cards and money along the lines.
Provide one game board for each player.
Photocopy enough money so there are four pages' worth for each player. At the beginning of the game, each player receives one of each of the following bills: $10, $20, $50, $100. The rest of the money is placed on the bank board for use during play.

Play

Each player rolls the die to find out who plays first; whoever gets the largest number on the die plays first. Play then rotates counterclockwise.

ACTIVITY 4. BOARD GAME (CONT.)

The number on the die also determines what that player is going to collect, as follows:

Number on the Die	Type of Collection
1	Baseball cards
2	Antique furniture
3	Paintings
4	Stamps
5	Coins
6	Player's choice of above

Players travel around the board, moving forward the number of spaces on the die. If a player lands on a space with a symbol on it, that player takes a card from the pile with that symbol and follows the instructions on that card.

If a player lands on a "Flash" space and draws a card that sends him or her across the speed zone, the player moves through the center bar of the dollar sign to the next nearest shaded space at the end of the speed zone.

A player who does not have enough to pay the total owed must pay all he or she has to the bank and then skip one turn.

The game ends when the first person finishes a trip around the board and lands on "Finish." The player does not have to have an exact roll of the die to land on "Finish."

All players then count their money. The person with the most money (NOT the first player to finish) wins the game.

STAR CARDS FOR COLLECTING CAN COUNT GAME

(Photocopy, cut, and place facedown on center board.)

You purchase a piece for your collection. It cost you $50 but is worth $100. Receive $50 from the bank.	You purchase a piece for your collection. It cost you $50 but is worth $100. Receive $50 from the bank.	You purchase a piece for your collection. It cost you $50 but is worth $100. Receive $50 from the bank.
You find a piece for your collection at a garage sale. You buy it for pennies. Receive $100 from the bank.	You find a piece for your collection at a garage sale. You buy it for pennies. Receive $100 from the bank.	You find a piece for your collection at a garage sale. You buy it for pennies. Receive $100 from the bank.
You inherit part of a collection from crazy Uncle Ed. Receive $200 from the bank.	You receive a piece for your collection as a gift. Receive $100 from the bank.	You trade something you have for a new piece for your collection. Receive $100 from the bank.

MOON CARDS FOR COLLECTING CAN COUNT GAME

(Photocopy, cut, and place facedown on center board.)

You insure your collection. Pay the bank $100.	You insure your collection. Pay the bank $100.	You insure your collection. Pay the bank $100.
You insure your collection. Roll the die and pay the bank 10 times the number on the die.	You insure your collection. Roll the die and pay the bank 10 times the number on the die.	You insure your collection. Roll the die and pay the bank 10 times the number on the die.
Someone steals part of your collection. Pay the bank $100.	Your collection was damaged when you spilled water on it. It loses some of its value. Pay the bank $100.	Part of your collection was broken or torn. It loses some of its value. Pay the bank $50.

SUN CARDS FOR COLLECTING CAN COUNT GAME

(Photocopy, cut, and place facedown on center board.)

Everyone goes garage sale shopping and finds a piece for their collections. Everyone receives $100 from the bank.	Everyone goes garage sale shopping and finds a piece for their collections. Everyone receives $100 from the bank.	Everyone goes garage sale shopping and finds a piece for their collections. Everyone receives $100 from the bank.
Everyone's collections are appraised higher. Everyone receives $50 from the bank.	Everyone's collections are appraised higher. Everyone receives $50 from the bank.	Everyone's collections are appraised higher. Everyone receives $50 from the bank.
All players find they have something another player needs for his collection. Everyone trades. All collections increase in value. Everyone receives $20 from the bank.	All players find they have something another player needs for her collection. Everyone trades. All collections increase in value. Everyone receives $20 from the bank.	You go to a thrift store and find what everyone needs. All players receive $10 from the bank; you receive $20 from each player.

From *Fun with Finance: Math + Literacy = Success* by Carol Peterson. Santa Barbara, CA: Libraries Unlimited. Copyright © 2009.

FLASH CARDS FOR COLLECTING CAN COUNT GAME

(Photocopy, cut, and place facedown on center board.)

Advance to nearest speed zone. Cross zone and land on next STAR space after zone. Take a Star card AND receive $100 from the bank.	Advance to nearest speed zone. Cross zone and land on next STAR space after zone. Take a Star card AND receive $100 from the bank.	Advance 1 space.
Advance 1 space.	Advance 1 space.	Advance 3 spaces.
Advance 3 spaces.	Take an extra turn.	Take an extra turn.

THINK ABOUT

Some collections come and go in popularity. During the 1990s many people in America collected POGs. POG stands for "passion fruit, orange, guava." POGs were decorative cardboard tops on juice bottles that originally came from Hawaii. The collecting turned into a game, and many kids spent their allowances buying, collecting, and displaying the various styles and patterns of POGs. But today, not many people even remember POGs, nor do they have any value, because there is no longer a demand for them.

When you are thinking about what type of collection you want for an investment, consider what will continue to have value in the future.

FIND OUT MORE

Resources in Your Community

Find out whether a parent or family friend of a student works in a museum, owns a rare coin or bookstore, or has a fine personal collection. Ask that person to visit the class to share experiences or answer questions.

Web Sites

- Visit the Collectors' Information Bureau at collectorsinfo.com.
- Decide what type of collection you are interested in learning about and search the Web using that keyword, such as "U.S. postage stamps," "U.S. Buffalo nickels," or "Hummel figurines."

Careers

Related jobs include museum owner or worker; antique dealer; appraiser; insurance agent; rare coin, book, or stamp shop collector or owner; and art dealer.

CHAPTER 12

ஸ் $ ௧

Future Focus

Subject Matter: Financial planning; goal setting

Math Standards Addressed:
- Number Sense: computing numbers; multiplication
- Data Analysis: tables; charts; graphs
- Percentages

Literacy Standards Addressed:
- Vocabulary and Concept Development
- Reading Comprehension
- Spelling

Written and Oral English Standards Addressed:
- Listening and Speaking Applications
- Verbal Communication
- Research and Technology

WHAT IS FUTURE FOCUS?

This chapter is about planning for the future. What? You have plenty of time to think about the future, right? Yes, you do, but if you don't have an idea what you want your future to be like, you have less chance it'll end up that way. After all, the future keeps plugging along until it becomes the present. Then before you know it, it's the past, and your new future is already on its way out. So let's look at what we can do to think about our financial future while it still is part of the future.

SETTING/PROPS/COSTUMES

This play has four scenes for seven readers. Several friends—Doug, Nicole, Jacob, and Chandra—are together. Their friend Quizy (an alien from another planet) is with them. They're discussing their futures. Props could include calculators, paper, and pencils Costumes are not needed. Quizy's clothing and appearance is limited only by students' imagination!

Pronunciation guides may be provided in the script in square brackets. The words are divided into syllables. The syllable to be stressed is in capital letters. For example, the pronunciation guide for Quizy's name would be [QUIZ-ee]. The reader should use the pronunciation guide but not read it aloud.

CHARACTERS

NARRATOR 1

NARRATOR 2

DOUG

NICOLE

JACOB

CHANDRA

QUIZY (an alien visitor who collects empty tissue boxes)

Thinking Ahead

Scene 1: What's It Worth?

NARRATOR 1: What kind of work do you want to do when you get older?

NARRATOR 2: I'm not sure. How about you?

NARRATOR 1: I don't know, either.

NARRATOR 2: Maybe Quizy and his friends have some ideas.

NICOLE: What do you want to be when you grow up?

QUIZY: I want to be rich.

DOUG: How rich?

QUIZY: Very rich.

CHANDRA: Then what do you want your net worth to be?

QUIZY: Oh, I don't care about that.

JACOB: Why not?

QUIZY: I don't need any hair nets.

NICOLE: We're not talking about hair nets.

QUIZY: I don't need any fishing nets.

DOUG: We're not talking about fishing nets.

QUIZY: I don't need any butterfly nets.

CHANDRA: We're not talking about butterfly nets.

QUIZY: I don't need a ping-pong net.

JACOB: We're not talking about ping-pong nets.

QUIZY: I don't need a basketball net.

From *Fun with Finance: Math + Literacy = Success* by Carol Peterson. Santa Barbara, CA: Libraries Unlimited. Copyright © 2009.

NICOLE: We're not talking about basketball nets.

QUIZY: I don't need a tennis net.

DOUG: We're not talking about tennis nets.

QUIZY: I don't need badminton nets.

CHANDRA: We're not talking about badminton nets.

QUIZY: I don't need volleyball nets.

JACOB: We're not talking about volleyball nets.

QUIZY: What kind of nets then?

NICOLE: Net worth.

QUIZY: What is a net worth?

DOUG: It's not a net.

CHANDRA: "Net worth" just means how much money you are worth.

JACOB: If you added up all the money you owned.

NICOLE: Plus all your investments.

DOUG: Plus the worth of all of your stocks.

CHANDRA: Plus the worth of all of your bonds.

JACOB: Plus the worth of all of your real estate.

NICOLE: Plus the worth of your businesses.

DOUG: Plus the amount of money you have in your savings account.

CHANDRA: All added up together.

QUIZY: That's going to be a lot!

JACOB: I hope so.

NICOLE: Then you subtract your debt.

DOUG: Any loans you have from others.

CHANDRA: Money you owe to other people.

JACOB:	Or to banks.
NICOLE:	On your real estate, for example.
DOUG:	Or your car loan.
QUIZY:	Or my spaceship?
CHANDRA:	Or credit card debt.
JACOB:	The amount you have minus the amount you owe.
NICOLE:	That equals your net worth.

Scene 2: Investments

NARRATOR 1:	There sure are lots of different kinds of nets.
NARRATOR 2:	I never knew about net worth.
NARRATOR 1:	I didn't either.
NARRATOR 2:	Let's learn more.
QUIZY:	I don't have any investments.
DOUG:	What do you think you'd like to invest in?
QUIZY:	I want to have lots of empty tissue boxes.
CHANDRA:	Empty tissue boxes?
QUIZY:	And fill all of them up with cash.
DOUG:	OK, but if everyone else saves their empty tissue boxes,
CHANDRA:	They won't be worth very much.
QUIZY:	So what do I do?
JACOB:	You need to diversify [dih-VERSE-ih-fy].
QUIZY:	What does that mean?
NICOLE:	It means you need to invest in several different things.
DOUG:	That way if one of the things loses value . . .

CHANDRA: You'll still have the possibility that the other things will be worth something.

QUIZY: So I should also save empty toilet paper tubes.

JACOB: Or you could buy some real estate.

NICOLE: Or start a business.

QUIZY: A business selling empty tissue boxes!

DOUG: Or a business selling something that people might really want.

CHANDRA: And you could buy some stock in other people's companies.

QUIZY: Like tissue paper companies.

JACOB: And keep some money in the bank for an emergency.

QUIZY: Like if I run out of tissue boxes?

NICOLE: Or if you get sick.

QUIZY: If I get sick, I'll really need those tissues.

DOUG: If you get sick, you won't be able to work.

QUIZY: Work? You mean I should get a job, too?

NICOLE: It would be smart to have a job.

CHANDRA: That way you could have an income.

QUIZY: Income?

JACOB: Yes, when you work, you receive a paycheck.

NICOLE: You can use your paycheck to pay your bills.

DOUG: And buy your food.

CHANDRA: And invest.

JACOB: To make your money work for you!

Scene 3: Careers

NARRATOR 1: I'd like my money to work for me!

NARRATOR 2: Me, too.

NARRATOR 1: I guess first we have to have some money so it can start to work.

NARRATOR 2: That means we need a job.

QUIZY: What kind of a job should I get?

NICOLE: What do you want to do, Quizy?

CHANDRA: I want to be an engineer.

DOUG: On a train?

CHANDRA: No, I want to build bridges and roads.

JACOB: Oh, you want to be a civil engineer.

QUIZY: That's very civil of you.

JACOB: I want to be a teacher.

NICOLE: Why do you want to be a teacher?

JACOB: I want to encourage other people to learn things.

QUIZY: But your teacher at school always looks like she's going nuts.

DOUG: Just because our class is a little energetic.

CHANDRA: But really she likes her job.

NICOLE: So what about you, Quizy?

JACOB: What do you want to do?

QUIZY: I want to be an engineer, too.

CHANDRA: Why?

QUIZY: I want to build a bridge from Earth to my planet.

DOUG: A bridge?

QUIZY: Yes, a train bridge.

NICOLE: Why a train bridge?

QUIZY: That way I could be a civil engineer AND a train engineer!

DOUG: You can't just say you WANT to be an engineer.

QUIZY: Why not?

CHANDRA: You have to go to college.

QUIZY: Is that where they build the bridges?

JACOB: No, that's where you get your education.

NICOLE: To become an engineer.

QUIZY: What do you mean?

DOUG: First you go to school to learn what you need to know.

CHANDRA: Then you get a job.

QUIZY: Do I have to go to college for all jobs?

JACOB: No. Some jobs you don't need to go to college for.

NICOLE: But some jobs you do.

DOUG: You definitely have to go to college to become an engineer.

QUIZY: Why?

CHANDRA: Because you have to learn enough so the bridges you build don't fall down.

QUIZY: Like in London.

NICOLE: London?

QUIZY: I heard the kindergarten class say London Bridge fell down.

DOUG: Right, Quizy.

Scene 4: College

NARRATOR 1: I always wondered why London Bridge fell down.

NARRATOR 2: I guess it wasn't built by an engineer!

CHANDRA: So if you want to build bridges, Quizy, you have to go to college for at least four years.

QUIZY: How do I get to college?

JACOB: First you have to apply.

NICOLE: You have to take some tests.

QUIZY: Before I even get into college?

DOUG: Yes, you have to prove that you're smart enough to take the classes.

QUIZY: But don't I go to school to become smart in the first place?

CHANDRA: Yes, but you still have to take the tests.

JACOB: Because college is hard.

NICOLE: And the college wants to know you can make it through.

DOUG: Or you'll be wasting your time.

CHANDRA: And the teachers' time.

JACOB: Then you have to pay money to go to college.

QUIZY: How much?

NICOLE: A lot.

QUIZY: But don't I want to go to school so I can EARN a lot of money from a job?

DOUG: Yes, but it still costs a lot of money to go to college.

CHANDRA: It's like an investment.

QUIZY: Education is an investment?

JACOB: Yes, it's an investment in your future.

NICOLE: A good education helps ensure your future earning power.

QUIZY: I like power.

DOUG: So first you need to go to college.

QUIZY: Do I HAVE to go to college to become rich?

CHANDRA: No. College will just help you earn more money at your job.

QUIZY: But I can still get rich if I don't go to college.

JACOB: Yes, but there's a secret to getting rich.

QUIZY: I won't tell.

NICOLE: It's OK to tell. In fact it's good to tell everyone this secret.

DOUG: It's not a secret because we don't want anyone to know.

QUIZY: How is it a secret then?

CHANDRA: It's a secret because not enough people know it.

QUIZY: What is the secret?

JACOB: Spend less than you make.

NICOLE: And save the rest.

DOUG: Then invest part of what you save.

CHANDRA: Make your money work for you.

JACOB: And plan for the future.

NICOLE: Have a goal.

DOUG: Have a plan to achieve your goal.

CHANDRA: Make your goal achievable.

JACOB: Monitor your plan as you head toward your goal.

NICOLE: Continue to make adjustments to your plan until you reach your goal.

QUIZY: Wow. That sounds complicated.

DOUG: The most important part is to spend less than you make.

QUIZY: You're sure it's not a secret to keep?

CHANDRA: No. It's a secret to share.

QUIZY: Sharing is good.

GLOSSARY

Career: A job that a person trains for and undertakes as a permanent calling.

Diversification: A typical goal of investors is to not have all investments of one type. For example, a diversified portfolio would include stock, bonds, real estate, and cash so that if one part of the portfolio lost money (for example, if all of your stocks became worthless), the other investments would keep their value.

Financial portfolio: The total of a person's financial investments, including cash, real estate, and other investments.

Goal: An end result you want to achieve.

Investments: Using money to increase wealth.

Liquidate: To transfer investments into cash.

Net worth: The amount a person is worth. It is calculated by adding up everything a person owns, including cash, investments, and real estate, and subtracting what is owed to others. The balance is called "net worth."

DOING TO UNDERSTAND

The following activities are included as handouts:

1. Financial Goals
2. Building a Portfolio
3. Retirement
4. Setting Goals
5. Board Game

ACTIVITY 1. FINANCIAL GOALS

Set financial goals for the future. Select a career you might be interested in. Check online resources and newspaper want ads to learn what a reasonable salary would be for that career. What would your first financial goals be? To save for a house? Start a business? Pay for higher education? Invest in mutual funds or stocks? What would you begin to save for first? Second? Third?

ACTIVITY 2. BUILDING A PORTFOLIO

This book has introduced many types of investments and ways to become financially responsible. Create your ideal diversified portfolio. Consider the different types of finances: cash savings, stocks, bonds, commodities, real estate, and collections, and anything other ideas you might have. Create a picture of how much of your finances you would want in each area. Create a pie chart showing those percentages. For example, if you wanted to have 20 percent of your finances in savings, 10 percent in stock, 10 percent in bonds, and 60 percent in real estate, you would create a pie chart divided into those percentages.

Now think about what would happen if part of your portfolio grew and part of it became worth less. For example, say your cash remained 20 percent of your portfolio and your real estate also stayed 60 percent, but your stock became 14 percent and your bonds became 16 percent. Create a new pie chart to show your new percentages.

What would you need to do to return your portfolio to its proper proportions? You would liquidate (sell) some of your stocks and bonds and place that money partly in cash and partly in real estate, so that the 20 percent, 10 percent, 10 percent, and 60 percent proportions were kept. The VALUE of the investments in all four categories would be higher, but the goal of portfolio management is to maintain proper proportions.

As a class, discuss your pie charts and portfolios and why each person chose those investments and those percentages.

ACTIVITY 3. RETIREMENT

Go to an online future planning site. Determine how much money you will need to have saved for the future to retire at various ages. Talk about what you have learned about compound interest and the importance of saving, investing, and being financially responsible as early as possible.

ACTIVITY 4. SETTING GOALS

Read the "Think About" section (p. 315). Discuss how to set a goal. Have everyone determine a goal and go through the exercise of planning how to achieve and monitor the goal and the plan. The goal could be short term (one week); intermediate term (several months), or long term (years in the future). It doesn't have to be financial for this exercise. It should just focus on the process. You can think about goals by using the Goal Setting Worksheet (p. 307).

Then use the Goal Tracking Worksheet (p. 308) to help you plan and follow how you would work to achieve your goals.

GOAL SETTING WORKSHEET

My long-term goals (will take more than one year) are:

1. _____
This goal is important because _____
The date I want to accomplish this goal is _____
The first thing I will do to work toward this goal TODAY is _____
_____

2. _____
This goal is important because _____
The date I want to accomplish this goal is _____
The first thing I will do to work toward this goal TODAY is _____
_____

3. _____
This goal is important because _____
The date I want to accomplish this goal is _____
The first thing I will do to work toward this goal TODAY is _____
_____

My short-term goals (will take less than one year) are:

1. _____
This goal is important because _____
The date I want to accomplish this goal is _____
The first thing I will do to work toward this goal TODAY is _____
_____

2. _____
This goal is important because _____
The date I want to accomplish this goal is _____
The first thing I will do to work toward this goal TODAY is _____
_____

3. _____
This goal is important because _____
The date I want to accomplish this goal is _____
The first thing I will do to work toward this goal TODAY is _____
_____

MAKE SURE THAT ONE OF THE FIRST THINGS YOU DO IS SET OUT A PLAN OF HOW TO ACHIEVE EACH GOAL AND DATES FOR GOAL REVIEW

GOAL TRACKING WORKSHEET

GOAL:

DATE SET:

TARGET DATE TO REACH GOAL:

STEPS TO REACH GOAL:

Goal review date:

Did I reach my goal? If not, what changes will I make so I can reach my goal? If yes, go to the next step.

STEPS TO ACHIEVE GOAL:

Goal review date:

Did I reach my goal? If not, what changes will I make so I can reach my goal? If yes, go to the next step.

STEPS TO ACHIEVE GOAL:

Goal review date:

Did I reach my goal? If not, what changes will I make so I can reach my goal? If yes, go to the next step.

STEPS TO ACHIEVE GOAL:

Goal review date:

Did I reach my goal? If not, what changes will I make so I can reach my goal? If yes, go to the next step.

ACTIVITY 5. BOARD GAME

Goal Game

The object of the Goal board game is to reach your financial goals and have the most money at the end of the game. This game can be played in small groups of two to four. To play you need:

   a calculator

   a pencil and paper

   small game pieces for each player

   1 die

   1 game board (see appendix 1) for each player

   1 center board (see appendix 1)

   1 bank board (see appendix 1)

   the Star, Moon, Sun, and Flash cards from the handouts (pp. 311–314)

   paper money (see appendix 1)

Set Up

Photocopy one set of cards for each game played. For example, a group of four players will need one set of Star cards, one set of Moon cards, one set of Sun cards, and one set of Flash cards. Place the piles of cards facedown in their boxes on the center board. When players have drawn all the cards in one pile, they should be shuffled and replaced, facedown on the center board, to reuse.

   ☆ STAR CARDS move the game forward

   ☾ MOON CARDS move the game back

    SUN CARDS help all players

    FLASH CARDS speed a player ahead

   Cut all cards and money along the lines.
   Provide one game board for each player.
   Photocopy enough money so there are four pages' worth for each player. At the beginning of the game, each player receives one of each of the following bills: $10, $20, $50, $100. The rest of the money is placed on the bank board for use during play.
   Use pencil, paper, and calculators, if needed.

Play

All players begin with five goals. Each player writes on a paper the numbers 1, 2, 3, 4, and 5. As they move through the game, players cross off the numbers as they achieve their goals.

Each player rolls the die to find out who plays first; whoever gets the largest number on the die plays first. Play then rotates counterclockwise.

From *Fun with Finance: Math + Literacy = Success* by Carol Peterson. Santa Barbara, CA: Libraries Unlimited. Copyright © 2009.

ACTIVITY 5. BOARD GAME (CONT.)

Players travel around the board, moving forward the number of spaces on the die. If a player lands on a space with a symbol on it, that player takes a card from the pile with that symbol and does what the card says.

If a player lands on a Flash space and draws a card that sends him or her across the speed zone, the player moves through the center bar of the dollar sign to the next nearest shaded space at the end of the speed zone.

A player who does not have enough to pay the total owed must pay all he or she has to the bank and then skip one turn.

The game ends when the first person finishes a trip around the board and lands on "Finish." The player does not have to have an exact roll of the die to land on "Finish."

At the end of the game, all players can purchase goals. Pay the bank $200 for each of the five goals left unachieved. You can pay for as many goals as you can afford.

All players then count their money. The person who has achieved the most goals AND has the most money (NOT the first player to finish) wins the game.

SUN CARDS FOR GOAL GAME

(Photocopy, cut, and place facedown on center board.)

Goal review. All players are making progress. Everyone receives $20 from the bank. ☆	Goal review. All players are making progress. Everyone receives $20 from the bank. ☆	Goal review. All players are making progress. Everyone receives $20 from the bank. ☆
Goal review. All players have had trouble reaching goals. Everyone pays the bank $50. ☆	Goal review. All players have had trouble reaching goals. Everyone pays the bank $50. ☆	Goal review. All players ADD one goal to their number! ☆
Goal review. All players ADD one goal to their number! ☆	Goal review. All players ADD one goal to their number! ☆	Goal review. All players receive $100 from the bank. ☆

From *Fun with Finance: Math + Literacy = Success* by Carol Peterson. Santa Barbara, CA: Libraries Unlimited. Copyright © 2009.

MOON CARDS FOR GOAL GAME

(Photocopy, cut, and place facedown on center board.)

Goal review. You've had some trouble. Pay the bank $50.	Goal review. You've had some trouble. Pay the bank $50.	Goal review. You've had some trouble. Pay the bank $50.
Goal review. You haven't been working on your goals. Pay the bank $100.	Goal review. You haven't been working on your goals. Pay the bank $100.	Goal review. You haven't been working on your goals. Pay the bank $100.
Goal review. You have a great idea. ADD one goal to your total.	Goal review. You have a great idea. ADD one goal to your total.	Goal review. You have a great idea. ADD one goal to your total.

STAR CARDS FOR GOAL GAME

(Photocopy, cut, and place facedown on center board.)

You're making progress! Receive $100 from the bank.	You're making progress! Receive $100 from the bank.	You're making progress! Receive $100 from the bank.
You're making progress! Receive $100 from the bank.	You're making progress! Receive $100 from the bank.	You're making progress! Receive $100 from the bank.
You review your goals and need to make some changes. Take an extra turn.	You review your goals and need to make some changes. Take an extra turn.	You review your goals and need to make some changes. Take an extra turn.

FLASH CARDS FOR GOAL GAME

(Photocopy, cut, and place facedown on center board.)

You achieve one of your goals! Cross one goal off and receive $100 from the bank. If you've already achieved all of your goals, receive another $100 from the bank. 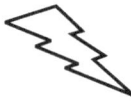	You achieve one of your goals! Cross one goal off and receive $100 from the bank. If you've already achieved all of your goals, receive another $100 from the bank.	You achieve one of your goals! Cross one goal off and receive $100 from the bank. If you've already achieved all of your goals, receive another $100 from the bank.
You achieve one of your goals! Cross one goal off and receive $100 from the bank. If you've already achieved all of your goals, receive another $100 from the bank. 	You achieve one of your goals! Cross one goal off and receive $100 from the bank. If you've already achieved all of your goals, receive another $100 from the bank.	You achieve one of your goals! Cross one goal off and receive $100 from the bank. If you've already achieved all of your goals, receive another $100 from the bank. 
You achieve one of your goals! Cross one goal off and receive $100 from the bank. If you've already achieved all of your goals, receive another $100 from the bank. 	You achieve one of your goals! Cross one goal off and receive $100 from the bank. If you've already achieved all of your goals, receive another $100 from the bank. 	You achieve one of your goals! Cross one goal off and receive $100 from the bank. If you've already achieved all of your goals, receive another $100 from the bank. 

THINK ABOUT

Have you ever made a New Year's resolution? Have you decided to get something done that you'd always wanted to do but never got around to it? What happened? Did you accomplish it, or did you forget about that resolution by February?

Goals are about more than saying you want to get something done. In order to move forward, you need to write down your goals, work toward them, and review them from time to time. Here's a good way to help you form your goals and achieve them.

First, make them specific. Saying "I want to earn more money this year" is fine, but it doesn't give you anything to work toward. Instead, say "I want to earn enough money to buy an MP3 player." With that, you know exactly what you are working toward.

Make the goal measurable. Specifically, how much are you trying to save? Learn enough about what your goal is so that you also know what you need to reach it. Decide also what time frame you are looking at. Do you want to have your MP3 player in time for your family's road trip in July? If so, how many months do you have before you want to achieve your goal? How much do you need to save each month until then?

Your goal must also be within your reach. If you are 12 years old and you want to buy your own home in two years, your goal is probably not within your reach, nor would it really mean anything to you to achieve the goal, because legally you can't own real estate anyway until you are older. But saving money to buy an MP-3 player is achievable if you have a way to earn money.

But it's not enough to just set goals. You also need to work toward them and review them. Break your goals down into time periods. Say you have a goal to buy an MP-3 player in six months and you have a lawn mowing job each week. How much will you need to earn and save each month? At the end of each month, review your progress. Are you still on track toward your goal? Are you ahead? Are you behind? If you're behind, think of ways you might be able to earn additional money to bring you back on track. Then implement those plans and review your progress again the next month.

By seeing forward progress, reviewing your plan, and making changes if you need to, you have a better chance of being successful in reaching those goals.

FIND OUT MORE

Resources in Your Community

Find out whether a parent or family friend of a student works in financial planning. Ask that person to visit the class to share experiences or answer questions.

Web Sites

- To see how much money you would need to retire, use the MSN retirement calculator at http://moneycentral.msn.com/retire/planner.aspx.
- Or try the Yahoo retirement calculator at http://finance.yahoo.com/calculator/retirement/ret-02.
- For help setting goals, search the Web using keywords "goals" or "goal setting."

Careers

Related jobs include financial advisor, consultant, and life coach.

Appendix 1: Board Game Pieces

Appendix 1 includes the following reproducible handouts:

Player Board

Bank Board

Center Board

Dollar Bills

Five Dollar Bills

Ten Dollar Bills

Twenty Dollar Bills

Fifty Dollar Bills

One Hundred Dollar Bills

These reproducible pages are intended to be used for the board games in *Fun with Finance*. Specific instructions for each game are provided in each chapter. You may wish to photocopy the paper money on different colors so that monetary values can be easily discerned. The Center Board is provided so that the Sun, Moon, Star, and Flash cards can be photocopied on one side and then placed facedown during play.

Players may use various items as game pieces, such as small paperclips, pebbles, erasers, or slips of paper. Game pieces do not have to be different because each player will be playing on his or her own game board. One die per player or per group is also needed.

Games will usually be played in small groups. Alternatively, students may play together as a class, during which there may be a discussion of the principles involved and terms that come up during play.

PLAYER BOARD

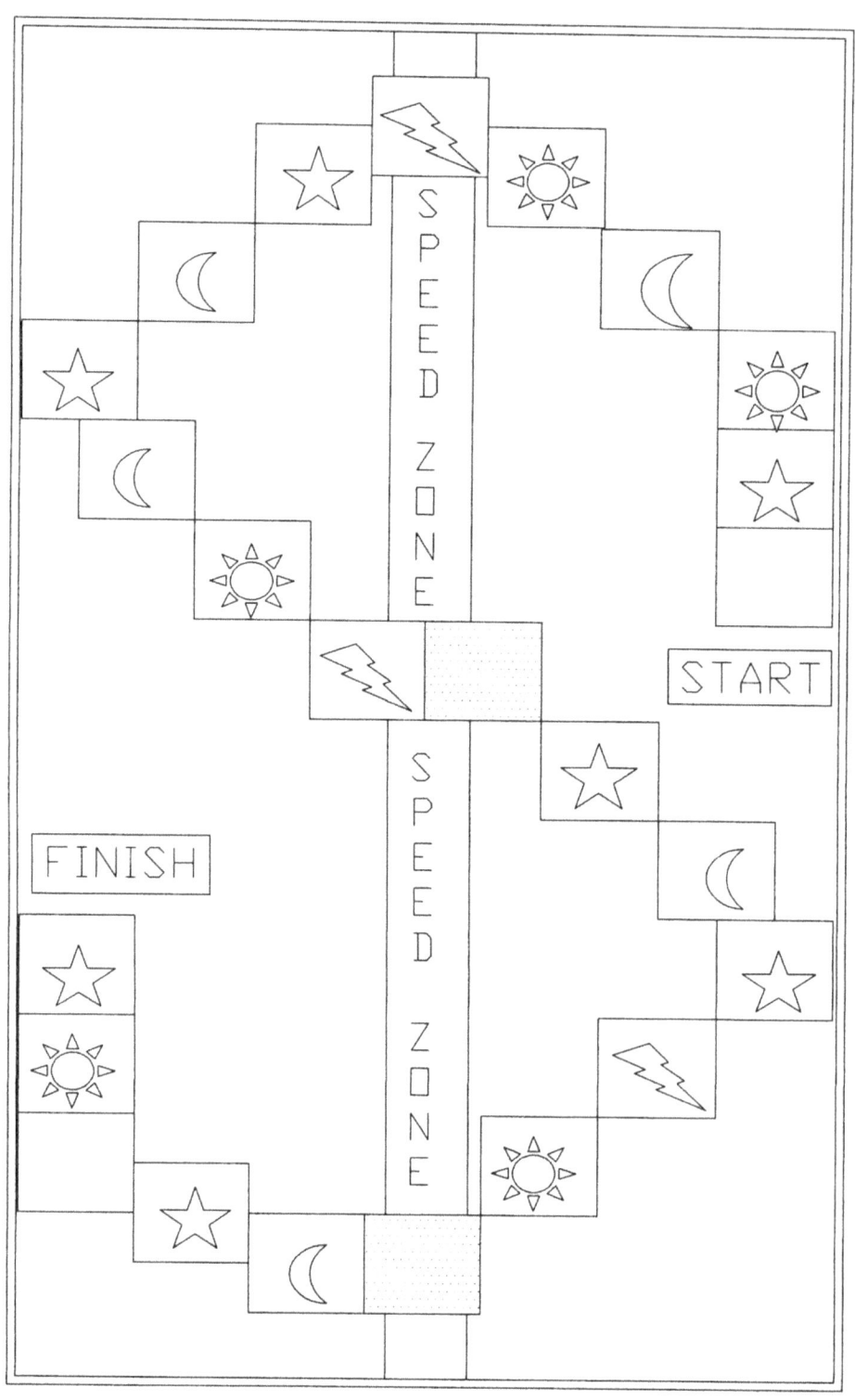

BANK BOARD

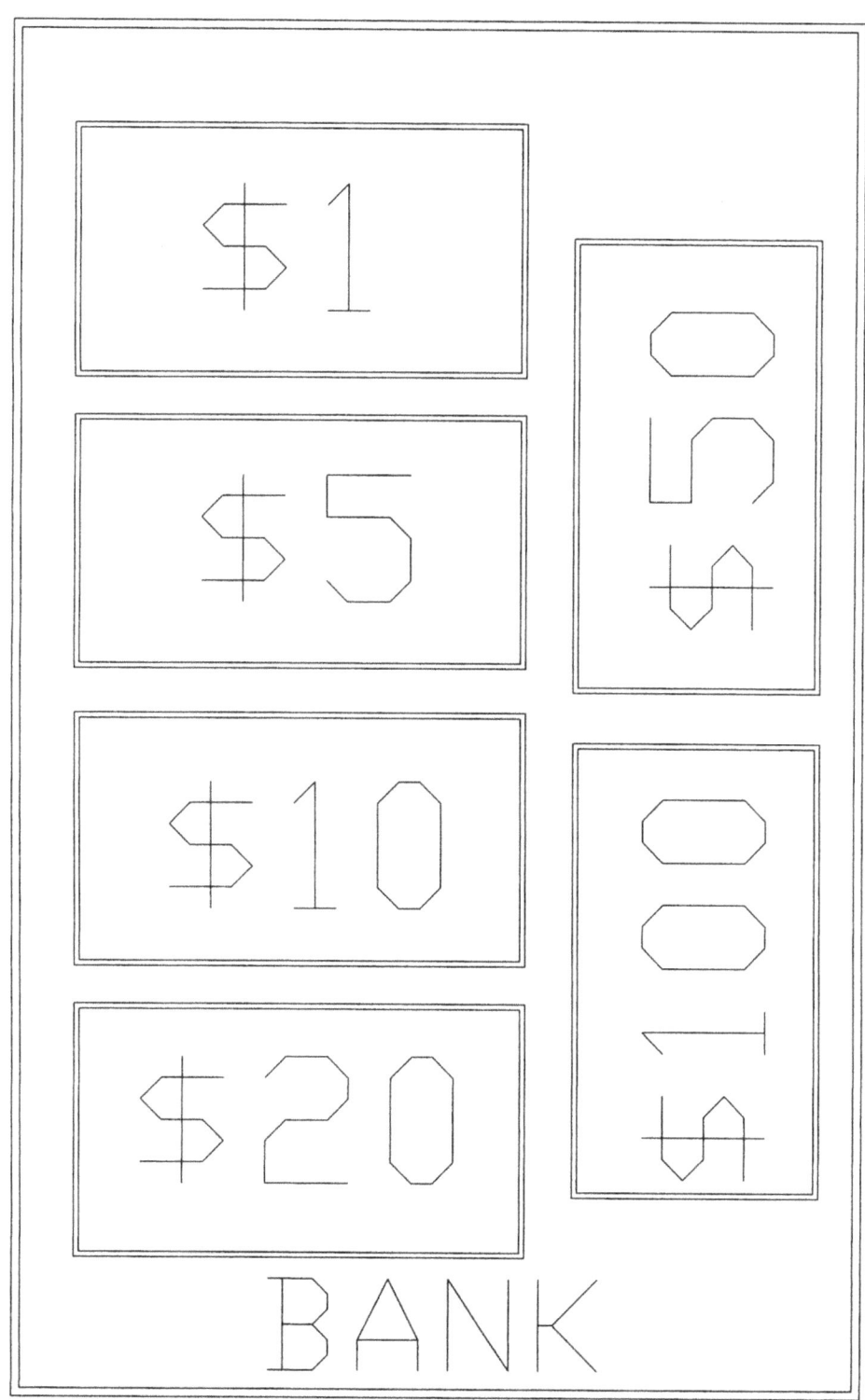

CENTER BOARD

DOLLAR BILLS

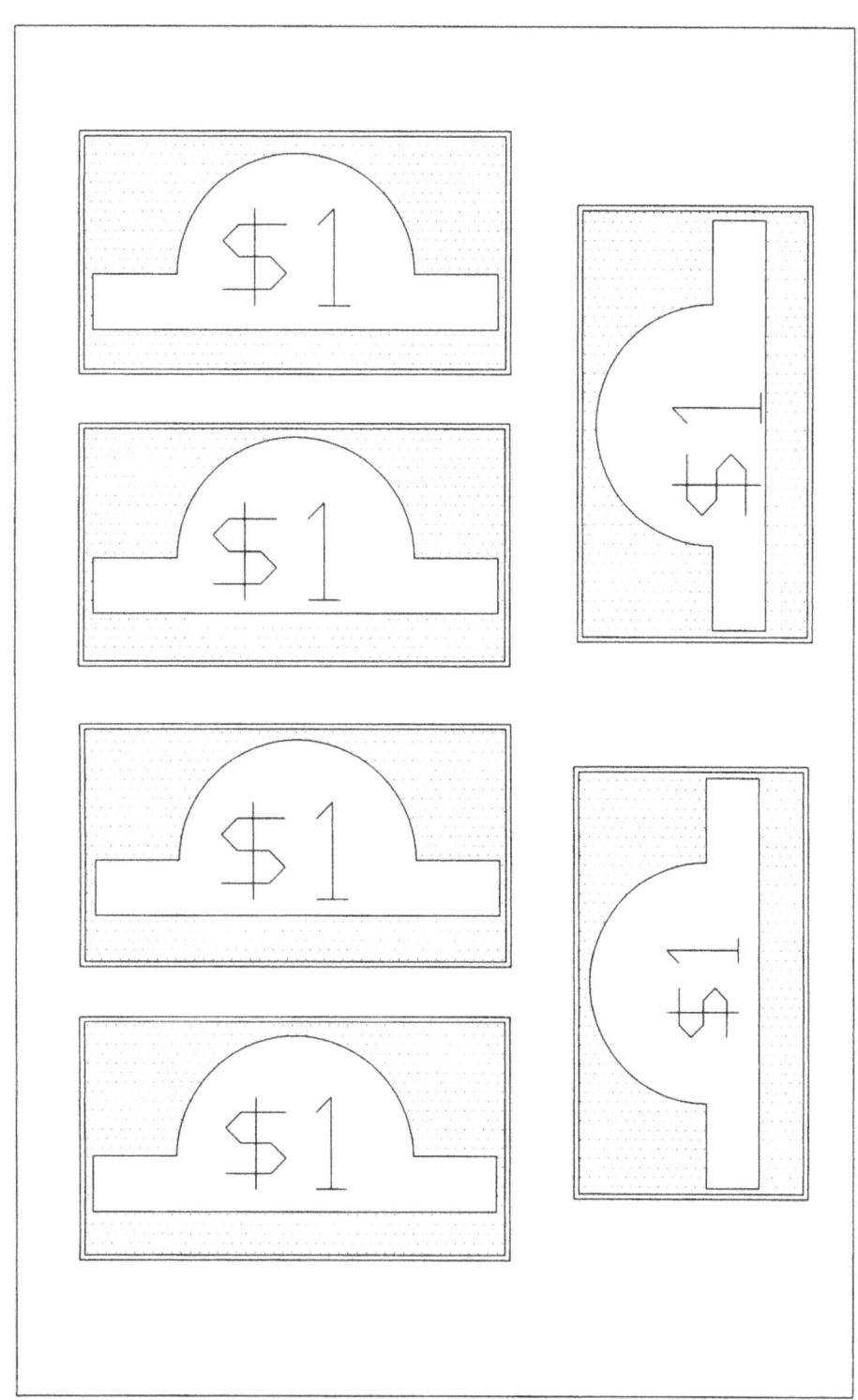

FIVE DOLLAR BILLS

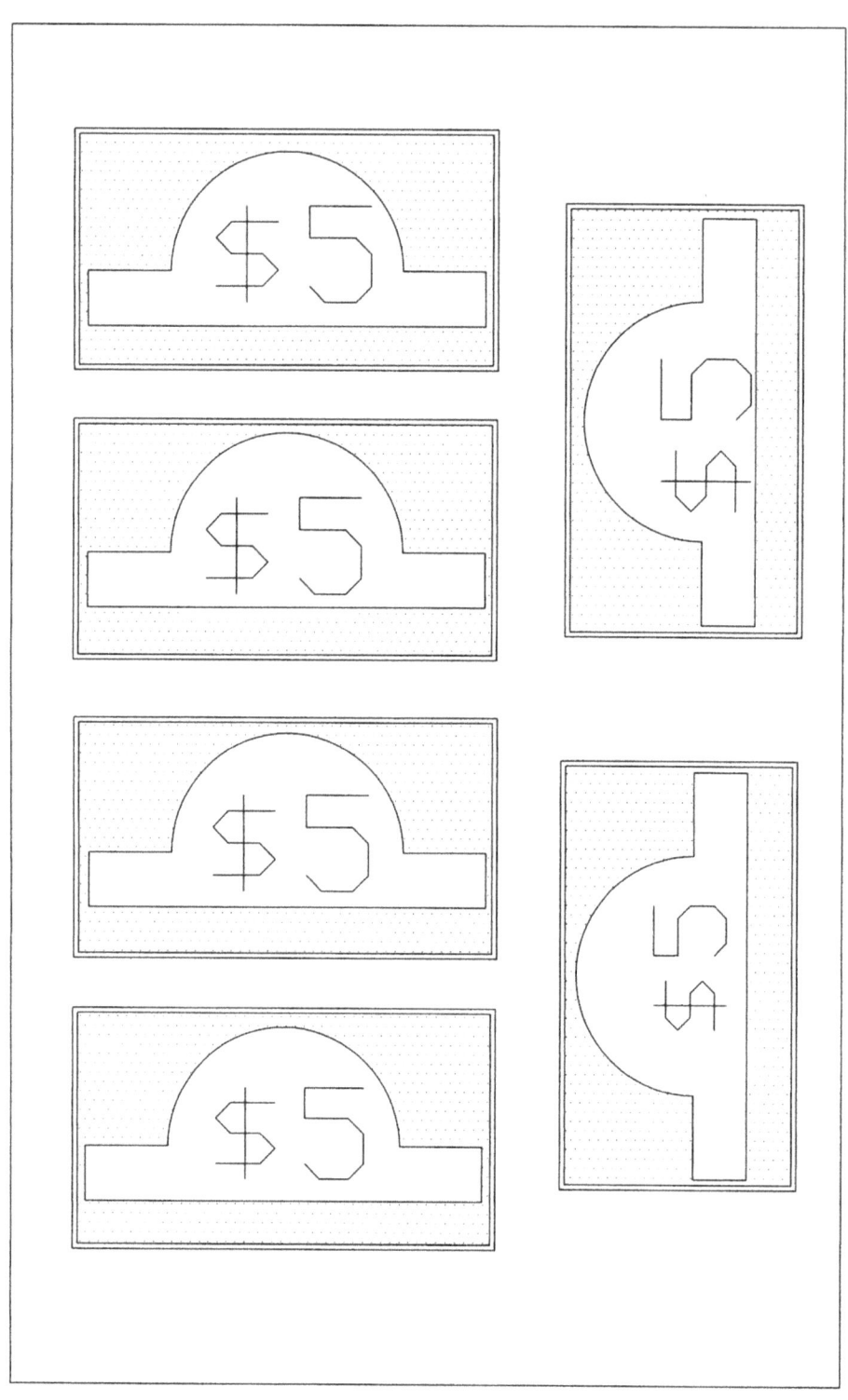

TEN DOLLAR BILLS

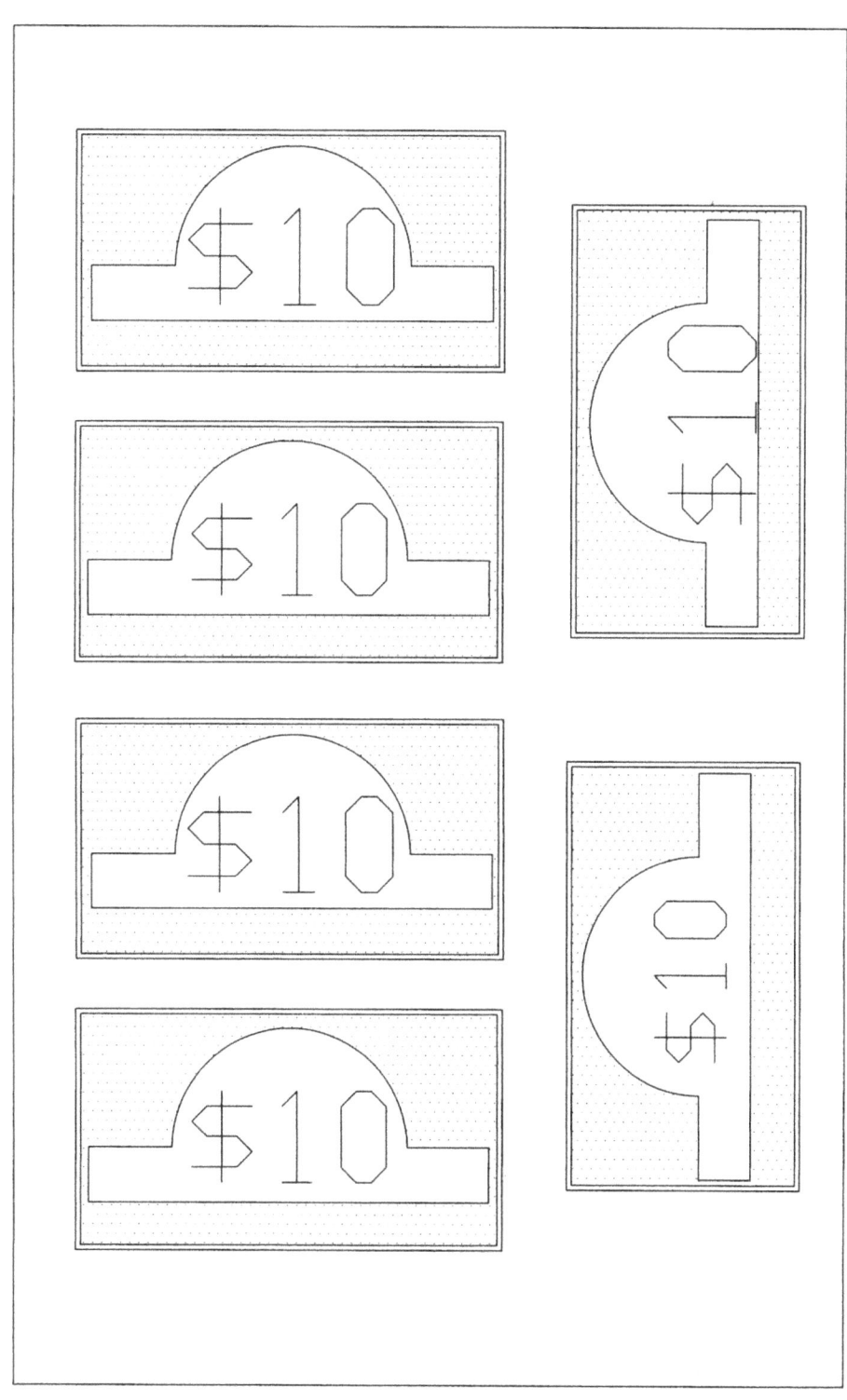

TWENTY DOLLAR BILLS

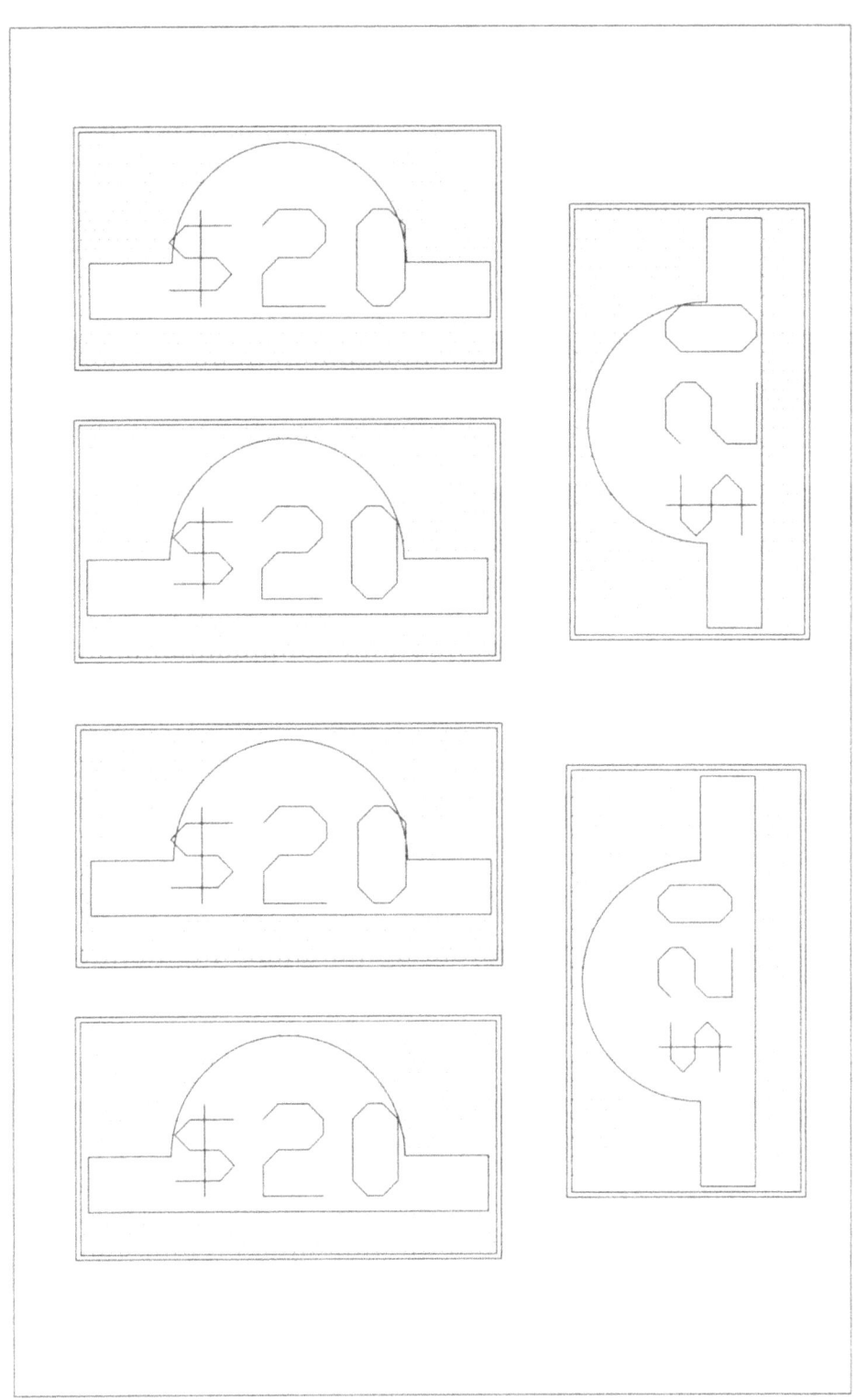

FIFTY DOLLAR BILLS

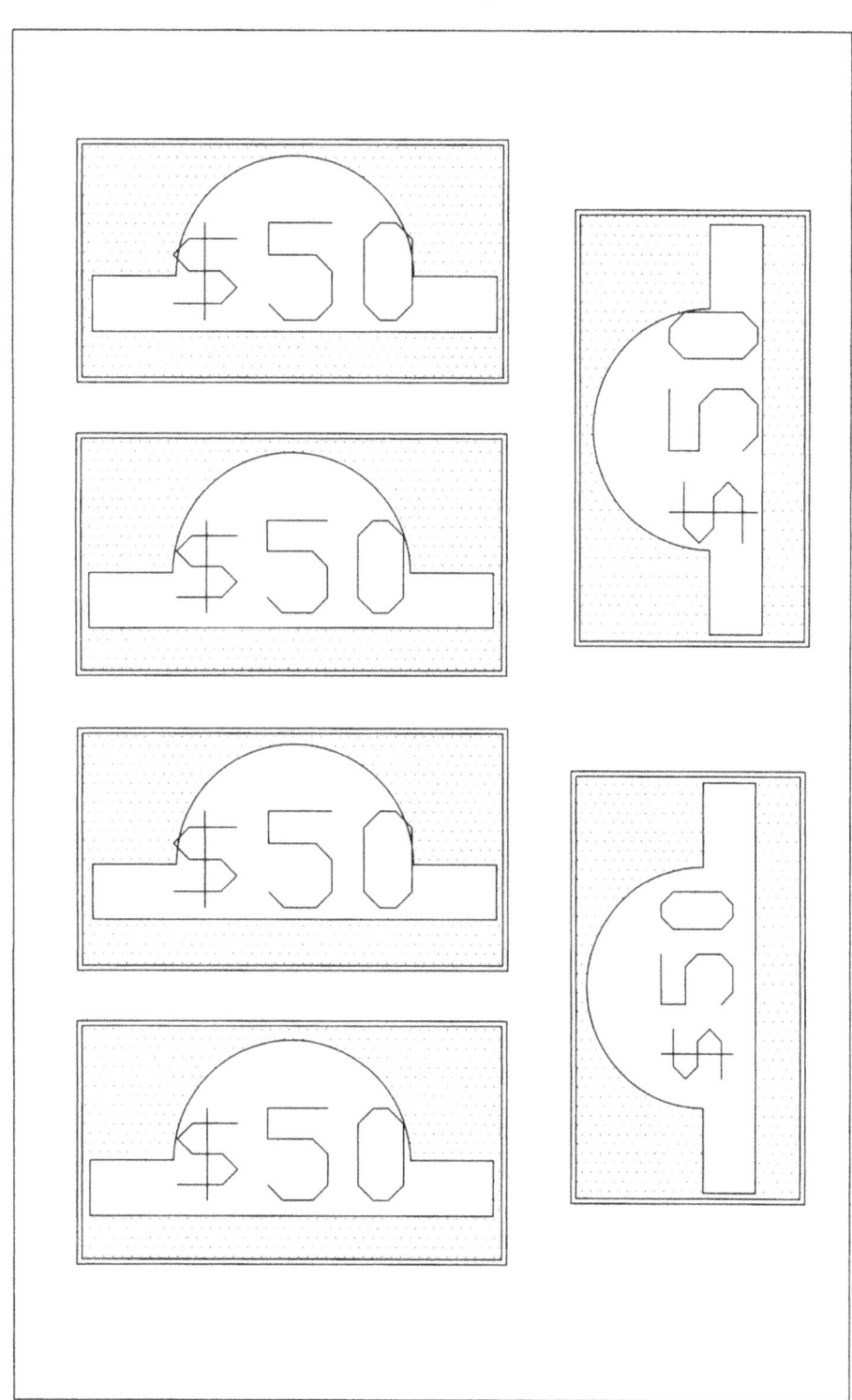

ONE HUNDRED DOLLAR BILLS

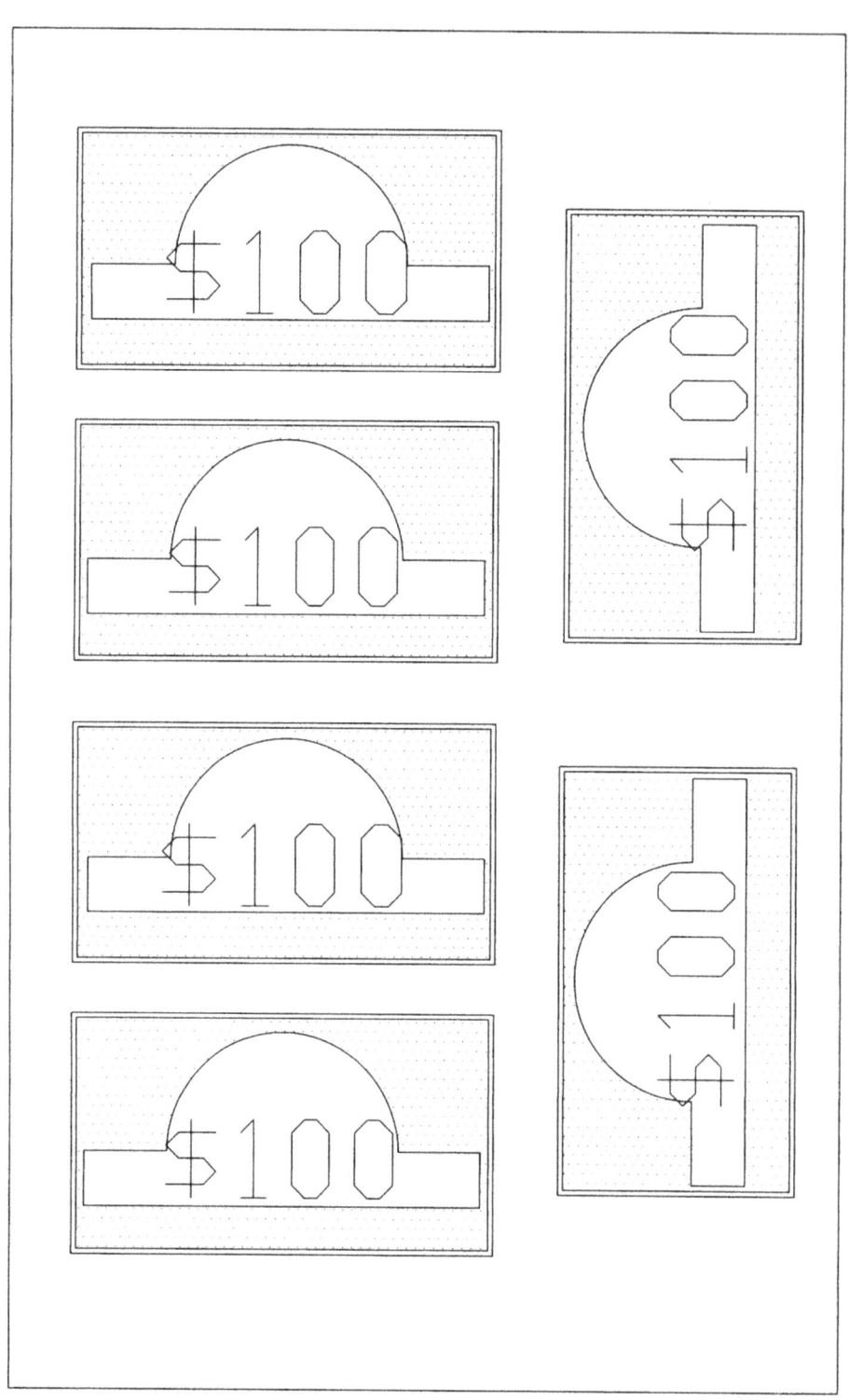

Appendix 2: Tables

Tables are used to organize information so it can be understood more easily. Tables organize information in horizontal (side to side) rows and vertical (up and down) columns. You may remember that rows go side to side by thinking of rows of seats in a movie theater. You may remember that columns go up and down by remembering that columns on a building go from the ground up to the roof. The spot where information in a row and in a column meets is called a cell. The table and each row and column should have a title to tell the reader what information the table shows.

Tables are often created first, and then the information from the table is used to create a graph or a chart. The graph or chart then helps a person understand how one piece of information relates to another and to all of the information as a whole.

If you are using Microsoft Word, you may easily create a table on a computer by left mouse clicking "insert" then "table." Then choose how many rows and columns you need. The number of rows and columns depends on how many pieces of information you want to show. Remember to have enough rows and columns to also show the titles of the information you are showing.

Here is an example of a table:

Illustrations Used in *Fun with Finance*

Chapter Number	Tables	Pie Charts	Bar Charts	Line Graphs

To complete this table, you would go through the book and count up the numbers of tables, charts, and graphs you find. You would then put those numbers in the appropriate spaces.

Appendix 3: Pie Charts

A pie chart is a type of graph. It is in the shape of a circle that is divided into pieces like pie slices. Each pie piece represents information related to the rest of the pie. Pie charts are used to show the sizes of parts that make up the whole of some information.

For example, if we have information that we want to graph, first we would create a table.

Favorite Desserts

Favorite Desserts	Number of People
Cake	10
Pudding	6
Ice Cream	9
Pie	4
Other	1

The total number of people who had favorite desserts was 30. We would then take that information and create a pie chart like this:

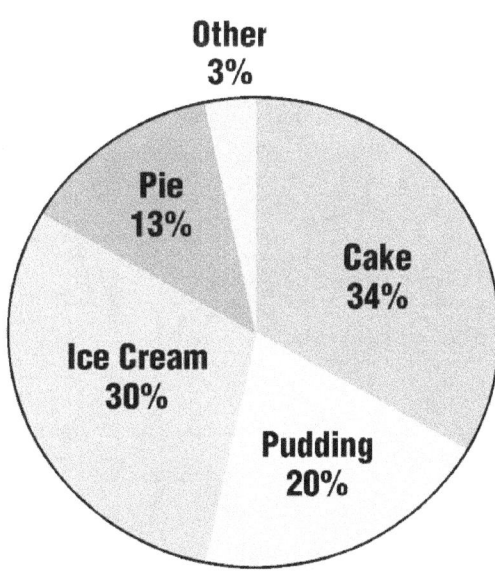

330 Appendix 3: Pie Charts

The pie chart shows what percentage of the entire 30 people interviewed like which types of desserts. The total, 30, equals 100 percent of all people asked.

We could also use the information to show the actual numbers of people who liked each dessert on the pie chart instead of their percentages. The percentages would still be seen visually on the pie chart, because the size of the slices represents those percentages. But the information about the number of people in each pie slice could be shown like this:

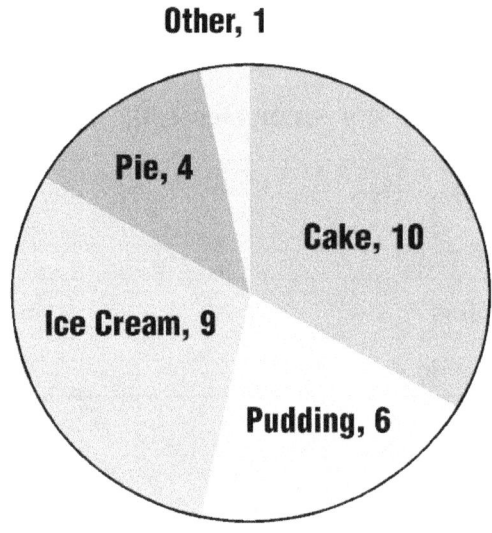

Favorite Desserts of 30 People Asked

Pie charts may also have a "legend," which is like a code that tells the reader visually what the pieces of information refer to. Sometimes you will find similar legends on a map, for example, showing that blue lines refer to rivers and black stars indicate capital cities. Here is an example of the percentage pie chart with a legend:

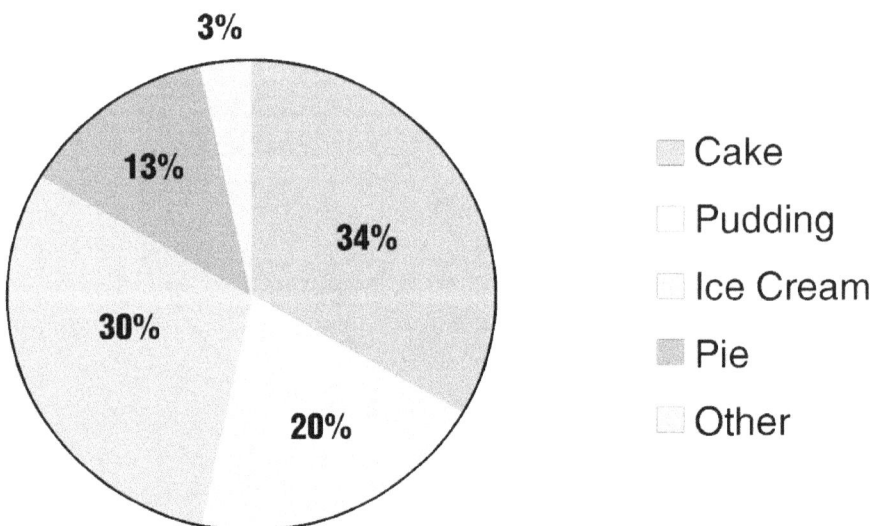

Appendix 4: Line Graphs

Line graphs are used to show how two sets of information are associated and how they change in relation to each other. Line graphs can also be used to show how information changes over time. For example, time might be shown on one side of the graph and the information itself along the bottom.

Line graphs are often created by using a grid. A grid is a set of horizontal (side to side) and vertical (up and down) lines. The points where the lines connect can be used to show specific points of information on the graph. These points of information are then joined together by a line, as in a connect-the-dot drawing. The line easily shows how the information increases or decreases based on changes.

If we have information that we want to graph, first we would create a table:

Favorite Desserts

Favorite Desserts	Number of People
Cake	10
Pudding	6
Ice Cream	9
Pie	4
Other	1

We would then create a line graph to show that information:

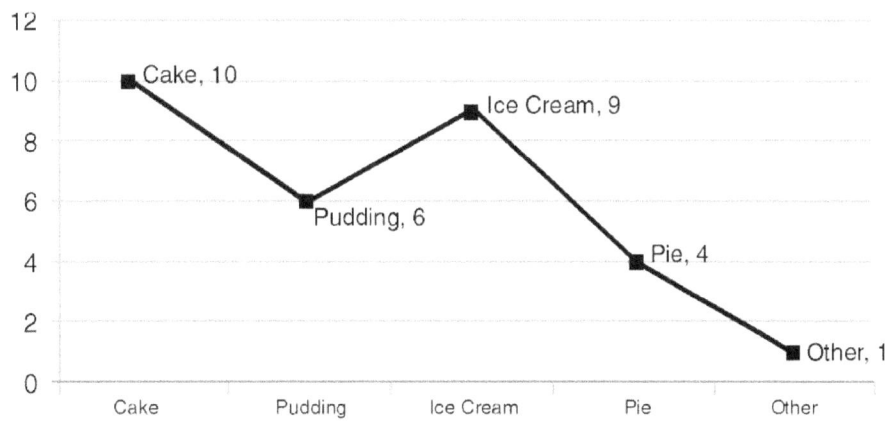

Favorite Desserts of 30 People Asked

Appendix 5: Bar Graphs

A bar graph (also sometimes called a bar chart or a column chart) is often used to compare groups of information. The bars can be drawn up and down or from side to side. Bar graphs let people compare data quickly. Bar graphs can help us understand trends based on categories.

The bar graph, like the line graph, has two axes. One axis shows groups of information. The other axis shows amount or frequency of the groups of information. The bars on a bar graph can show data either horizontally or vertically.

The information on both axes must be labeled so the reader of the bar graph can tell the type of information that is being counted and how the information is grouped. The information is then represented by rectangular blocks. Each group of information has its own bar. The bars can be shown horizontally or vertically.

For example, if we have information that we want to graph, first we would create a table:

Favorite Desserts

Favorite Desserts	Number of People
Cake	10
Pudding	6
Ice Cream	9
Pie	4
Other	1

We could then create a column-type bar graph, like this:

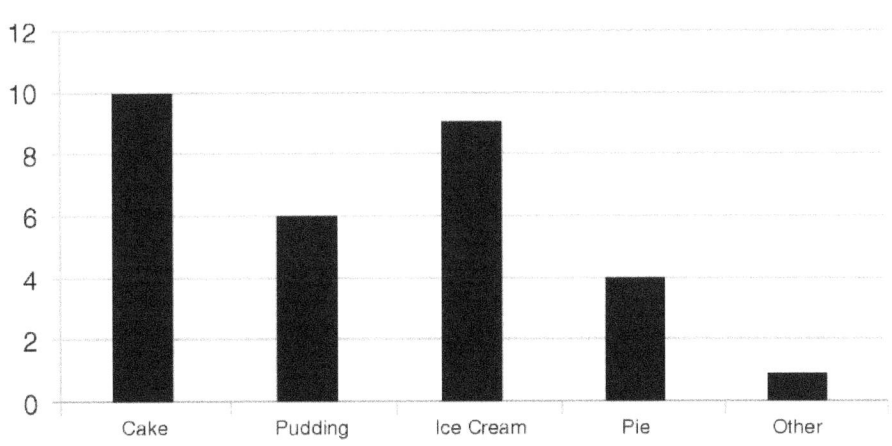

334   Appendix 5: Bar Graphs

Or we could create a horizontal bar graph, like this:

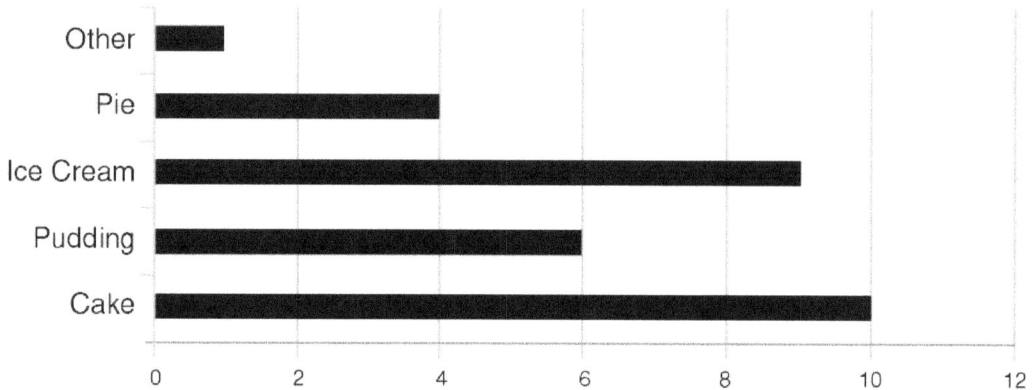

Appendix 6: Curriculum Standards

Although the terminology used in curriculum standards varies by state, generally the states addresses similar standards. The following may be helpful to teachers in understanding which curriculum standards are covered in *Fun with Finance*. The page numbers indicate where a principle of finance or activity addresses that standard.

MATH	PAGE NUMBERS
Number Sense: computing numbers, decimals, fractions, percents; positive and negative numbers	19, 20, 22, 23, 49, 56, 58, 74, 75, 76, 77, 79, 99, 100, 105, 128, 130, 131, 133, 157, 158, 159, 161, 194, 215, 217, 235, 261
Statistics, Data Analysis, Probability, Graphs, Mathematical Reasoning	20, 49, 74, 75, 77, 99, 100, 101, 103, 128, 130, 131, 158, 185, 186, 187, 211, 212, 216, 236, 237, 239, 280, 282, 304, 327, 329, 331, 333
Measurement and Simple Geometry	186
Rates, Proportions, Percentages	74, 75, 76, 87–97, 99, 100, 102–103, 128, 130, 304

LITERACY	PAGE NUMBERS
Vocabulary and Concept Development	2, 18, 30, 73, 98, 126, 139, 184, 209–210, 235, 258, 279, 291, 302
Reading Comprehension	3–17, 35–47, 65–72, 87–97, 143–155, 171–183, 199–208, 227–234, 251–257, 271–278, 293–301
Spelling	18, 48, 73, 98, 126, 156, 184, 209–210, 235, 258, 279, 302

WRITTEN AND ORAL ENGLISH	PAGE NUMBERS
Writing Strategies: Organization and Focus, Research and Technology	31, 50–52, 54, 55, 61, 84, 111, 139, 158, 168, 195, 213, 214, 223, 236, 237, 240, 247, 259, 260, 267, 281, 289, 303, 305, 307, 315
Listening and Speaking Strategies and Applications	3–17, 35–47, 53, 65–72, 78, 84, 87–97, 143–155, 171–183, 199–208, 227–234, 238, 251–257, 271–278, 293–301, 305, 306
Verbal Communication	53, 78, 130, 131, 132, 157, 158, 187, 238, 305, 306

SOCIAL STUDIES	PAGE NUMBERS
Chronological and Spatial Thinking	212, 238
Economics and Historical Interpretation	2, 19, 128, 271–279
Geography	8–10, 19, 21
History and World Culture	3–21, 22

Appendix 7: Books about Money or Math

FOR KIDS

The Best of Times. By Greg Tang. Scholastic, 2002.

40 Fabulous Math Mysteries Kids Can't Resist. By Marcia Miller and Martin Lee. Teaching Resources, 2001.

Funny and Fabulous Fraction Stories. By Dan Greenberg and Jared Lee. Scholastic Teaching Resources, 1999.

Grapes of Math. By Greg Tang. Scholastic, 2004.

Graphing the Universe. By Deborah Underwood. Heinemann-Raintree, 2009.

Graphing Transportation. By Deborah Underwood. Heinemann-Raintree, 2009.

Growing Money: A Complete Investing Guide for Kids. By Gail Karlitz. Price, Stern, Sloan, 2001.

Kid's Guide to Money: Earning It, Saving, It, Spending It, Growing It, Sharing It. By Diane Mayr. Adams Media Corporation, 2002.

Kiss My Math: Showing Pre-Algebra Who's Boss. By Danica McKellar. Hudson Street Press, 2008.

Math Appeal. By Mind-Stretching Math Riddles. By Greg Tang. Scholastic, 2003.

Math on Call: A Mathematics Handbook. By Andrew Kaplan, Carol Debold, Susan Rogalski, and Pat Bourdreau. Great Source Education Group, 2004.

Math Potatoes: Mind-Stretching Brain Food. By Greg Tang. Scholastic, 2005.

Money Sense for Kids. By Hollis Page Harman. Barron's, 2005.

Motley Fool Investment Guide for Teens: 8 Steps to Having More Money Than Your Parents Ever Dreamed Of. By David Gardner. Fireside, 2002.

Mummy Math: An Adventure in Geometry. By Cindy Neuschwander and Bryan Langdo. Henry Holt, 2005.

Power of Un. By Nancy Etchemendy. Front Street, 2000.

Real World Math: Money and Other Numbers in Your Life. By Donna Guthrie. Millbrook Press, 1998.

Rich Dad Poor Dad for Teens: The Secrets About Money That You Don't Learn in School! By Robert T. Kiyosaki. Warner Books, 2004.

Safari Adventure: Charts, Graphs and Tables. By Deborah Underwood. Heinemann-Raintree, 2008.

Sea Sums. By Joy N. Hulme. Hyperion, 1996.

Sea Squares. By Joy N. Hulme. Hyperion, 1991.

Totally Awesome Money Book for Kids. By Adriane G. Berg. Newmarket Press, 2002.

Ultimate Kids' Money Book. By Neale S. Godfrey. Simon & Schuster, 1998.

Wild Fibonacci. By Joy N. Hulme. Tricycle, 2005.

FOR TEACHERS

Making Allowances: A Dollars and Sense Guide to Teaching Kids About Money. By Paul W. Lermitte. McGraw-Hill, 2002.

Raising Financially Fit Kids. By Joline Godfrey. Ten Speed Press, 2003.

Silver Spoon Kids: How Successful Parents Raise Responsible Children. By Eileen Gallo, Jon J. Gallo, and Kevin J. Gallo. McGraw-Hill, 2001.

Teaching Money Applications to Make Mathematics Meaningful. By Elizabeth Marquez and Paul Westbrook. Corwin Press, 2007.

Appendix 8: Readers Theatre

Readers theatre is a form of play presented through oral reading. It is most typically used in two formats: nontheatrical and performance reading. No matter which format you choose, the parts are read, not memorized. It is "readers" theatre, after all.

NONTHEATRICAL READING

In a nontheatrical setting, students simply read scripts aloud as a group. The scripts are a reading resource. One way to read scripts is in "circle reading," in which all students read the various parts by taking turns around a circle. Each student reads one line, followed by the next student, who reads the next line. In circle reading, no one student reads all of the lines of any one role. Scripts may also be used in "instant reading," in which students are assigned parts and the play is read once from their seats. Alternatively, students may be assigned parts, read through the script silently, and then read it through aloud once.

THEATRICAL PERFORMANCE READING

An alternate focus for readers theatre is theatrical performance. Here roles are read standing in front of the classroom or on a stage. Performance might include simple costumes and props, rehearsal, stage direction, facial expression, gestures, and sound effects. Even in a performance setting, however, scripts are not memorized. The emphasis is on encouraging literacy through *reading*.

Plays in a theatrical setting might be performed as "cooperative reading." This format breaks a classroom into groups. Scripts are rehearsed individually by reading aloud and are rehearsed once or twice as a group. Each group then performs the entire play for the others.

A play may also be a "staged reading," in which a specific area of the classroom is selected as the "stage" or an actual stage is used, if available. Entrances and exits are included and rehearsed. Plays might then be presented to other classes in the same grade level or to other grade levels within the school.

Each script includes performance suggestions for props, action, gestures, stage entrances, and exits for optional use in a theatrical performance format. If a nonperformance format is used, they may be ignored, or one student may be assigned to read them aloud.

TIPS FOR SUCCESS

The 12 scripts have varying numbers of parts. Each script includes two narrators. If there are many students, consider having a different narrators for each scene. If the class is small or students are divided into groups to present to each other, you may want to assign students more than one part. Some of the same characters are found throughout the 12 scripts: Doug and Nicole (a brother and sister), their friends, Jacob and Shandra, and a friendly extraterrestrial named Quizy. The character of Quizy can be played up or played down as the reader desires.

One way to introduce characters to the audience at the beginning of the play is to line up the characters facing the audience. Students then introduce themselves in turn. For example, "I am playing the part of Doug." Alternatively, each student may carry the script in a folder with the character's name printed on the front in large letters for the audience to see.

REHEARSAL

Encourage students to follow along as others read. Have them rehearse their parts in pairs and help each other with words. For performance theatre, first practice the play a few times seated in a circle. Then have readers rehearse the play with gestures, expression, and movement. Finally, rehearse the play in the staging area with entrances and exits, using proper stage directions. Don't worry too much about entrances and exits. If the stage area is small and there is no room for a "backstage," readers may enter the performance area by walking through or around the audience.

PERFORMANCE

Photocopy scripts as needed. Make sure each reader has a script with the character's name highlighted. Encourage readers to speak loudly. Remind students that the more familiar they are with the part, the more professional the performance will be (and the better their literacy and self-confidence will be). Do not, however, encourage memorization. This is "readers" theatre. Costume and prop suggestions are included for each script. Remember, however, that one hand should be free to hold the script.

Instruct students to talk to the audience, rather than to each other, to help project their voices and make the audience feel part of the play. Tell them to hold the scripts away from their faces, so their facial expressions can be seen and their words are not muffled.

Encourage eye contact between the readers and the audience. Although the readers will have to look down at the scripts from time to time, they may want to focus on a point at the back of the room, slightly above the audience. When characters speak to each other, they should continue to speak to that point above the audience, as if that is the location of the other character.

READERS THEATRE TERMS

You may want to introduce students to the following theatrical terms, especially if you are using the performance format of readers theatre.

Backstage and offstage: The area that is not the stage

Cast: People reading the play

Downstage: The portion of the stage in front of the reader

Dress rehearsal: Practicing the play as it will be performed, using costumes and props

Narrator: Person who explains the action or setting

Performance: Reading the script to an audience

Readers: Students who provide the action and the drama

Rehearsal: Practicing the play

Script: The play being read

Stage: The area where the play is read

Stage left: The portion of the stage to the reader's left

Stage right: The portion of the stage to the reader's right

Upstage: The portion of the stage behind the reader

Bibliography

Clason, George S. *The Richest Man in Babylon*. New York: Penguin Group, 1926.

Dayton, Howard. *Your Money Counts*. Gainesville, GA: Crown Financial Ministries, 1996.

Eker, Harv T. *Secrets of the Millionaire Mind: Mastering the Inner Game of Wealth*. New York: Collins Business, 2005.

Kaplan, Andrew, and Ann Petroni-McMullen. *Math on Call*. Wilmington, MA: Great Source Education Group, 1998.

Kiyosaki, Robert T., and Sharon L. Lechter. *Rich Dad/Poor Dad: What the Rich Teach Their Kids That the Poor Do Not*. New York: Business Plus, 2000.

Natenberg, Sheldon. *Option Volatility & Pricing*. New York: McGraw-Hill, 1994.

Ovason, David. *Secret Symbols of the Dollar Bill*. New York: Perennial Currents, 2004.

Ramsey, Dave. *Total Money Makeover*. Nashville, TN: Thomas Nelson, 2003.

Tracy, Brian. *Focal Point*. New York: American Management Association, 1994.

Index

accounts payable, 69, 73
accounts receivable, 69, 72, 73
agent, 171, 184
antique, 279

baht, 8, 18
balance, 126, 159
bankruptcy, 116, 117, 126
banks, 87–89
   bonds, 237
bear market, 198, 207
bill (bond), 226, 232, 235
bills, 115, 156
board games, 23, 56, 79, 105, 133, 162, 188, 217, 241, 261, 283, 309, 317–26
bond measure, 235
bonds, 225–26, 229–34, 235, 239, 247
   bank, 237
   corporate, 235, 247
   municipal, 235, 238, 247
   savings, 236, 240, 247
borrower, 180, 184
broker, 198, 205, 253
budget, 118–20, 126, 141, 142, 143–57
bull market, 198, 207
business, 63, 65–67
   fictitious, 63, 68
   setting up, 67–70, 78
   small, 71–72
buyer, 173, 175, 181, 184

call, 209
careers, 31, 55, 61, 84, 111, 139, 158, 168, 195, 223, 247, 267, 289, 297–98, 302, 315
category, 147, 156
charts, 49, 99, 100, 103, 186, 189, 209, 216, 284. *See also* pie charts; tables
check stub, 77
checkbook, 156, 159–61
checking account, 156, 159
collecting, 269–70, 271–78
collections, 279–80
commodities, 249–50, 251–57, 258, 259–60

community resources, 31, 61, 84, 111, 139, 168, 195, 223, 247, 267, 289, 315
company, 63, 68
corporation, 63, 68, 73
credit, 114, 132
credit bureau, 126, 132, 139
credit rating and credit score, 126, 132, 133, 134, 139
credit report, 116, 127, 132
creditor, 126, 132
currency, 6–7, 18, 19, 30
currency converter, 19, 31
curriculum standards, 1, 33, 63, 85, 113, 141, 169, 197, 225, 249, 269, 291, 335–36

debt, 114, 126, 130, 131
   getting out of, 120–25
debtor, 126
deductions, 75, 76, 77
defensive sectors, 258
diversification, 302
diversify, 209, 295
dividend, 197, 203
dollar, 5, 10, 13, 18, 19, 20, 21, 22, 24, 25, 26, 27, 28, 29, 30
Dow Jones Industrial Average, 209
down payment, 129, 177
drachma, 7, 18

economics, 256, 258, 279
economies, 4–6, 11–13, 18, 30. *See also* currency
employee, 48, 70, 84
employer, 48, 64, 73, 84
employer identification number, 78
employment, 34
escrow, 176, 178, 179, 180, 182, 184
escrow officer, 176, 180, 184
euro, 5, 6, 7, 9, 10, 15, 18, 19, 24, 25, 26, 27, 28, 30
European Union, 18
exchange rate 12, 18, 19
expiration, 209

family finances, 115–25
FICA, 75, 84
financial portfolio, 302
Flash Cards, 29, 60, 83, 110, 138, 167, 193, 222, 246, 266, 288, 314
foreign exchange, 15–16
Forex, 15, 16, 30
franc, 6, 7, 15, 18, 21, 30
fundamental analysis, 213
fundamentals, 209
future focus, 291, 293–301
futures, 250

goals, 302, 303, 306–8
graphs
    bar, 333–34
    line, 331
gross pay, 48, 49, 73, 74, 84
gulden, 21

income, 150, 296
    passive, 184, 194
income tax, 75, 84
index, 209
industry, 209, 212
inspector, 184
institutional investors, 209
insurance, 76, 279, 282
interest, 90–97, 104, 128, 130, 131
    compound, 92–93, 98, 100, 101, 103
    simple, 91, 98, 99, 101, 103
interview, 45–47, 48, 53–54
investment collection, 269–70
investments, 154, 169, 295–96, 299, 302
    return on, 194
investor, 228, 235
issuer, 235

laddering, 239
ledger, 156, 161
lender, 184
letter
    cover, 52
    thank you, 54
liquidate, 302, 304

margin, 209
mark, 7, 18
maturity date, 235
money, 2

Moon Cards, 26, 58, 81, 108, 136, 165, 191, 220, 244, 264, 286, 312
mortgage, 126, 128–29, 184
mottos, 22
mutual funds, 209

net pay, 48, 49, 73, 77, 84
net worth, 294, 302
note, 235

offer, 173, 184
options, 197, 209, 223
overdrawn, 156, 160

partnerships, 63, 68, 73
    general, 73
    limited, 73
paycheck, 77, 296
payment, 235
payroll deductions, 48, 49
percentages, 98
peso, 21
pie charts, 329–30. *See also* charts
pound, 5, 9, 10, 13, 18, 30
portfolio management, 215, 304
premium, 279
principal, 98
put, 209

rate, 235
readers theatre, 339–42
real estate, 169, 170, 171–83, 184, 185–87, 194
recording, 182, 184
resistance, 210, 214
resume, 40–42, 48, 51
retirement, 305
return on investment, 194
Roman numerals, 22
roundel, 22
ruble, 7, 18, 24, 25, 26, 27, 28
rupee, 7, 18, 20

saving(s), 85–86, 98
secondary market, 279
sector, 258
seller, 173, 175, 181, 184
shareholder, 203
Social Security, 75
    number, 78

sole proprietorship, 70
Star Cards, 25, 57, 80, 107, 135, 164, 190, 219, 243, 263, 285, 311
stock exchange, 204
stock market, 16, 197, 223
stocks, 197, 202–8
sucres, 21
Sun Cards, 27, 28, 59, 82, 109, 137, 166, 192, 221, 245, 265, 287, 313
supply and demand, 256, 258, 270, 274, 277, 279
support, 210, 214

tables, 20, 216, 237, 239, 260, 282, 327. *See also* charts
taxes, 75, 84
T-bill, 237
technical analysis, 214
technicals, 210
term, 235

termites, 184
ticker symbol, 200, 210
treasuries, 235, 236
trend, 210

unemployment insurance, 76, 84
U.S. Treasury, 31
utility, 156

value, 235

wages, 74
Web sites, 31, 61, 75, 84, 111, 139, 168, 195, 223, 240, 247, 267, 289, 315
workers' compensation insurance, 70, 84

yen, 8, 15, 18, 24, 25, 26, 27, 28
yuan, 8, 18

zero coupon, 235

About the Author

CAROL PETERSON is an active investor in the stock, futures, and bond markets and holds a real estate broker's license. Her experience as a legal assistant established her understanding of types of business entities and bankruptcy law. She and her husband owned a business, for which she managed payroll, taxes, insurance, and accounts payable and receivable. She is passionate about the need to train our kids to be good financial stewards.

Fortunately Carol never outgrew her fourth-grade sense of humor. This humor fuels her writing and her desire to "Make Learning Fun" for both kids and teachers.

www.ingramcontent.com/pod-product-compliance
Lightning Source LLC
Chambersburg PA
CBHW080541230426

43663CB00015B/2668